RAVEN 23

ALSO BY GINA KEATING

Netflixed: The Epic Battle for America's Eyeballs

RAVEN 23

HOW THE DEPARTMENT
OF JUSTICE BETRAYED
AMERICAN HEROES

GINA KEATING

BROADSIDE BOOKS

Without limiting the exclusive rights of any author, contributor or the publisher of this publication, any unauthorized use of this publication to train generative artificial intelligence (AI) technologies is expressly prohibited. HarperCollins also exercise their rights under Article 4(3) of the Digital Single Market Directive 2019/790 and expressly reserve this publication from the text and data mining exception.

RAVEN 23. Copyright © 2025 by Raven 23 Productions, LLC. All rights reserved. Printed in the United States of America. No part of this book may be used or reproduced in any manner whatsoever without written permission except in the case of brief quotations embodied in critical articles and reviews. For information, address HarperCollins Publishers, 195 Broadway, New York, NY 10007. In Europe, HarperCollins Publishers, Macken House, 39/40 Mayor Street Upper, Dublin 1, D01 C9W8, Ireland.

HarperCollins books may be purchased for educational, business, or sales promotional use. For information, please email the Special Markets Department at SPsales@harpercollins.com.

hc.com

Broadside Books™ and the Broadside logo are trademarks of HarperCollins Publishers.

FIRST EDITION

Designed by Michele Cameron

Library of Congress Cataloging-in-Publication Data has been applied for.

ISBN 978-0-06-337060-9

25 26 27 28 29 LBC 5 4 3 2 1

This book is for Hannah, Quinn, Lily, Willa, Eileen, Christian, and Reagan.

Never take your own revenge, beloved, but leave room for the wrath of God, for it is written, "Vengeance is Mine, I will repay," says the Lord. But if your enemy is hungry, feed him, and if he is thirsty, give him a drink; for in so doing you will heap burning coals on his head.

—ROMANS 12:19–20

AUTHOR'S NOTE

——— ★★★ ———

A portion of the proceeds from this book will go to financially support four American heroes whose lives were devastated by America's criminal justice system: Dustin Heard, Evan Liberty, Paul Slough, and Nick Slatten.

CONTENTS

★★★

Introduction: The Case of the Vanishing Insurgents	1
Chapter One: Catch-23	5
Chapter Two: Sometimes They Really Are Out to Get You	19
Chapter Three: What Actually Happened in Nisour Square	41
Chapter Four: The Frame-up Begins	54
Chapter Five: The Government Is (Almost Always) Out to Get You	67
Chapter Six: Allies in Unlikely Places	83
Chapter Seven: Judges Make All the Difference	90
Chapter Eight: How WikiLeaks Revealed That Hillary Clinton Made the Raven 23 Men Political Prisoners in Their Own Country	102
Chapter Nine: The Guilty Conscience of American Warmongers	117
Chapter Ten: Judge Lamberth Tightens the Knot	128

CONTENTS

Chapter Eleven: Verdict — 146

Chapter Twelve: How to Get a Pardon — 152

Chapter Thirteen: The Persecution of Nick Slatten — 163

Chapter Fourteen: Government Killing Machines — 182

Chapter Fifteen: Sentencing — 192

Chapter Sixteen: Mordor — 204

Chapter Seventeen: Pete Hegseth — 212

Chapter Eighteen: Never Read the Comments — 219

Chapter Nineteen: How to Get Donald Trump's Attention — 228

Chapter Twenty: Bravo Zulu — 234

Chapter Twenty-One: The Way Forward — 242

Acknowledgments — 251

Notes — 257

Index — 265

RAVEN 23

INTRODUCTION

THE CASE OF THE VANISHING INSURGENTS

WHAT DO YOU DO when the entire world believes a story that you can see is false? When no one is interested in the truth? At the beginning of my investigation into the Raven 23 case, I thought I knew what the world was like. The reality of the corruption, abuse of power, and malice I saw in America's institutions persuaded me of something I didn't believe before: that evil exists.

The men of Raven 23 could have faded into the obscurity they craved after their unlikely pardons, but they wanted the truth told. And we who took the journey to free them wanted those who imprisoned them to know: We saw what you did. We will not forget.

It started with a false story. The events in Nisour Square, where four Blackwater mercenaries opened fire in an Iraqi intersection, constituted one of the most notorious incidents of the Iraq War. According to the official story, the mercenaries fired unprovoked into a crowd of civilians, leaving chaos and death in their wake, and attempted to cover it up. That accounting helped shape a narrative that US mercenaries were corrupt and vicious killers, that our government was comparatively upstanding and willing to prosecute even its own citizens, and that the sort of men who worked for Blackwater were just thugs looking for trouble.

But what if I told you that nearly every "fact" in the official story was a lie? That the men were, in fact, fired upon by insurgents that no government wanted to admit existed? That far from holding our own accountable, the US Department of Justice cooked up a flimsy story to condemn Americans because it wanted to win diplomacy points with foreign leaders and earn plaudits from a media universe that hated the war?

Thanks to WikiLeaks, we know that behind the scenes, Secretary of State Hillary Clinton, Vice President Joe Biden, and Attorney General Eric Holder pushed for convictions because of political pressure from a corrupt Iraqi government that they wanted to make appear legitimate.

It sounds crazy. Yet that was what happened. I saw it with my own eyes.

You've probably heard the government's version of events. "Shoot first, justify later." That was what the government claimed happened on Sunday, September 16, 2007, in Baghdad, Iraq. To refresh your memory, here's the "official" story that gripped international headlines for a decade.

It was a clear day in Baghdad. Twenty-one-year-old Ahmed Haithem Al Rubia'y and his mother, Mahassin, were driving to one of her work locations. Mahassin was a doctor, and her son, in his third year of medical school, was well on his way to following in her footsteps.

Their path went through Nisour Square, normally a busy roundabout that saw hundreds of Iraqis traverse it daily. But today was different. Traffic wasn't moving. Ahmed craned his neck to see why. It wasn't hard to identify the problem. Huge military vehicles sat at one end of the circle, damming up traffic. On top of the vehicles, armed mercenaries toted massive guns. More men peered out of the windows. The nineteen-man convoy was called Raven 23, and its members worked for the private security contractor Blackwater USA.

The men of Raven 23 were paid by the US government to protect its diplomats.

But the Blackwater convoy was not protecting anyone in the traffic circle that day. Their shift leader disobeyed orders to head out of the US-controlled Green Zone that morning. The squad was full of bloodthirsty thugs, eager to kill anything not American. And that was exactly what they did, without a hint of provocation.

The men fired at Ahmed and his mother, killing them. Peppering Ahmed's vehicle with bullets, they then turned to shoot into the crowd. Two men fired grenades into the vehicle, causing it to ignite.

"When the shooting stopped, they had killed fourteen and injured another eighteen. Every man, woman, and child out there that day that either died or suffered an injury posed no threat to these men whatsoever. . . . They shot them anyway." That's what a federal prosecutor said, capping off the official story in court. Every version of this story insisted on one fact: The Raven 23 men were shooting at nothing and no one. There were no insurgents in Nisour Square.[1] So when, many years later, President Donald Trump pardoned the men of Raven 23, the media reacted with outrage.

"Shock and Dismay After Trump Pardons Blackwater Guards Who Killed 14 Iraqi Civilians" was the NPR headline. The *Los Angeles Times* said that the pardon "sparks outrage in Iraq." *The Guardian* called what happened in Nisour Square "one of the lowest episodes of the US-led invasion and occupation of Iraq." Internationally, the reaction was the same. UN "experts" described the pardon as an "affront to justice."

The US bureaucracy got in on the act. CNN published an article by an FBI agent, Thomas O'Connor, who had investigated the scene and said that the men "were undeserving of pardons" and that "there is no forensic evidence of anyone shooting at the Blackwater team."[2] He didn't mention that his investigation of the scene had happened three weeks after the event.[3] Nor did he mention that army investigators *had* found forensic evidence of insurgents: piles of new AK-47 shells. Dozens of eyewitnesses mentioned the insurgents' presence.[4]

But federal prosecutors made sure that their star witness—Raven 23 turret gunner, Jeremy Ridgeway—would carry the unit's tale. Soon after Ridgeway took a plea deal, the insurgents curiously vanished from the official story, and the legacy media parroted that story all the way through the multiyear saga of the Raven 23 case.

This book reveals why.

CHAPTER ONE

─── ★★★ ───

CATCH-23

The press was to serve the governed, not the governors.

—US SUPREME COURT JUSTICE HUGO BLACK,
NEW YORK TIMES CO. V. UNITED STATES

NOT EVERY STORY is Watergate—but you still have to show up to your beat every day, sometimes for years, to know it when you see it.

All the President's Men did not have an entirely positive effect on journalism because it lured a lot of failed writers into the field. I spent many years doing monotonous beat checks, knocking on doors, and conducting stakeouts so I could recognize a story when I saw it. But many Woodward and Bernstein wannabes did not have that grounding; they got into the business stringing while studying abroad in college and returned to the United States with very little day-to-day experience of covering a beat or creating relationships. When members of this species become editors, they often insist that something is nothing—or vice versa.

One editor, an Ivy League alumnus, ruined my carefully tended relationship with an independent Hollywood studio by claiming that it was trying to cover up problems in its earnings report. He kept pointing to boilerplate legal language that appears in every company's earnings report and insisted that I include a caution in my story. I refused, and we had a screaming match that ended with his inserting the error into my story and sending the studio's stock price tumbling. He had to correct it, but the CEO, who had been friendly enough to give me the company's embargoed earnings figures every quarter, refused to speak with me again.

With my "Watergate"—the Raven 23 story—the beginning couldn't have been more unlikely. The case fell into my lap thanks to a redneck named Joe Bob, a stolen newspaper, and Jessica Simpson, a Shih Tzu. It started in Taft, Texas, at breakfast on April 14, 2015, and ended 2,079 days later with four presidential pardons.

It was a Tuesday; warm and breezy as spring in south Texas usually is and still dark as I let my dog, Jessica Simpson, out into the backyard and went about making coffee, eggs, bacon, and toast for my boyfriend, Joe Bob, before he went to work on the oil platforms on Corpus Christi Bay. He worked as a gauger, maintaining the machinery and pipelines that measure and route oil and gas from offshore wells to onshore storage tanks.

I am an investigative journalist who moved from Los Angeles to Corpus Christi to write my first book, fell in love, and never made it back to the West Coast. To a big-city liberal like me, Joe Bob was a cultural challenge to all of my stereotypes.

The first time my Aunt Molly met Joe Bob, she told me, "He's for sex." As if that was a bad thing. My mother cornered him in my kitchen the second time she met him and warned, "Don't interfere with her writing." He ignored her.

The first time I visited his house, I asked why he needed six firearms. He stared at me in horror. (After surprising a rattlesnake outside our house a few years later, I got it.) Joe Bob never had a lot of money or leisure time, so he made his fun with whatever and whoever was at hand. He could make an evening out of a garden hose, a trampoline, and a bottle of good scotch. He smoked in the house until I made him quit.

He was terrified of the huge roaches that hung out in South Texas bathrooms, so twice a year, he crawled under the house wearing coveralls to spray chemicals that were probably banned under the floorboards.

"Hiring it done" showed a lack of character; he fixed his broken stuff no matter how long the parts sat in piles or how high the chances were of his falling off the garage. His biggest thrill was considering what generator to buy in case of a zombie apocalypse or the Democrats taking back Texas. Both of those obsessions were exacerbated when he discovered YouTube.

Joe Bob was a keen observer of people and customs, an ardent gatherer of esoterica, and a champion (and dirty) debater. His habits and beliefs were foreign and fascinating to someone who had spent her professional life in offices and public buildings in Austin and Los Angeles and whose recreation encompassed gossipy parties or whatever show, play, opera, or in-crowd events were available to the liberal, educated, and aspiring. Somehow, though, he came from a place I recalled deep in my bones—the tiny factory town in Missouri where my mom and her brothers and sisters had been born and grown up and eventually left and my grandparents and great-grandparents and so on had been born, grown up, and died.

In that place, my grandfather arrived at the same time every workday morning for breakfast at the Liberty Creamery Cafe, ordered the same breakfast, and related or digested whatever stories were making the rounds with the same group of men. Then he headed off to get dirty at Shapiro Bros., the scrapyard he ran with his brother, Earl. He wore a blue button-down shirt, khakis, and steel-toe boots to work every day, year after year, and drove a white Chrysler sedan long after he could afford to buy his own airplane. In a small town, you succeed by being reliable and not standing out. In that place, you were who you were. There was no hiding it, no changing it, and no bullshitting people. They knew what they knew.

As I set the plate in front of Joe Bob, Jessica Simpson hurled herself at the screen door. I pushed it open, and she dragged in a copy of the local newspaper by its plastic sleeve. It was almost as big as she was. I had no idea where she had found it; our backyard was fenced, so either someone had thrown it over the fence or she had somehow escaped and stolen it from a neighbor's yard. Either way, I was mortified.

Joe Bob picked up the newspaper, unwrapped it as he sat at the table, and told the dog, "Sweet! Now go find a *New York Times*."

"That's not funny," I said. "She stole that, and I meant to give it back." He didn't answer. He was immersed in an article titled something like "Blackwater Guards Sentenced in Fatal Iraq Shootings."

The article told of the sentencing of four men employed by the military contractor Blackwater who had fatally shot or injured thirty-four civilians in a Baghdad traffic circle in 2007 while protecting a US diplomat. The international press had dubbed the incident "the Nisour Square massacre" and compared it to the Vietnam War's infamous My Lai massacre. I had never heard of Nisour Square.

He pointed to a name in the story: Dustin Heard of Maryville, Tennessee. "I think that's my friend's kid," he said. "He grew up across the street from me. There is no way that kid did what they're saying he did."

Joe Bob grew up in Olney, Texas, about sixty miles south of the Texas-Oklahoma border and two hours west of the Dallas–Fort Worth metroplex. We had visited his parents and high school friends a few times in the three years we had been together, but I'd never met Stacey Heard, the friend he was talking about—Dustin Heard's father.

I was skeptical. So Joe Bob knew Dustin's dad, but he had known Dustin only as a kid. How could he possibly be so sure that

Dustin was innocent? But Joe Bob insisted. He knew exactly why Dustin couldn't have done what the papers said he had.

The paper's portrait of Dustin, while not in so many words, inferred a vicious character who was reckless with weaponry. It was a picture of panic and carelessness. Joe Bob found it baffling because the one thing he remembered about Dustin was that even as a child, he'd never taken a shot without meaning to kill. Once, when Joe Bob and Stacey had been young dads living across Bloodworth Street in Olney from each other, they had taken Dustin, then about six years old, out to shoot birds. At that young age, Dustin had spent most of his time with his step-grandfather, Arlen Crosthwaite, who ran oil field leases. "Arlen was very conservative, and you just didn't shoot at nothing," Joe Bob said. "Dustin already showed a propensity to listen to Arlen, and he was very serious. He didn't shoot at every little thing. He was already incredibly responsible."

Dustin's parents were still in high school when he was born. Stacey was eighteen years old, and Dustin's mother, Donna, was seventeen. They lived in a trailer out in the country after they married, and Joe Bob and the other high schoolers used to go out there and party.

On that occasion, Joe Bob, Stacey, and Dustin wandered around in the countryside for a little bit and couldn't find any birds or anything else to shoot. "Dustin had to identify a target," Joe Bob told me. "He was so young, and we thought, 'Wow, that's what you were supposed to do.'"

It was remarkable because Joe Bob and Stacey, then about twenty-three years old, were still acting like kids, plinking at cans when they couldn't find anything else. "Dustin was highly skeptical of that and asked, 'Why would you do something like that?' Stacey was proud of him," he said.

The reason Joe Bob was so sure that Dustin was not guilty in Nisour Square stemmed from that incident. "At that age, demonstrating discipline like that, he wasn't going to go blasting away [in Nisour Square]," he said. I did not doubt that Joe Bob knew Dustin Heard pretty well; everyone in Olney knows everyone else or knows of them. The town floats lonely on a grassy, mesquite- and pumpjack-dotted plain with just about three thousand souls along for the ride.

Still, Dustin Heard had barely graduated from high school when Joe Bob moved to south Texas. I wondered what kind of man he had grown into; I would later learn that Dustin had enlisted in the US Marine Corps just in time for the September 11, 2001, attacks on New York and Washington, DC, and joined Blackwater, the infamous mercenary company founded by Erik Prince, an ex-Navy SEAL and conservative scion of a Michigan auto parts fortune, as soon as his tour of duty with the marines ended in 2004. At the time, I'd never heard Dustin's name, but I thought I knew the type: another gung ho warmongering red stater.

At least, that was what my yellow-dog Democrat brain said silently.

But Joe Bob's hunch would reveal more oddities about the case. By the time he returned from work that day, he had talked to Stacey Heard and learned that Dustin had been sentenced to thirty years in prison on numerous voluntary manslaughter and attempted manslaughter charges. Then there was the single, bizarre charge of using an assault weapon in the commission of a felony—a strange charge for a war zone, I thought. Kind of like calling movers to haul away your stuff and then accusing them of theft.

His codefendants Evan Liberty and Paul Slough had received the same sentence as Dustin, and a fourth man, Nicholas Slatten, had been sentenced to life in prison for murdering one person.

I had to admit that it sounded strange: How can the government legally or morally justify imprisoning the combatants it trained, paid, and armed to destabilize a country because a number of people died in the chaos? Did no one see that coming? I wondered bitterly.

"You've got to do something!" Joe Bob told me.

"Me?" I said, startled. "What am I supposed to do?"

"I don't know—write a story. Something's not right about this," he said.

Maybe, maybe not, I thought. The Iraq War was over, and, like most Americans, I had no desire to rehash any part of it—even less because I am a lifelong liberal and I hated the Iraq War. I put solar panels on my home in California in 2004 to protest what I considered an immoral and wasteful war of opportunity motivated by the oil industry.

I am not touching this—they probably got what they deserved, I thought but did not say. However, God and Joe Bob saw it differently.

What followed was a painful six-year journey that dismantled the cynic I had become and reminded me of the curiosity and compassion I'd had in abundance when I'd started my professional life as an unpaid intern at KRIS-TV in Corpus Christi in 1984. Since the day I walked into the newsroom at KRIS-TV, I have made my living as a journalist or in a news-facing role. I have never wanted to do anything else.

When Joe Bob asked me to "write a story," I knew it would take a lot more to change the minds of people who could do something about the sorry situation. The case had already gotten plenty of attention in media outlets all over the world, and curiously, they were all peddling the same story: Blackwater, mercenaries, massacre. I knew from experience that convincing major news outlets to change that mantra would be a tough sell, given how they spent more time matching one another's stories—even quoting one another as sources—rather than engaging in actual reporting.

A quick read of the trial coverage suggested that for the most part the Washington, DC, press corps had talked exclusively with

Department of Justice prosecutors for their stories and had not bothered to get any input—on or off the record—from the defense lawyers or the defendants' large community of supporters, including their former military and Blackwater colleagues. The reporters had been either lazy or scared of pissing off their government sources—not a real revelation, I thought.

Although I had covered scores of civil and criminal trials in state and federal courts over the years, I recalled reading about some complicated rules governing how US personnel who committed crimes in Iraq would be prosecuted. It seemed a chore to figure out how it all worked—on top of everything else that screamed, "Don't get involved."

"I'm a business writer," I reminded Joe Bob. "I know nothing about foreign policy or the military. You know that I was totally opposed to the Iraq War—especially using mercenaries to fight a war over oil. I won't do it. No way." Plus, I had spent two decades living and working in California, and I doubted that families from four small rural towns would want to speak to a liberal and a member of a profession that had described their loved ones as war criminals and monsters.

By the time Christmas rolled around, I had moved to Austin to pursue a master's degree in writing—to teach, maybe write novels or movies, and put some distance between me and daily journalism. After covering the aftermath of the September 11, 2001, hijack attacks on the market and companies in LA, as well as the 2008 banking meltdown, and going through an expensive divorce, I was burned out and wanted to start over doing something a little less fraught and a lot more fun.

I hadn't thought much about the Raven 23 case since leaving Taft, but it had remained on the front burner for Joe Bob. He asked me to meet him in Olney; he had engineered a meeting with Stacey Heard, he said. Because I missed him, I said I would come.

Dustin's young wife, Kelli, an elementary school teacher, and their two children, nine-year-old Hannah and five-year-old Quinn, were visiting Stacey and his wife, Lawana, for the holiday. Kelli was just thirty, pretty and tiny with long, straight honey blond hair, a round face, and exhausted green eyes. We talked that first evening at the Heard family's hunting lodge, sitting around a firepit after she put the children to bed. She described how she had collapsed in her classroom the day in 2014 when Dustin had been convicted; he had told her not to bother making the nine-hour drive between Maryville and Washington, DC, to hear the jury's verdict read. He would drive himself home when it was over.

She had a master's degree in education but told me that she could not figure out how to explain to Hannah and Quinn why their father was in prison and would not come home until they were grown.

The Heards and the other families—and apparently their lawyers—believed that the Department of Justice had pursued the case to appease Iraqi civilians angered by the civil war unleashed by the US-led ouster of Saddam Hussein.

Kelli told me that their Washington, DC, defense lawyers had said that no jury could convict Dustin, Evan, Paul, and Nick on the evidence—or lack thereof—that the government had presented. They had been fighting for their lives and their comrades' lives in an armed conflict using weapons and rules of engagement given to them by the US government. In fact, the Raven 23 defense attorneys had put on only a handful of the seventy witnesses during the five-week trial. They were certain that the prosecutors could not overcome a jury's reasonable doubt about what had happened in the Nisour Square traffic circle that day.

Kelli was compelling, and I wanted to believe her. But the shootings of almost three dozen people—including a child—in broad daylight in a crowded traffic circle would be hard to square for any jury. Plus, the jury sat in the courtroom for two months, closely watching the defendants and weighing the witnesses' testimony. Something must have convinced them that the government's theory—that the Blackwater men had freaked out and started shooting wildly—made sense.

What I had heard about Blackwater was not positive; the stories made it sound as though guards were swanning around Baghdad in their Oakley sunglasses and Columbia quick-dry outfits, armed to the teeth and acting as though they owned the place. I wasn't alone. Journalist Terry McCarthy had gone to Baghdad in 2003 as *Time* magazine's Baghdad bureau chief and had been working as the Baghdad correspondent for ABC News at the time of the Nisour Square massacre. He told me that military contractors had killed an Iraqi man and boy walking past the bureau when they had gotten too close to the vehicle carrying a State Department official who was visiting American journalists. "They smoked him and the [boy]," he said. "They were innocent civilians . . . and they didn't stop. They just kept going."[1]

I wondered what kind of man would volunteer to return to Iraq after surviving a tour of duty in the most dangerous city on Earth. Warmongers, that's who. Men who needed the chaos of battle to feel normal. Not well-balanced individuals.

Also, why would the DOJ choose to make examples of those particular four men? It was a little strange that the defense had not tried harder to refute the government's case. That made me wonder. Erik Prince could surely afford good lawyers, and I felt positive that manslaughter and murder convictions would be bad for Blackwater's business. So why hadn't he fought harder? Something was wrong, but I didn't know whether that sweet young mother had been taken in by her murderous husband or whether the government was up to something.

I told the Heard family that I'd look at the trial transcript and see if anything stood out.

By the time I showed up, the Raven 23 families and their communities—Olney, Texas; Dickens, Texas; Sparta, Tennessee; and Rochester, New Hampshire—had been fighting the federal government for seven years. The families and their communities had sold T-shirts, baked goods, and whatever else they could think of to raise money for trips to see their men in prisons in Memphis; Schuylkill, Pennsylvania; El Reno, Oklahoma; and Wildwood, Florida.

The Raven 23 men had had the misfortune of having their trial splashed in international headlines as popular approval of the wars in Iraq and Afghanistan reached its nadir. A June 2014 Gallup poll showed that 57 percent of Americans believed that the United States had made a mistake in sending troops to Iraq, and 49 percent felt the same about troops in Afghanistan. The only time that disapproval rating had been higher was in late 2007, when it had risen above 60 percent, peaking at 63 percent in 2008. "A quicker souring on the military action than had occurred in the 1960s after the nation's initial involvement in Vietnam," Gallup said in its analysis.

The families were executing a lonely counterattack, intent on taking on the world's most powerful government and the international media because there was nothing else they could do. I still wasn't sure what had happened in Iraq, but if what Kelli and Stacey Heard told me was true, the government's prosecution of the four Blackwater guards had been tainted in a way I had never seen before. Their predicament terrified me. What if the same thing happened to me or someone I loved? Who would sacrifice everything they had to bring me home?

That selfish thought, combined with my natural loathing of authority, spurred me to page through the case files that Stacey Heard had put into my hands at Christmas 2015. By the following spring, it was clear that something was rotten in the prosecution of the Raven 23 case.

I could not figure out how the case had even made it to trial, let alone to a jury. There was a lot of evidence that the Raven 23 convoy had come under heavy fire upon entering Nisour Square; transcripts of the radio communications between the convoy and the Tactical Operations Center, photos of AK-47 shell casings, Iraqi witness statements, and bullet strikes on the vehicles showed that they had been involved in a firefight.[2]

The Second Amendment of the US Constitution affords every American the right to self-defense. As far as I was concerned, that entitled the Blackwater men to stand on the roofs of their armored vehicles, if they felt so inclined, and shoot the people who were shooting at them. Believing that your life or property or the life or property of someone else is threatened is an absolute defense to manslaughter and murder under US law.

As a wire service reporter, I had seen Los Angeles gang members beat similar charges by claiming self-defense. A bloodbath at a car wash in Inglewood between rival gangs wielding automatic weapons stood out in my mind. If that defense had worked in the context of Los Angeles's gang wars, why did it not seem to apply to an actual war zone?

But again, I'm not a lawyer, so maybe I didn't understand something about federal criminal procedure since most of the criminal cases I had covered had been brought in state courts. Maybe all of those irregularities were allowed under Paul Bremer's Coalition Provisional Authority, which had created the system in which Americans were tried in US federal courts for alleged crimes that had occurred in Iraq. I was certainly no expert on those byzantine rules—and I didn't want to become one.

I kept going back through the court documents, wondering if I was missing something. In the spring of 2016, I felt paralyzed about what to think about the strange conduct revealed in the court documents and trial transcript of both the prosecutors and the judge. Frankly, I was still hung up on the fact that the men had worked for Erik Prince, a person I considered a notorious war profiteer and right-wing nut job. Then Nick Slatten's sister, Jessica, emailed me an amicus brief written on behalf of the Blackwater defendants by the National Association of Criminal Defense Lawyers (NACDL) for their appeal.

The NACDL is the premier professional bar association for US criminal defense lawyers. It weighs in on high-profile cases to advance "the mission of the criminal defense bar to ensure justice and due process for persons accused of crime or wrongdoing." Although it bills itself as nonpartisan, I do not know many conservative defense attorneys. These are my people, I thought, and I was anxious to see how they had interpreted this perplexing case. I immediately read through the forty-two-page brief, hoping for some rational explanation of what looked a lot like government misconduct.

In its brief, the NACDL lawyers asked the federal appeals court to reverse the convictions of Dustin, Evan, Nick, and Paul for what they described as a litany of "serious errors" and "prosecutorial overreaching and unfairness" in what they called a "textbook case of prosecutorial vindictiveness."[3] My mind raced as I read through the descriptions of questionable behavior by both the judge and prosecutors; what I had suspected as I'd read the trial transcript had actually occurred. I could not ignore it any longer. I had to act.

What was worse, a few months earlier, on October 21, 2015, Attorney General Loretta Lynch had presented awards to the team of prosecutors who had tried the Blackwater case.[4] She had *promoted* T. Patrick Martin, Jonathan Malis, Gregg Maisel, Kenneth Kohl, Jay Bratt, John Crabb, Jr., Christopher Kavanaugh, David Mudd, and Yvonne Bryant, although it was publicly known by then that the prosecutors failed to turn over exculpatory evidence to defense attorneys on at least four occasions during the trial.[5]

Those individuals, described in the NACDL amicus brief as "vindictive" violators of the Constitution, had been honored for their "immense sacrifices," "plac[ing] themselves in harm's way," and "outstanding work [that] is an inspiration to public servants everywhere."

The concept was simply too much to bear. I asked the families if they could put me in touch with Dustin, Evan, Nick, and Paul and if I could visit them in the four separate federal prisons where they were serving what amounted to life sentences. I wanted to lay eyes on them, decide what kind of men they were, and hear what they had to say about Nisour Square. Then I'd figure out what to do.

CHAPTER TWO

✯✯✯

SOMETIMES THEY REALLY ARE OUT TO GET YOU

The enemy is anybody who's going to get you killed, no matter which side he's on.

—JOSEPH HELLER, *CATCH-22*

WHERE I COME FROM, evidence of the New Deal abounds. My Missourian grandfather was a Franklin Delano Roosevelt Democrat who gave generously to the cause; he flew his lawmaker friends around in his airplane, gave money to their campaigns, and expected favors in return. There was a system. He worked it and it worked for him.

From him, I learned that the government is about people—the people who run it and the people it is supposed to serve. Call me a Pollyanna, but until the Blackwater case, I had never viewed the US government as some kind of evil monolith.

The worst corruption I had personally seen up to that point was the Rampart scandal that engulfed the Los Angeles Police Department in 1999. Just like any other partners in crime, government agencies are perfectly capable of lying and covering up for each other for reasons that make no sense to anyone but them. The Rampart scandal broke when a defense attorney named Stephen Yagman filed several civil rights lawsuits against the LAPD with stories of corruption. He insisted that police officers had been planting weapons and drugs on his clients, beating them up, and committing all manner of civil rights violations—and then lying about it on the witness stand.

But just because Yagman had "broken" the story, that didn't mean it was truly public. No one in the media believed Yagman, mainly because his clients were gang members and convicted felons. His legal briefs were full of seemingly fantastical allegations about an LAPD crime syndicate operating out of the Rampart station. It just didn't make sense. One corrupt department, sure, but a syndicate of them, operating in unison?

No one would report on it, leaving journalists with egg on their faces when the police officers involved in the illegal activity started turning state's evidence. Yagman didn't look so stupid after all, and we journalists learned an important lesson: Competing government agencies will lie and obfuscate for one another to cover their collective asses. The reality was that what had seemed like haphazard collusion was actually a deep web of loyalties and favors owed. The LAPD, Los Angeles City Council, and Los Angeles County District Attorney's Office each had its motives for looking the other way in a scandal that many people had known about and that had extended to cops dealing drugs and robbing banks.

The nonparticipating officers at the Rampart station were afraid to report their lawless colleagues for obvious reasons. The LAPD was already under federal scrutiny over excessive force allegations but thought it could handle the problem in-house. But the corruption ran too deep. Other agencies had their own motivations for avoiding an exposé. The Los Angeles Police Protective League—the police union—was not going to turn on its members, and the DA's office did not want to see perhaps hundreds of cases nullified by the testimony of lying cops.

The overarching reason that no one had looked into the allegations sooner was that no one had wanted to question a narrative that made the government look good. The official narrative was that crime was under control. The Rampart anti-gang unit, whose unfortunate acronym was CRASH (Community Resources Against Street Hoodlums), seemed to be tamping down the gang violence that plagued the city's poorest neighborhoods. That the CRASH unit had accomplished that by becoming a street gang did not seem relevant, I suppose.

So even though they were at cross-purposes, the agencies had reason to back one another up. Somehow, the noble purpose of protecting citizens of the Rampart neighborhood had been perverted by their would-be protectors.[1]

As I began questioning the official narrative about Nisour Square, I remembered that story, and also something told to me by Joseph Low IV, a former US marine, a member of and instructor in the Judge Advocate General's Corps, and the head of the elite Trial Lawyers College in Sheridan, Wyoming. He had spent the Iraq War years defending US servicemen and -women accused of war crimes. In his most notorious case, he had had murder charges dismissed against Marine Sergeant Jermaine Nelson. Nelson and two comrades were accused of murdering unarmed Iraqis during a house-to-house battle in Fallujah in 2004. The men had not hidden the shootings; they had happened during the bloodiest urban warfare since the Vietnam War in a battle to push insurgents out of the city. But the Marine Corps and federal prosecutors inexplicably pursued murder charges against the men after one of them mentioned the shootings in a job interview with the Secret Service three years later. It was as though the government was waging a separate war in the court system against its military veterans.[2]

"Whenever you give someone a lot of power and there is no consequence of the abuse of it, then you have ensured that that's exactly what's going to happen," Low told me when I called him to discuss the Blackwater case. "Especially if they get promoted and heralded and their careers advanced for being able to do what you are reportedly paying them to do, which is get a conviction. Remember, no prosecutor has ever been singled out, given an award, promoted, made a statue of for dismissing a case or losing it."

In the Blackwater case, I could not identify the government's purpose in pursuing a criminal case in the Nisour Square shootings with such zeal. The more I looked into the case, the more the government revealed itself as something dark that I had not seen before.

In May 2016, Joe Bob and I met in Austin and hit the road in my yellow compact car, bound for the Federal Correctional Institute Memphis to visit Dustin Heard. After that, we would head to Schuylkill, Pennsylvania, to see Evan Liberty and return to Texas via the federal prison in El Reno, Oklahoma, home to Paul Slough.

We'd already started to see evidence of government obfuscation. It had taken me a couple of months to complete the paperwork required for Joe Bob and me to be admitted to the prison as friends of the inmates. I had first applied to enter as a journalist so I could take a recording device and pen and notepad into the prisons with me. The Bureau of Prisons immediately denied my request, so I reapplied under my maiden name as a family friend and was approved.

The Bureau of Prisons sent pages of information about protocols, including a strict dress code and procedures for navigating the daylong visits. I read the rules to Joe Bob as he drove, remarking that my two meetings with Queen Elizabeth II and Prince Philip in Austin in 1991 had been casual in comparison. Outside Little Rock, my car blew a tire. We had it towed to an auto mechanic's shop and spent the night at a hotel to wait for the low-profile tire to be delivered the next morning.

I started to get nervous; the BOP limited visiting hours to weekends and Mondays, 8:30 a.m. to 3:30 p.m., and I had no way to let Dustin know that we would be late. Plus, it was my only chance to talk to him without the government listening in on our conversations. Since I had asked to visit, each of the men had added me to his email list. We had traded emails a few times, but their access to the prison computers was limited and all communication was monitored, so they had been guarded in what they wrote. With their appeal pending, the DOJ had begun ratcheting up the pressure on them to take plea deals to avoid another trial. They were not allowed to speak with one another directly but passed messages through family members.

Stacey Heard had told me that his cell phone was acting strangely, dropping calls and erasing his contacts. That did not surprise me. In 2002, my cell phone had been hacked in Los Angeles by associates of "private eye to the stars" Anthony Pellicano after I had written a series of stories about Anita Busch, an entertainment journalist who had investigated some of Pellicano's clients and then been harassed by his goons in a crackpot version of a gangster film. They had left a dead fish and a rose on her car windshield with a note demanding that she "STOP!"

Anita's colleagues in the entertainment press thought she was inventing the threats for attention and said so publicly, basing their idiotic conclusion on what they described as her "high-strung" and "demanding" personality. When her two attackers appeared in LA federal court in jumpsuits and manacles for their arraignment, I noted in my story that she had gotten the last laugh. After Pellicano went to prison for, among other things, possessing enough C-4 explosives in his office to take down an airliner and illegally tapping the phones of hundreds of people, I won a few thousand dollars in an ensuing lawsuit against AT&T. After that incident, I operated as if I always had an audience.[3]

We arrived in Memphis just before 2:00 p.m. on Saturday—the cutoff time for visiting. Joe Bob dropped me off at the visitors center and parked the car. I had memorized Dustin's inmate number, which I needed to complete the visitor paperwork. I hurriedly filled it out, showed the guard at the desk my driver's license, and exchanged some cash for tokens that I could use to buy food and drinks from the vending machines in the visiting area. Things were going smoothly, I thought, and soon I would finally hear what Dustin Heard had to say about Nisour Square.

I walked through the metal detector, dressed in the baggy jeans and a button-down shirt I had purchased from Walmart for the occasion, fearing that my skinny jeans and V-neck T-shirts would violate the prohibition against "revealing or tight clothing." The metal detector shrieked, and another stone-faced guard stopped me. "Are you wearing an underwire bra?" she asked.

"Well, yes," I said. "There wasn't anything in the rules about that."

"You can't go in wearing that," she said.

"What if I just take it off?" I asked. Or I had a sports bra in my car that I could change into, I said, feeling slightly hysterical at losing an entire visiting day between the blown tire and my bra.

She shook her head and told me to come back in the morning. It took every ounce of self-control to keep walking out the door instead of using my normal tactic of trying to argue or wheedle my way inside. I could not imagine how the families endured the expense and tension of the visits or the guards' capricious attitude toward visitors who had to jump through bureaucratic hoops like circus dogs to see their loved ones.

That evening, we met up with Kelli, Hannah, and Quinn Heard and Kelli's mom, Gail, at the hotel they had recommended. A year into her husband's incarceration, Kelli could afford to make the six-hour drive with the kids from Maryville to FCI Memphis only about once a month on her elementary school teacher's salary.

The next morning, we lined up just after 8:00 a.m. with dozens of other families, mainly women with very young children, and waited about an hour for the guards to open the visitors center. It was clear that most had been through the same drill I had the day before and were just as wary of the prison staff as I was. Neither Joe

Bob nor I had ever been inside a federal prison, and for one frantic moment, I thought about what I could do if the guards wouldn't let us out at the end of the day.

We waited for another hour, sitting on benches and the floor. At last the guards admitted us in groups to a large room with aged linoleum flooring, a raised guard platform on one end, a bank of vending machines and microwave ovens along the back wall, and rows of plastic molded chairs facing one another across the middle.

We sat in the chairs and waited. A few minutes later, a door on the far wall opened, and the prisoners filed in wearing khaki uniforms and heavy-soled shoes. The children saw Dustin first, and all of his attention was on them as he approached. He hugged them tightly for a moment and nuzzled Kelli briefly before the guards ordered the inmates and visitors to stop touching each other and sit. Dustin shook Joe Bob's hand, and I introduced myself.

Dustin was then and remains physically imposing despite being a short guy with some serious health issues stemming from combat and prison. He had joined the Marine Corps at age nineteen. To stay in shape during his leave, he would run from Olney to the town of Jean and back—about twenty-two miles down two-lane State Highway 114—with truck traffic whizzing past. As a younger man, he'd liked to party as much as the next guy, but "there are only so many trips you can make to Wichita Falls without getting burned out," he later told me. Fishing was his solace both before and after he went to war, and he dreamed of a future when he would again chug out on a Tennessee lake in his bass boat and cast into the placid waters over and over again.

His parents' families, the Heards and the Tatums, are related to about half the county, so Dustin had never wanted for love or attention. He had many cousins and close friends at Olney High School. He grew up loyal and had no tolerance for people who were not.

"I'm one of those guys that [a relationship] is a one-time and done thing," he told me some years later during a phone call from prison. "If somebody is going to be with me, be with me. If not—then don't."

That applied to his business and personal lives. He trusted his own judgment absolutely. That was a good trait when it came to his decision to join Blackwater and do whatever it took to come home to his wife and kids.

I had read in the pretrial motions about a fight between the defense attorneys and the government over allowing the jury to hear the Blackwater team's nicknames for one another. The team called Dustin "Extreme," a moniker that was not explained in the trial transcript and probably did not sit well with the jury.

The prosecutors made a big deal about Dustin's nickname in particular and wanted to tell the jury about it, but the judge said no. Nevertheless, Assistant US Attorney T. Patrick Martin told the jury during opening statements that "Defendant Heard . . . liked to put armor on." When the defense attorney and judge told him to shut it down, Martin replied that "it was a nickname he was happy to have."

"Extreme" sounded pretty bad, especially when the person with that nickname had later shot a bunch of innocent civilians, so that had to be among the first things I asked him.

I watched Dustin visit with his wife and mother-in-law, pose for photos, and lead his children to the family area and sit down on a chair to play with them. He wore a curly red beard, and his hair was longer than in pictures of the trial and swept back from his face, which was rounder from the steroid shots he was taking for chronic back pain from combat injuries and surgery. He walked and moved stiffly for a man in his mid-thirties, his arms held out slightly in front of his body. His attention seemed completely focused on Hannah and Quinn as he hugged and wrestled with them, unless one noticed his eyes, slewing left and right under downcast lids, always on guard. He was polite to me, and he and

Joe Bob talked about people they knew in Olney and memories of Dustin's childhood. I managed to shoehorn in a question about the nickname "Extreme": Where had it come from?

Dustin looked surprised but answered easily. When he had served alongside marines who had fought in Fallujah, he explained, he had gotten into the habit of stacking his truck with as much ammunition as he could fit into it in case they got ambushed. After being trapped in alleys during some Blackwater missions with insurgents shooting down at him from buildings, he had started buying top-quality body armor to cover the part of him that stuck out of the turret. He did not pay attention to the teasing he got from his teammates over his battle preparation. And as Baghdad became more violent, the other guys changed their tune, he said. In short, the nickname, when explained, fit better with Joe Bob's memories: He was *extremely* well prepared.

The next day, Joe Bob and I visited Dustin again, this time on our own, and I got down to business, asking what I needed to know about the incident and the trial. He answered rapid-fire, his eyes on mine. I wanted to watch him for any hint of mendacity, cruelty, or delight in the violence of war. He instead radiated the calm of a man who knew his business and did it without fuss or the need for adulation.

"I don't understand how this happened," I told him after he confirmed everything that I had read in the court papers. "How did this go from being a gunfight with Iraqi militia to the four of you in prison?" I don't know anything about foreign policy or battle strategy, I told him, but I've covered more than my share of criminal trials and peered into the investigative, prosecutorial, and judicial operations of government. And none of this adds up. What's the government's motive for spending seven years and millions of taxpayers' dollars to send four innocent veterans from Flyoverland to prison?

"Our attorneys told us it was political theater," he said. "The government did not have enough evidence to convict us but had to put on a trial to appease the Iraqi government."

I asked about the victims. News reports and Iraqi government accounts released that day had stated that there had been no more than a dozen casualties in Nisour Square that day. How had the body count gotten so high?

He told me that all but one of the men who had fired their weapons that day had killed gunmen who were shooting at the Blackwater convoy—not civilians. That amounted to a body count of eight to twelve, he said. The defense attorneys had decided not to challenge the inflated number of victims so as not to appear "insensitive" to the jury. I later learned that the decision had also been tactical; whether they were convicted of killing one or all the alleged victims, the gun charge with its mandatory thirty-year sentence would be applied. So paring down the body count held little advantage. The defense needed the jury to like the Raven 23 men enough to free them.

But that inaction allowed prosecutors to expand the casualty list to fit the definition of a "massacre" without having to prove that the victims on that expanded list had died in Nisour Square, on the same day as the incident or that they were dead in the first place. Two of the purported victims were reported missing in the days before or after September 16, 2007. Their bodies were never found. A man killed two miles away at Baghdad International Airport was also added to the list, as were people whose death certificates said they had been killed on different days. Dustin said he had urged his attorney with increasing urgency to challenge the victims list as the trial went south but was ignored. "We were not tried by a jury of our peers," he said. Seven years after the war and three years after US troops had officially left Iraq, the government painted Baghdad in the war's most violent year as the equivalent of Times Square, he said, a bustling and chaotic but peaceful place. And the Beltway jury bought it.

We discussed the trial errors enumerated in the NACDL amicus brief, and he urged me to look into the testimony of the Iraqi witnesses, especially the testimony of a man who had revealed on the witness stand that an Iraqi policeman had coached him and other witnesses to say that they had seen no Iraqi gunmen in the square that day. Dustin also wanted to get recordings of the Iraqi witness testimony vetted by an independent translator to make sure that the court-appointed translators were not shaping their statements to fit the prosecutors' narrative.

What did the judge have to say about that? I asked him.

Dustin snorted. "He was sleeping through most of the trial," he replied. "When our attorneys objected to anything, he threatened to throw them in jail."[4]

That did not sound particularly farfetched to me. I spent a little over a year working at the Los Angeles *Daily Journal*, the largest legal daily newspaper in the United States. As part of my job, I had to do a certain number of judicial profiles each month so that our lawyer subscribers could research the judges who heard their cases. After interviewing many attorneys who regularly appeared before the federal bench in Los Angeles, I quickly realized that I would never get straight, on-the-record answers about the legal competence of those "little gods" who had lifetime tenure and could be removed only through impeachment. I ended up doing a story on the Los Angeles federal bench highlighting how frequently the Ninth Circuit Court of Appeals had overturned each of the Central California District Court judges and included some of the appellate justices' damning comments about the lower courts' competency. That story led to many tips from attorneys about frankly insane conduct by some members of the federal bench—but my one story did little to make real change. There were no actual reforms or widespread public acknowledgment of the judges' immense and unchecked power and how capriciously they often wielded it.

Most upsetting to Dustin were the plea and immunity offers

the government had continued to dangle as his appeal worked its way through the court system. He had finally told his attorney to give the prosecutors a message: "Go fuck yourselves." He wasn't taking a plea deal, and he wasn't going to testify against his brothers to get a lighter sentence. None of them had done anything wrong, he said.

At the end of our visit, as the guards called the inmates to line up on one side of the room, Dustin asked me to give his regards to Evan Liberty, Paul Slough, and Nick Slatten. Dustin had not spoken with Evan, Paul, or Nick since they had been sentenced a year earlier. The BOP had classified them all as high-risk prisoners because of their military training and sequestered them from the regular prison population at first. Their notoriety had spread and led to challenges and invitations from prison gang leaders.

I noticed that Dustin had a dotted line and the words "cut here" tattooed around his neck. The tattoo and another line beneath his shirt that read "Give me a soldier's death," along with several scars on his neck, head, and shoulder were vestiges of an attack by another inmate wielding a piece of sharpened metal. "It means, 'Don't let me die in a fucking cage,'" he said of the tattoo.

He had not wanted to discuss the conditions at FCI Memphis in front of Kelli, he said. His death by violence would provoke no questions there, he intimated. The hair stood up on the back of my neck as I realized that he was right. He and the others were sitting ducks in those prisons, and I had to find out why the government wanted so badly for them to remain there.

At the end of the visit, Joe Bob and I lined up on the other side of the room and watched Dustin disappear into the lockup.

The next day, we got onto the road to Pennsylvania. We planned to stop at Gettysburg National Military Park while we waited for visiting hours at FCI Schuylkill the following weekend. Joe Bob, an amateur military historian, helped me understand the jargon and practices of military and battlefield life as I plowed through the court transcripts and filings in the passenger's seat. He especially wanted to see the famous Gettysburg battlefield, and he spent the thirteen hours driving between Memphis and Gettysburg regaling me with stories about the historic conflict.

We spent a day in the museum, and Joe Bob arranged for a tour guide with a PhD in history to drive us around the huge battlefield in the afternoon. The day was glorious, clear, and warm. As we listened to the guide describe the battle from the perspectives of the citizen soldiers who had fought with such deadly conviction on both the Union and Confederate sides, I thought about the men who were sitting in prison. Whatever I thought about the Iraq War, the four Raven 23 men had also offered up their young lives for a cause that was no less worthy to them.

I was torn about whether to believe Dustin's story. I knew, as I watched him walk back into the prison, that he did not belong in that line of convicts. Still, while my heart went out to him, I don't do conspiracy theories. Believing his story would mean accepting the frightening construct that the government had more than lost the plot—and a faceless bureaucracy had decided that those four guys from Nowheresville, USA, would somehow shoulder the blame for its stupendous fuckup in Iraq.

On September 11, 2001, the United States had sustained life-threatening wounds to its financial and government centers, after which many young men and women had heeded the call to respond to that attack with equally deadly force. Our leaders had pointed them to Iraq, and the troops had fought and died on that battlefield without question. Joe Bob and I had argued relentlessly about whether war had any merit, any redeeming value. Although he spoke passionately about the tactical intricacies of historical battles, the glorious valor of the warfighters, and the spoils of war, he had begged his son not to enlist after the 9/11 attacks. "Remember what happened in Vietnam," he told his boy. "Your government will fuck you." To me, every "preemptive" war was an utter waste of lives and treasure.

Judging the war's planners had been easy—and so, initially, was judging its fighters. After meeting Dustin and visiting Gettysburg, I began to change my mind. That so many returning fighters were being prosecuted over battlefield conduct while their leaders skated by unscathed seemed atrocious.

The next defendant we'd visit was Evan Liberty, a journey that led to even more revelations about the weakness of the prosecution's case and the inhumanity of the men's conditions. FCI Schuylkill lies about a hundred miles north of Gettysburg, deep in Pennsylvania's forested hills, down a winding highway in Minersville. Unlike at FCI Memphis, the parking lot was nearly empty. As we parked and walked up to the square, single-story visitors center, I recognized a man coming out through the double glass doors from photos of the trial. I called out to Evan's attorney, William Coffield, and introduced myself.

"Uncle Bill," as the Raven 23 defendants affectionately called him, had been visiting Evan to discuss the pending appeal. We talked for a few minutes, exchanged phone numbers, and as he walked away, I asked, "Why didn't you put on more of a defense?"

He turned back with a disconsolate look on his face. "We didn't think we had to," he said almost apologetically. "The government had no case."

Even in a prison uniform, Evan Liberty looked as if he had walked off a recruitment poster for the US Marine Corps. He was tall with close-cropped dark blond hair and square features. His demeanor was cool, zen even, as he talked about the experience of the trial and prison. He had an aura that I can only describe as spartan, disciplined, and clean that was completely at odds with the grubby prison visitors room. He had a calm, centered way of existing in space that was at odds with his gruff Yankee way of talking—abrupt, funny, and practical. He had a New England accent—not as profound as his parents' but noticeable—kind of like a wise guy from the classic films. He told me and Joe Bob that he had had some trouble with the other inmates challenging him when he had first arrived, until a copy of Erik Prince's 2013 book, *Civilian Warriors: The Inside Story of Blackwater and the Unsung Heroes of the War on Terror*, which discusses the Nisour Square incident, began circulating among the prison population. A mystique had grown up around Evan's fighting prowess, encouraged by his association with Prince and Blackwater. He thought it was ridiculous, but he was grateful that the other inmates were leaving him alone.

At that first meeting, he seemed unbothered by his prison experience—as though he were just hanging out and seeing what was going to happen next. He said he spent his days reading, doing the same workout he had done while in the Marine Corps (with necessary modifications for lack of equipment and space), and drilling Spanish vocabulary. Later, he told me that he had to think about prison as though it were another deployment to stay sane.

He also told me and Joe Bob that he had lost about thirty pounds in prison because the food was terrible. When he said that, I thought he just didn't like the institutional cooking. In fact, he was mightily battling a sort of obsessive-compulsive disorder around food. He did not admit to the depth of his anxiety until I had known him for years. He was extremely rigid and structured, especially about food and his body, and maintaining his rituals was how he survived mentally in prison. He later told me about the lengths he had gone to get fresh food—actually smuggling veggies and fruits from the kitchen in his clothes and devising a way to cook eggs on a metal desk in his cell with an extension cord.

His mom and dad, Deb and Brian, had told me that he had been a normal boy who loved sports and the outdoors. He had distinguished himself as an athlete since elementary school, and they had expected him to go to college on an athletic scholarship. But Evan had secretly visited a marine recruiter at age sixteen and persuaded his parents to let him go to boot camp at seventeen. He had risen quickly through the ranks and become a Marine Security Guard shift commander at nineteen. He had guarded the US embassies in Cairo and Guatemala with distinction, leaving the marines only because he could not get a posting to Iraq.

Evan had never drunk alcohol or done drugs, even as a teenager. He had started running road races with his parents at eight years old and by ten was running a six-minute mile. He had started working out as soon as he was allowed to when Deb took him to the day care at her gym.

Like Dustin, Evan described having been offered plea deals before and after his conviction—offers he had immediately turned down. He had returned to the United States from Colombia, where he lived with his wife, to face trial. "I didn't do anything wrong," he told me when I asked whether he regretted not taking a plea and returning home for trial. "Why would I plead guilty to something I didn't do?"

He hoped that the appeal would result in a new trial, and for good reason. As the NACDL had pointed out, there had been several reversible errors committed by both the judge and prosecutors. Evan said he was going to make no waves, stick to his routine, and get out. It was just a matter of time.

I hoped he was right. The appeal centered on some technical issues rather than the simple argument that they had been ambushed and fired their weapons in self-defense. Rather than attack the underlying convictions, the Raven 23 defense team argued that prosecutors could not try the men under a statute called the Military Extraterritorial Jurisdiction Act, which had been designed to try US citizens who worked for the Department of Defense in federal court for crimes committed abroad. It seemed like a decent argument; Blackwater's contract was with the Department of State, not the DOD, and Deputy Secretary of Defense Gordon England testified at their trial that the Blackwater men did not work for his agency, nor did the US military have any authority over the State Department's private protection squads.

The defense also planned to argue that the trial judge had allowed prosecutors to illegally "venue shop" to get a favorable jury pool in Washington, DC. No jury drawn from Maryville, Tennessee; Rochester, New Hampshire; or Olney, Texas, would have convicted military veterans on the evidence the prosecutors proffered at the 2014 trial, nor would those jurors have given a damn that Erik Prince was a conservative Christian and generous Republican donor.

Last, the defense asked for a review of the trial judge's ruling that prosecutors had committed a harmless error when they had failed to alert the defense that a key prosecution witness—an Iraqi traffic cop—had changed his story radically between his trial testimony and a posttrial victim impact statement. In a normal case, that should have been enough to overturn the verdicts or at least win a new trial.

The following weekend, I made a solo trip to El Reno, Oklahoma, where the federal prison that housed Paul Slough sits on an empty plain just outside the town, and strangely, beside a golf course. Paul, then thirty-five, had an earnest, open face, upturned nose, and ginger hair that instantly recalled for me the *Happy Days* character Richie Cunningham. That first day, we sat and talked for several hours about the case, eventually drifting into the constitutional law and American history that Paul had been studying. He talked to me about his Christian faith and his study of the Bible. He had a kind laugh and a formal, old-fashioned way of speaking and otherwise was quiet and stoic. It seemed that he grieved for more than he could say, and I didn't ask. It was difficult to imagine that thoughtful, restrained man in the noise and heat of the battle that I had read about in the court documents.

I would come to know Paul as the most inward looking, tenderhearted, and idealistic of the four Raven 23 men, and the government's betrayal hurt him more than any of the other three. Rather than fight outwardly against the lies and manipulation as Dustin did, Paul struggled internally to make sense of it—trying somehow to find a hero's journey in it.

His parents, Rick and Vivian West, described the boy they had informally adopted when he was thirteen years old as hardworking and eager to learn and please, a kid who was loyal and slow to anger, a kid who loved the ranching life in tiny Dickens, Texas, and just wanted a chance to excel and be loved.

The trial had forced Paul to realize that not everyone—even the leaders he looked up to—held the same ideals and values. And that his young life, given in service to his country, could be held so cheaply and used for ends that he could not comprehend.

"As a citizen, as a warrior, as a soldier—when you go into service of your nation, you agree to uphold the Constitution against all enemies foreign and domestic, and you go in with full faith against enemies that your country has identified as such," he told me. "It was so mind blowing that the government wasn't just lying to the American people—they had been lying for generations, and it was staggering to see it in real time."

Raised in a conservative family, he expected to serve in some way—as President John F. Kennedy had said every citizen should do. "I don't know of anything different that I could have done that day. I responded the way they trained us. The befuddling thing was we didn't change . . . the narrative changed," he told me.

The following day, I arrived to find his wife, Christin, and three-year-old daughter, Lily, in the visitors room. I had spoken and emailed with Christin, but it was the first time we had met. I immediately vibed with her candor and recognized that her charisma and easy beauty, along with Lily's angelic face and adorable precociousness, would be an enormous asset in any public relations effort to free the men.

I did not stay long. Christin drove eight hours round trip each weekend to the prison to give Lily time with her daddy, and every moment was precious. Lily had been eighteen months old when her father had gone on trial, and she had no memory of him other than in prison. It was as though Lily, as well as Dustin's children, Hannah and Quinn, were players in some bizarre theater brought to the world's stage by the US government—caught in an amber unreality until their fathers were not just freed but exonerated by the appeals court.

My last trip, to FCI Coleman, had me flying to Florida to meet with Nick Slatten. I was supposed to meet Nick's mother, Reba, and his sister, Jessica, at a motel near the prison, but a few days before I was to fly out, I received a letter from the Bureau of Prisons canceling my visit. Nick remained a cipher for several months simply because the BOP made it so difficult for me to speak with him.

The youngest of the Raven 23 men, Nick had had the most misfortune heaped upon him. He had gone from a talented teenage army marksman from the Tennessee woodlands to a man sentenced to life in prison for a crime he could not possibly have committed, if one believes the laws of physics.

I saw Nick in person only once during that time—at his sentencing. He was tall and rangy with a shaved head, blue eyes, and a cautious look. He was the fifth generation in his family to serve in the military, joining the army's 82nd Airborne Division almost as soon as he graduated from White County High School in Sparta, Tennessee. His family had lived in the same area for those five generations, raising cattle and horses, hunting and tending the land. When he wasn't helping his dad with the animals, Nick would get lost in the woods, caves, and hills around his home, hunting and exploring on his own. He especially loved the company of the older generation, sitting for hours on the porch to hear them tell stories of the old days.

In the many phone calls we had over the years, I thought he had attained a masterful level of emotional restraint: He had gone from being hopped up on prescription PTSD meds and threatening to shoot a man in an altercation in a feed store parking lot before his trial to, as a prisoner, sitting unbothered as men tried to goad him into attacking a suspected Muslim terrorist sitting in front of him.

Whenever I asked how he was doing when he called from prison, he would invariably say, "I'm blessed." I believed him. His life in prison was taken up with working on his case, doing mixed martial arts, reading the Bible, and ministering to fellow inmates. He talked freely of his own weaknesses and chose every day not to give way to cynicism, trying to get stronger in his conviction to love and forgive. His voice, movements, and speech were deliberate and even; he once told me he called out to Jesus every morning before his feet hit the floor, like a shield against the memories and fears and trauma of the past decade. Prison, he said, had made him more present. "My walk with Jesus is the greatest change," he told me. "He took a heart of stone and made it flesh. Filled me with His love so love is what usually comes out of me. I used to push away anyone who tried to love me. I give all the credit to Jesus."

The men were limited to something like 360 minutes of phone time per month, doled out in fifteen-minute increments. When they could access the prison telephones, they understandably wanted to speak with their loved ones. We exchanged emails after those initial visits, but I still had no idea what I could do for them.

The news coverage of the incident and trial had been so negative that former colleagues I spoke with at major news outlets had no interest in the story and, frankly, talked to me as though I were crazy for wanting to revisit it. Later, when my literary agent in California said he would not represent a book about the Raven 23 case for personal and "moral" reasons, I approached other agents who had successfully sold military-related projects to publishers. All of them turned me down as well.

However, several journalists understood the gravity of the story and its importance to every American. As I researched the news coverage about Nisour Square to figure out how to attack the government's misinformation campaign, I found an excellent series by Harrison Thorp, the editor of *The Rochester Voice*, in Evan Liberty's hometown. From what I could tell from reading his coverage, he had come to the story with the same doubts I had.

"When I first read about it, I saw the four faces of the defendants, and I gotta tell you, I said, 'Boy, these guys don't look like monsters, but I guess they did it because the overwhelming press report was that they had done it,'" he told me. "They were reckless, maverick Blackwater thugs, and they finally got what was coming to them."

Thorp first tried to find someone who knew the Liberty family, but for several months after the verdict, he hit dead ends. Finally, he tracked down Brian Liberty, Evan's father, at a golf tournament. "I went to the Rochester Country Club to do a story on SimGolf . . . and there was a guy with a T-shirt that had 'Raven 23' on it. And I said, 'Are you related to anybody with Raven 23?' . . . and he said, 'I'm Evan's father.' And we sat down and had a long talk."

As he dug into the case, Thorp recognized many of the same problems with the trial that I had. He was particularly incensed by the fact that the DOJ had charged the men with using the automatic weapons issued to them by the State Department, allegedly to commit crimes. The gun charge, designed to lengthen the sentences of drug dealers in the 1980s, carried a thirty-year mandatory minimum sentence. It proved to Thorp that the Raven 23 defendants had been railroaded. "That's when I was all in," he said.

In follow-up stories, he queried Rochester's congressional representatives, mobilized the community to sign a petition to free

Evan and his comrades, and pushed back against the misinformation the government was peddling in the appeal.

The headlines coming out of Rochester were brash and breathtaking: "The Long and Twisted Prosecution of Evan Liberty and Raven 23," "The Pesky Facts That Show Political Bias, Deceit in Evan Liberty's Prosecution," "Veep Biden's Promise for 'Iraqi Justice' Threw Evan Liberty, Raven 23 Under the Bus."

I went back to the court documents to boil down a decade's worth of legal wrangling into the story of what had really happened in Nisour Square at ten minutes to noon on September 16, 2007. I started with the written statements the nineteen men in the Raven 23 convoy had made to State Department investigators two days afterward. Those were supposed to be kept confidential as part of their personnel files. The interesting thing about the statements was this: The contractors could not be fired or prosecuted for anything they said—unless they lied to investigators. So I presumed that those statements were likely the most truthful accounts of what each man had seen that day. Even more interesting was the fact that nearly every one of them said they had either seen or heard incoming enemy AK-47 and small-arms fire.[5]

The statements were pretty dry and filled with military lingo, so I tracked down several members of the team, including Thomas Vargas and Edward Randall, the vehicle commander and driver of the rearmost or "follow" vehicle, to get more details. I spoke with Blackwater managers Nick Poulos and Keith George, who had been manning the Blackwater Tactical Operations Center (TOC) that day, to find out what they had heard and what had happened after Raven 23 had returned to the Green Zone. I combed through emails that the government had seized from Raven 23 team members to find out what the men had been saying about the shootings to one another and their friends and families right after it happened.[6]

When I put it all together, it went something like this.

CHAPTER THREE

★★★

WHAT ACTUALLY HAPPENED IN NISOUR SQUARE

The past was erased, the erasure forgotten, the lie became the truth.

—GEORGE ORWELL, *NINETEEN EIGHTY-FOUR*

IT WAS A SUNDAY, a workday for Iraqis, whose businesses, banks, and government offices are open from Saturday through Thursday. It was hot and sunny. A few minutes before noon on September 16, 2007, a massive explosion jolted the Green Zone, the US-controlled area at the center of Baghdad, and soldiers within the zone could see a plume of smoke rise about a mile northwest of its cement blast walls.

Across town, the radio chatter began immediately in the Blackwater compound: A car bomb had detonated about twenty-five yards from a complex of offices called the Izdihar financial compound, where a US diplomat was meeting with her Iraqi counterparts. The State Department had immediately ordered Raven 4, the Blackwater personal security detail, to return her to the Green Zone.

The diplomat, Rodeina Fattah, worked for the United States Agency for International Development (USAID), the agency tasked with rebuilding Iraq's shattered public services. She had been handing out scholarships that day. When Fattah and Raven 4 had left the Green Zone earlier that morning, Raven 22 and Raven 23 had been placed on standby for exactly the situation they faced now.

Dustin Heard was in his trailer, getting dressed to work out in the compound's gym. Raven 22 was called to Patriot Parking Lot first to arm and load up, but a short time later, Dustin's radio crackled to life: "Two-three, two-three to the trucks!" Time to go to work, he thought. He shucked off his gym clothes and put on a fire-retardant flight suit and body armor.

Dustin didn't care that his teammates called him "Extreme" for the amount of armor and ammunition he took along on each mission. As those ugly months wore on with heavier fighting and more casualties, he looked like a prophet. His nickname was no worse than Nick Slatten's moniker, "Stewie," from the bigheaded baby in the *Family Guy* cartoon, or "Otis," given to Paul Slough after the town drunk in *The Andy Griffith Show* and the fact that, bearded, he resembled the Otis Driftwood character in the Rob Zombie film *House of 1000 Corpses*. Evan Liberty was called "Libo" for obvious reasons, and a turret gunner named Jeremy Ridgeway was tagged "Mancow" for his apparent aversion to physical training and the weight he had gained.

Dressed and armed within five minutes, Dustin joined the rest of the team in Patriot Parking Lot and began loading the follow vehicle—the last in line—where he would take up his usual position in the rear turret along with driver Eddie Randall, fire team member Dean Wagler, and tactical commander Tommy Vargas, with Ridgeway in the front turret.

That morning, as usual, Blackwater's intelligence analyst Mia Laczek-Johnson had briefed the teams and reviewed the safest routes through Baghdad. One of the preferred routes from the Izdihar compound back to the Green Zone went through a traffic circle called Nisour Square in the affluent Mansour neighborhood.

Mia also told the Raven teams to be on the lookout for a white Kia sedan, a possible car bomb. Intelligence reports did not specify its target or where in Baghdad it was located, she said.[1] White Kia sedans were among the most common vehicles in Iraq and so were often flagged on the BOLO list. She also reminded them that the insurgency had put a bounty on their heads—$50,000 for each dead Blackwater guard. Because of that threat, Blackwater employees had been told to stop wearing clothing or hats bearing Blackwater's black-and-red bear paw insignia or to cover it with a US flag patch.

After Raven 22, the team on duty, took off to help take Fattah to safety, Raven 23 sat in the Patriot Parking Lot and waited. For Dustin, that was the hardest part of his job. It was not the fear of battle, he later said; it was the waiting, knowing that people were in trouble. "It just eats at you while you're sitting there. It's like a dog on a leash. You let go of the leash, and then they go."

The four vehicles idled loud and hot at Checkpoint 12, the nineteen men nervously swapping jokes on an internal communication channel. In the lead vehicle, driver Corey Wainscott and Daniel Childers sat up front with fire team member Dustin Hill in the back, and Mark Mealy and Donald Ball manning the front- and rear-facing turret guns, respectively.

The emergency response vehicle (ERV) carried driver Jeremy Skinner, medic Kevin Rhodes, and fire team member Jeremy Krueger inside and Matthew Murphy and Adam Frost in the front and rear turrets. In the command vehicle, third in line, shift leader Jimmy Watson, a US Marine veteran nicknamed "Hoss," sat up front beside driver Evan Liberty. Watson was talking to the Blackwater TOC on a secure channel that the rest of the team could not hear. Inside the command vehicle, Nick Slatten readied his SR-25 sniper rifle, making sure there was a round in the chamber, and prayed to God to keep the team safe and make him fight better than his enemy. Paul Slough waited in the vehicle's single turret.

"Lead's up."

"ERV's up."
"Command's up."
"Follow's up."

They were ready to go as soon as the TOC gave Watson the go-ahead. Dustin Heard, in the follow vehicle's rear-facing turret, noticed that the front turret was empty; Ridgeway was missing. Typical, he thought. Ridgeway had been in country about nine months and had earned a reputation as a talented marksman but also an oddball. He was disorganized, told improbable tales about his battlefield prowess, and was frequently late to missions.

Watson told the convoy to roll out; the rest of the team would not learn until they limped back—bullet riddled and dragging the command vehicle—that Watson had disobeyed the TOC's order to hold Raven 23 at Checkpoint 12. Watson, who received government immunity to testify, later said at the 2014 trial that he did "not believe they gave me that order" but also that TOC's order "would mean hanging out at the checkpoint until I make a decision, . . . until I, not [TOC commander] Nick Poulos, . . . make a decision on what's going to happen, because . . . he's in an office, . . . and I'm in charge of the team and what we're going to do." Watson represented his choice as one taken in the absence of other input, but in fact, Poulos had ordered him to stay at the checkpoint. The other members of Raven 23 did not know that they were proceeding out contrary to orders. Later, Watson would become a key witness in the government's effort to portray his brothers in arms as lawless vigilantes.[2]

Dustin Heard told Vargas to leave without the front turret gunner. But Ridgeway, then thirty-six years old, showed up and climbed into the turret as the vehicle slow rolled toward the parking area's exit.

The trip to Nisour Square was short—about a tenth of a mile down a one-lane serpentine alley with tall blast walls on either side, not an easy maneuver in large, armored trucks. Insurgents would sometimes dig out chunks of concrete, bury explosives in the holes, and cover them with fresh concrete. It was the equivalent of riding through a shooting gallery.

Traffic poured into Nisour Square from four divided roadways in the north, south, east, and west. There were no lanes, no stoplights, just Iraqi traffic cops trying to keep the cars flowing around a large empty fountain in the center of the traffic circle. A car bomb had demolished part of a tunnel that fed into the traffic circle, and months later, it was still under reconstruction. The Blackwater convoy drove in from the north and took up positions on the south side of the circle. The four vehicles sat in a semicircle, blocking the southern lanes of traffic, so that Raven 4 and Raven 22 could whisk Fattah through the northern end of the traffic circle and into the Green Zone through Checkpoint 12. There were a square cement structure that served as a bus shelter about a hundred meters down a road south of the circle and a kiosk immediately south of the circle for Iraqi police to shelter in.

"Lock it down," Watson told the men over the internal communications channel. It was eleven minutes after noon, according to Blackwater radio logs.

Mealy, standing in the turret of the first vehicle, scanned his surroundings looking north-northwest. He saw armed Iraqi National Police and Iraqi Army personnel stationed around the traffic circle and a uniformed Iraqi policeman in the kiosk. He wasn't doing much to help stop traffic, he noted. He scanned the rooftops of the buildings surrounding the circle; there were armed men there, too. An Iraqi army convoy of armored vehicles and armed men drove through.

He waved them off. Off to his left, he saw an Iraqi soldier in what he later described as a "fighting position" behind a wall of sandbags.

He glanced back over his shoulder, to the south, and saw four of the seven turret gunners, Paul Slough, Dustin Heard, Jeremy Ridgeway, and Donald Ball, waving to motorists approaching the circle from the south. They were displaying their weapons and motioning the drivers to stay back.

Two things happened almost at once. First, Jimmy Watson, in the passenger seat of the third vehicle, heard *pop-pop-pop*—the sound of an AK-47, the weapon carried by insurgents. Mealy saw bullets skipping off the pavement. Somebody was shooting, but it wasn't clear where it was coming from.

Tommy Vargas, sitting in the follow vehicle behind the rest of the convoy, had the best view of what transpired next through the thick, bulletproof glass of his south-facing side window and front windshield.[3] Almost immediately, he saw bullets striking the ground toward the center of the convoy, aimed at the follow, command, and emergency response vehicles. Tracing the gunfire back to its source, he saw two men dressed in Iraqi National Police and Iraqi Army uniforms crouching behind a row of scrubby trees in a median about thirty-five to forty yards to the south. It was strange to see Iraqi army and police personnel together, and something was odd about the uniforms the men were wearing, he thought. Iraqi soldiers wore brown camouflage, and the Iraqi National Police uniforms consisted of white or light blue shirts and blue pants. But those uniforms were somehow . . . off, he thought. The soldier was wearing camouflage pants, but his brown T-shirt was untucked. Then they lifted AK-47s and began firing in his direction.

As he watched the rounds kick up debris from the pavement around the vehicles in front of him, Vargas hesitated calling out, "Enemy contact!" as he tried to determine whether the Iraqi gunmen were actually enemy combatants shooting at the Blackwater convoy or legitimate Iraqi law enforcement personnel shooting at someone behind the stopped traffic.

As Vargas called "Contact, contact, contact, nine o'clock, my left flank" over the internal communications channel, a 40 mm, "40 Mike-Mike," grenade launched by one of the Blackwater turret gunners hit the gunmen's position. Someone else in the convoy had seen the gunmen and had taken them out, he thought. But the spray of automatic gunfire continued, this time coming from behind the cars jammed up in the lanes south of the circle. Vargas saw the rear windshields of vehicles explode as the gunmen fired indiscriminately through the parked vehicles at the Blackwater convoy.

Watson then noticed two gunmen hiding between a flatbed "bongo" truck and a berm on the southwest side of the traffic circle. When they started shooting at the convoy, he called out the enemy contact over the radio.

Next, a white Kia sedan separated from the stopped traffic and drove slowly, at about five miles per hour, around the vehicles in front of it and aimed itself straight at the command vehicle.

Watson, who had been startled by Vargas's assertion that Iraqi police were firing at the convoy, alerted the Blackwater TOC that they were taking incoming fire from multiple points around the traffic circle. It was 12:12.

At 12:13, Watson called for backup from Blackwater MH-6 Little Bird helicopters. He heard the hiss of pen flares, small flares that Blackwater convoys used to warn drivers to stay away.

Eddie Randall, driving the follow vehicle, heard his turret gunners, Dustin Heard and Jeremy Ridgeway, run through the rules of engagement, hoping to alert the driver of the white Kia to back off. Paul Slough ordered the driver to stop in Arabic and English, tried hand signals, then sent water bottles and a pen flare arcing off the vehicle's windshield. They were halfway through the list of deterrent actions demanded by the State Department's rules of engagement, and still the driver kept rolling forward.

In the command vehicle's lone turret, Paul Slough was quickly losing any doubt that the white Kia was exactly what they had been warned of that morning: a vehicle-borne improvised explosive device. He fired his machine gun into the vehicle's grille, and as it continued its slow forward motion, aimed at the driver, and squeezed the trigger. The man died instantly, shot through the forehead. The woman in the passenger seat began wailing and cradled his body. The men would later learn that the Kia had not been a bomb, but what happened next made the threat level even harder to interpret.

One of the Iraqi officers standing in the nearby traffic kiosk ran to the driver's door. He yanked on it, but it was jammed. But to Eddie Randall, driving the follow vehicle, it looked as though the cop was pushing the suspected car bomb toward them. Up in the front turret, Ridgeway assumed the same thing and, he later told investigators, fired his M-4 rifle into the passenger-side windshield, killing the woman inside.

At the same moment, two gunmen began shooting at the convoy from the bus shelter about fifty meters behind the Kia. Paul Slough fired machine-gun rounds at where he saw the muzzle flashes until he got no answering fire. Seconds later, he saw a man in a blue shirt and black pants standing beside a large truck near the convoy and pointing an AK-47 at Dustin Heard. Slough engaged the man and killed him.

He turned back to the Kia. Its driver was dead, the windshield and front grille mangled, but it kept rolling toward the convoy. Four of the convoy's seven turret gunners—Heard, Slough, Ridgeway, and Ball—lit into the vehicle with their machine guns. Vargas noticed Ridgeway's explosive gunfire, believing initially that it was aimed at a couple of armed men standing behind the white car. But when Ridgeway did not let up, Vargas feared that he would melt the barrel of his weapon and render it inoperable. He called up to Ridgeway in the turret, "Cease fucking fire!" He elbowed the turret gunner's kneecap.

Sometime during these first few moments of the gun battle, sniper Nick Slatten, peering out a porthole in the side of the command vehicle, spotted two men in civilian clothing shooting at the convoy from the tree line through his scope. He heard the impacts of bullets landing on the side of the command vehicle. He fired one shot from his SR-25 rifle at the closest gunman. The gunman went down and did not fire again. He engaged the other shooter, who dropped out of sight behind a white truck.

In the command vehicle, Watson told Evan Liberty, the driver, to kick his door open. When Evan did so, Watson leaned over him and shot a magazine's worth of M-4 rounds into the Kia's engine. As the vehicle continued to approach, he shot an M203 grenade into the door. The vehicle stopped. The Kia was now fully engulfed in flames with the driver and passenger dead inside. The Blackwater convoy was still taking small-arms fire. Vargas was speaking into the radio to the Blackwater TOC, calling in muzzle flashes he saw in some bushes south of the traffic circle. Watson again ordered Evan to open the door of the command vehicle. This time, Evan shot at two men firing on the convoy from southeast of the circle.

Vargas told Randall to reposition the truck so turret gunners Dustin Heard and Jeremy Ridgeway could get tighter beads on enemy shooters to the south, near the bus shelter, and avoid flames that were leaping out of the burning Kia. At some point during the shooting, a tracer round skipped off the ground or the truck, hit the chin strap of Dustin Heard's helmet, and landed in the crook of his arm, burning a hole in his Nomex flight suit. Randall repositioned the truck and looked out the left-side window just as a hail of bullets hit the side of the vehicle and the fragments splattered off the flat steel surface.

As he scanned in front of him, Randall saw radiator fluid pouring out from beneath the command vehicle just as the TOC ordered them to disengage and return to the Green Zone. But the enemy fire had rendered the imposing command vehicle useless. The four crewmembers were trapped inside an eight-ton albatross. It was now 12:15, according to Blackwater's radio log.

Watson ordered the first and fourth trucks repositioned to shield fire team members from gunfire while they hooked up a tow strap between the second and third vehicles. "Please don't let me get shot," turret gunner Adam Frost pleaded as he climbed out of the second truck to hook up the strap.

At 12:18, Watson told the Blackwater TOC that Raven 23 was exiting Nisour Square. As the command vehicle was towed out, it passed a red bus stopped at the intersection. Gunfire erupted from the side windows of the bus. Paul Slough engaged the gunman who had hidden inside among the passengers, killing him. Inside the command vehicle, Nick Slatten watched through his scope as uniformed Iraqi police shot at the convoy as it drove out of Nisour Square.

At the convoy's tail end, Dustin Heard threw out smoke grenades to mask their retreat from the traffic circle. Eddie Randall looked in his rearview mirror and saw smoke filling the street. As they drove into oncoming traffic, Dustin Heard reported to Watson that the follow vehicle was still taking small-arms fire from the rear. Watson ordered him to shoot back. "Negative," Dustin said. "I don't have a target."

Randall also heard sounds from the other turret gunner, Ridgeway, discharging what he later calculated were more than a hundred rounds.

The traffic leaving Nisour Square was heavy, and the Blackwater trucks pushed civilian vehicles out of the way to avoid getting trapped in an ambush. The follow vehicle got pinned against a T-wall, and as Randall got it unstuck, it crushed the side of a sedan with an open sunroof. Vargas looked down through the sunroof and saw the sole occupant, an Iraqi man, bouncing around inside the car as the huge truck jostled past. He made an apologetic gesture, then sucked in his breath as bullets ripped into the car's interior. The man desperately tried to move from the driver's seat to the passenger's seat as bullets convulsed his body. Vargas thought he was taking fire from the enemy gunmen who were still shooting at the convoy. Then he focused on the sound of the machine gun firing from the front turret. He realized that Ridgeway was shooting the driver. He yelled up at the turret gunner, "Cease fucking fire! Cease fire!" He watched in horror as the driver took rounds to the jaw and face and to his body and legs. His body was mangled. The convoy limped back to the Green Zone through heavy traffic, towing the command vehicle and taking small-arms fire the entire route.

As Raven 23 arrived at the Patriot Parking Lot, Blackwater shift leader Nick Poulos was stuck in the TOC, trying to defuse a standoff between the Iraqi Army and Raven 22. Raven 22 had delivered Fattah safely to the Green Zone, then returned to Nisour Square to extricate Raven 23 but the two teams had missed each other.

Poulos called Watson on his cell phone and told him to stand Raven 23 down. "Stay in the parking lot, don't go anywhere," he told Watson.

"Fuck you. I'm going to go out if I need to help people, and I'm going to do what I need to do," Watson told him. Poulos asked his boss, Keith George, the Blackwater detail leader, to deal with Watson. "Watson is refusing to stand down," he told George. "Can you go and relieve him of his duty?" George met the team at the parking lot, noting fresh bullet impacts that looked like craters all over the armored vehicles.

T. J. Hill, a Blackwater mechanic, inspected the vehicles a short time later. He saw Evan Liberty looking at the steel doors of the command vehicle, and the two made note of five impacts on the side of the truck. The left rear tire had been shot out, and the engine had been disabled after the truck had taken rounds; that much seemed clear to the mechanic.

Hill popped the hood and stuck a hose into the radiator. He climbed into the engine compartment and saw water coming out the back of the radiator in a stream the size of a pencil. "Well, there's your problem," he told Liberty. The impact mark had left a crater typical of a bullet strike, he later said. It seemed pretty obvious to Hill that a bullet had hit the ground and bounced up, hitting the differential and then the radiator. That trajectory was consistent with a round fired from a grassy area southwest of the circle, where State Department investigators would find eight AK-47 shell casings days after the incident.

The follow vehicle also showed about a dozen fresh strikes on its steel plates. Dustin Heard was the only team member with injuries; the burns to his arms caused by the tracer round were serious.

The last order of business for Keith George at Patriot Parking Lot was relieving Watson of his command for good for taking the team into the Red Zone against orders from the TOC. It was a short conversation, with Watson protesting but handing over his weapons.

As George dealt with Raven 23, Poulos tried to mediate a standoff between Raven 22 and heavily armed Iraqi army and police personnel, who had blocked all avenues of egress from Nisour Square. Poulos contacted the State Department operations center and asked for US Army assistance from nearby Forward Operating Base Prosperity. The army arrived minutes later and escorted Raven 22 back to the Green Zone.

In the meantime, Army Captain Peter Decareau, from FOB Prosperity, began interviewing Iraqi civilians about what they had seen and photographing piles of AK-47 shell casings in several locations around the southern sweep of the traffic circle. He later handed over to an army investigator his interview notes, which documented statements from several Iraqi witnesses who had seen gunmen firing on the convoy, as well as photographs of enemy shell casings. As one defense attorney later told me, "He lost all those notes. The army burned them in a burn bag. . . . [Decareau] had written down the names and addresses of all the Iraqis who told him that [Raven 23 had taken incoming fire], and they were lost." He added, "I always thought that was an unusual feature of the case, that you have a credible army officer who is first on the scene, whose contemporaneous interviews support the defense theory of the case, and those notes were lost."

As luck would have it, an army drone flying over Nisour Square at noon on September 16, 2007, filmed the incident. Prosecutors asked analysts from the National Geospatial-Intelligence Agency to evaluate the images and footage in 2009 but inexplicably failed to ask the agency to preserve the footage for a possible trial. By the time of the trial, only forty-six seconds—in the middle of the footage—remained.

In the Green Zone, two contractors from a rival outfit heard the gun battle and climbed up to the top of an observation post overlooking Nisour Square. One of them pulled out a video camera and began filming the aftermath of the gun battle: the smoking Kia and the confrontation between Raven 22 and the Iraqi Army. Within an hour, the images were all over the internet and the international news.

CHAPTER FOUR

── ★★★ ──

THE FRAME-UP BEGINS

The first casualty when war comes is truth.

—US SENATOR AND CALIFORNIA
GOVERNOR HIRAM JOHNSON

THE HOPI NATIVE AMERICAN tribe has been credited with the wisdom that "he who tells the stories rules the world." When I worked at the Los Angeles *Daily Journal* covering law firms, a bearded gentleman who looked like a 1970s hippie walked into the *Journal* offices with a crazy story about how O'Melveny & Myers, one of the world's largest and most powerful law firms, was trying to paper over an environmental disaster at an unfinished high school in East Los Angeles. According to that man, O'Melveny had helped its client Kajima Urban Development win the contract to build the state-of-the-art Belmont Learning Center for another client, the Los Angeles Unified School District (LAUSD), but the project had gone off the rails when Kajima had allegedly failed to disclose or mitigate pockets of explosive methane gas beneath the ground. By the time that alleged omission was discovered, the budget for the Belmont Learning Center had already ballooned past $200 million and nobody could figure out how to make the half-constructed school safe enough to open. So there it sat beside the 110 Freeway, an eyesore dubbed "the world's most expensive high school" and a boondoggle by the media.

The LAUSD sued the law firm and Kajima, and state lawmakers called for a criminal investigation. O'Melveny faced potentially hundreds of millions of dollars in malpractice damages: in addition to writing the contracts, O'Melveny lawyers had sat on the selection committee that had chosen Kajima. The firm had a strong incentive to get the problem to go away, and according to my bearded visitor, it was mounting a campaign to convince the school district that the methane gas pockets shouldn't be a barrier to opening the school, forgive Kajima, and complete the project.

I had heard about the lawsuit but was skeptical about the story because the teachers' union and the LAUSD were in the midst of contract negotiations and I thought that perhaps it was some sort of bargaining tactic. However, I called O'Melveny and was surprised when the firm hooked me up with a $950-an-hour senior partner who invited me to his office and showed me a persuasive PowerPoint presentation that downplayed the risks to students and explained how the school could be opened safely. I knew as soon as I saw that dog-and-pony show that something was up. It turned out that the firm was holding "informational" meetings in the low-income community to convince parents to demand that the LAUSD complete the school.

I admired O'Melveny's determination to control the narrative around the school and wondered whether it would make a difference. I wrote about the campaign in a story that won investigative awards from the Society of Professional Journalists Los Angeles and the California Teachers Association.

O'Melveny's efforts worked. A few years later, construction began again at the Belmont Center site, and the school opened—at a cost of $400 million—in 2008. O'Melveny changed the horrific tale of an unscrupulous law firm and its greedy client endangering children with an exploding school into a story about two benevolent corporations that were trying to build a state-of-the-art high school for underprivileged children.[1]

The lesson is clear: Whoever controls the story controls the world. The US government understands this well. The government's narrative that in 2007, four Oakley-wearing, gun-toting, raghead-hating American mercenaries had mercilessly cut down dozens of innocent Iraqi civilians would dominate the news coverage of the Raven 23 case despite a different story told by the evidence. The government would demonstrate in the days and years after Nisour Square that it was willing to peddle total fabrications to make American warfighters look bad—and that it would enlist an eager and incurious media in shaping that narrative. The question was: Why?

As Dustin Heard sat in the chow hall nursing his scorched arm and trying to absorb what had just happened, a CNN special report banner flashed across the television screens mounted on the wall. The video had been shot from a tower in the Green Zone facing Nisour Square. The reporter on the scene quoted Iraqi officials as saying that American contractors had shot and killed a number of people in the busy traffic circle. The report showed video of Nisour Square as Raven 23 moved out and Raven 22 moved in, along with tight shots of bullet casings, the burnt shell of the Kia, Iraqi and American troops patrolling the scene, and a discarded magazine inscribed with the name "Liberty" on the pavement.

It is worth noting that American war zone reporters were mostly confined to bureaus located in heavily guarded compounds near the Green Zone in what ABC News Baghdad Correspondent Terry McCarthy called "extremely unsatisfying, frustrating and frankly less than ideal journalistic conditions." The bureaus often had to rely on Iraqi staff to cover stories in the Red Zone and feed the information to Western news desks. In addition to access and cultural context, the Iraqi correspondents also brought local biases to their reporting. "Depending on whom you sent out—and we all had crews from both sides—you would likely get different versions of the same story, depending if it's a Sunni or a Shi'a group," he told me. "It wasn't that they were lying. It was just that they would talk to their own people . . . and you would get different versions."

It is also worth noting that in Baghdad during that period, it was so dangerous for Western journalists to leave their bureaus that they were driven to assignments by private security guards in armored vehicles with thick bulletproof glass and were often limited to fifteen minutes on location.

"The streets were, of course, not policed, so militias on both sides were looking for targets of opportunity, and foreigners were right up at the top of the list," McCarthy told me. "Western crews were scared for their lives, [and] it just wasn't practical for them to do a lot of that work because they wouldn't last. Sometimes they would have to hightail it after five minutes or they would risk getting kidnapped or shot."

Some of the men in the chow hall began ribbing Evan Liberty about the magazines, which had apparently fallen out of the command vehicle when Watson told him to kick open the door. Paul Slough watched the report with dismay, thinking *They're saying we're guilty of something.* Several team members went back to their trailers and sent emails or made quick calls to loved ones after seeing the news report, assuring them that they were fine and that what was being played over and over on cable news loops was far more dramatic than what had occurred. "It was just another day at the office," Paul Slough told his wife, Christin.

In Rochester, New Hampshire, workmates of Evan Liberty's mom, Deb, took pains that she did not hear the news reports at the restaurant where she worked. "My coworkers noticed something about it on TV, and I didn't even notice that they had shut off all the TVs so I wouldn't see it," she said later. "I didn't know anything about it until later that afternoon when [my husband] Brian told me there was an incident, but Evan was okay. He didn't know much about it. I didn't realize how severe it was at that time."

Stacey Heard got a call from Dustin after seeing a report about a civilian "massacre" involving a Blackwater Tactical Support Team (TST). "I'm all right," Dustin told him. "That's not what happened."

In the first few hours after the shooting, Keith George shepherded each of the Raven 23 team members to interviews at the Presidential Palace with the State Department's Diplomatic Security Service (DSS). DSS Special Agent Theodore Carpenter oversaw those oral interviews, which detailed the actions that each team member had taken in Nisour Square, and then assembled the statements into a report. State Department procedures also required all Blackwater personnel involved in shooting incidents to prepare written statements. On September 18, 2007, they returned to the palace and submitted their accounts to the DSS in interviews that were characterized as part of the "After Action Report" rather than a State Department investigation.

The same day at Iraqi National Police (INP) headquarters, DSS investigators interviewed fourteen Iraqi nationals who claimed to have witnessed the Nisour Square incident. Several were INP officers or traffic policemen posted at Nisour Square at the time of the incident; these witnesses had been identified as such by the INP.

Over the following days, DSS investigators called Slough, Slatten, Ball, and Heard to ask them more questions focusing on specific details. On September 20, 2007, DSS investigators conducted an incident scene investigation at the traffic circle, taking photos, collecting physical evidence, and interviewing witnesses.

Yet another round of interviews followed to clear up discrepancies in the number and types of rounds fired at different threats. During that interview, the DSS investigator focused for the first time on the round count, which was off because Jimmy Watson denied having fired his weapon.[2] Paul Slough acknowledged having fired an M203 grenade at the white Kia sedan.

THE FRAME-UP BEGINS   59

What's interesting, given the later excoriation of the Raven 23 team, is that early accounts by both the media and the government supported their story. A volley of media accounts of the Nisour Square gun battle immediately followed the CNN report, with State Department officials asserting that Raven 23 had been engaged in a firefight and that its actions had been taken to neutralize a number of insurgent threats.

An account of the battle, filed from Baghdad on the day of the attack by *New York Times* reporter Sabrina Tavernise, listed a body count of eight—exactly the number of gunmen that Raven 23 members in the south-facing trucks had reported. "The Iraqi government said Monday that it had revoked the license of Blackwater USA, a private security company that provides protection for top American officials in Iraq, after shots fired from an American diplomatic convoy killed eight Iraqis," the *Times* report said. In that same statement, the Iraqi government condemned Blackwater for having caused a combined twelve fatalities and injuries in Nisour Square—just one-third of the casualties that would later be attributed to Raven 23 by US prosecutors. Where did the extra bodies come from?

A second *New York Times* story, written two days later by Tavernise, added the detail that two other deadly incidents involving US troops had occurred on the same day within a mile of Nisour Square and resulted in Iraqi casualties. "An official at Yarmouk Hospital, where the dead and wounded were taken, said 12 dead Iraqis had been taken in from three different incidents," the report said. "Thirty-seven more Iraqis were wounded."

The first sign that the US government planned to throw the members of Raven 23 under the bus occurred weeks after the incident when a source inside the State Department leaked the men's protected statements to ABC News, a violation of the Blackwater contractors' employment contract. Both Republicans and Democrats seized on the incident and the Blackwater shooters as a convenient distraction; most knew that they would soon have to answer to their constituents in the upcoming election for their votes authorizing the increasingly unpopular wars.

The State Department's investigative process had changed after Nisour Square, with the coming of Ryan Crocker as US ambassador to Iraq, Keith George told me. Unlike his predecessor, Zalmay Khalilzad, Crocker seemingly had an agenda: to make it look as though President George W. Bush's "surge" was working and that Iraqi Sunnis and Shi'as were fighting for their country rather than each other. "Ambassador Crocker was not a fan of Blackwater," he told me. "He made no bones about that, and he was probably more of the stereotypical State Department ambassador type: kinder, gentler, all we need to do is hug it out and we'll be okay."

On November 14, 2007, ABC News posted Paul Slough's September 18 written statement in its entirety on its website. Portions of the other guards' statements appeared in reports by ABC News, MSNBC/*Newsweek*, *The Washington Post*, *The New York Times*, *Time*/CNN, and other sources. The coverage became so overwhelming that many of the Blackwater guards set up Google News alerts to email them news stories about the gun battle.

The coverage ratcheted up the pressure on the State Department, especially after the Senate Armed Services Committee called Erik Prince to testify on October 2, 2007, about Nisour Square and other shootings involving civilians. Prince testified that his employees had been responding to hostile fire and the threat of a car bomb in Nisour Square. He came away from the hearing convinced that his company would be blamed for the US military failures in Iraq in a "rush to judgment." "Based on everything we currently know, the Blackwater team acted appropriately while operating in a very complex war zone on Sept. 16," he said.

The New York Times noted that the "lines of debate quickly formed along party lines" with Democrats hostile to the wealthy and conservative Christian Blackwater founder. Prince pointed out that thirty Blackwater employees had lost their lives protecting US diplomats in a "dangerous and hostile" environment, yet had not lost a single protectee.

I abhorred hiring mercenaries to fight wars simply because US lawmakers are too cowardly to reinstate a draft. But I had to admit that the US government certainly got its money's worth from Blackwater, which dealt with the chaotic aftermath of Bush's short-sighted decision to remove Saddam Hussein from power with no realistic plan to stabilize Iraq. Also, I knew that the Blackwater guards had gone to Iraq to perform a defensive role but increasingly found themselves fighting alongside US troops in a mission creep that proved to be their undoing in court.

Representative Henry A. Waxman, a California Democrat who headed the panel, chose to emphasize Blackwater's economic gains rather than the sacrifices of its men, all of whom were US military veterans. "Privatizing is working exceptionally well for Blackwater," he said. "The question for this hearing is whether outsourcing to Blackwater is a good deal to the American taxpayer."

A report by the committee's Democratic majority's staff contended that "Blackwater guards had engaged in nearly 200 shootings in Iraq since 2005, and in the vast majority of cases the guards fired their weapons from moving vehicles without stopping to count the dead or assist the wounded," *The New York Times* reported in October 2007. "In at least two cases, Blackwater paid victims' family members who complained, and the company sought to cover up other episodes," the report said.

Secretary of State Condoleezza Rice jumped on the bandwagon, demanding "a probing, comprehensive, unvarnished examination of the overall issue of security contractors working for her department in Iraq," David Satterfield, the State Department's senior coordinator in Iraq, said during the hearing.

In the midst of that political thumb sucking, Dustin, Evan, Paul, and Nick came home from Iraq with no definite plans for what would come next, their lives in a government-ordered holding pattern. But they believed and acted from the conviction that the investigation would soon clear up any doubt that they had acted according to the protocols set forth by their State Department contract and the international laws of war.

Evan returned to the United States by November 2007 and visited his family in New Hampshire. Attorney William Coffield contacted him and explained that Blackwater had hired him to represent the contractors who had admitted to firing their weapons in Nisour Square in a growing government investigation. "I assumed I would be cleared and go back to work in a matter of months," Evan told me. "The thing that stuck out to me was all the media attention, but I assumed it would be sorted out. There was no doubt that there was incoming fire, and I assumed that would come to light and we would all be able to go back to work as soon as possible."

Weeks turned into months, and the men were no closer to a resolution. Evan applied to the US Navy SEAL training program and was accepted but told to wait until the investigation ended. So he moved to Colombia to be with his soon-to-be wife, Paola, and started taking online college courses.

Paul took a job as a ranch hand back in Texas but fretted about not being able to return to Baghdad to complete the mission. He even considered reenlisting in the army but rejected the idea because Christin wanted to start a family. Paul seemed "lost," Christin thought.

Nick pondered applying to the Central Intelligence Agency to become a sniper or reapplying to the Army Special Forces but mainly stayed on the family farm, escaping the cloud hanging over him in the tranquility of the woods. He began a self-destructive spiral on booze and pills prescribed by his local physician to treat post-traumatic stress disorder.

Dustin had surgery to alleviate chronic pain from his combat-related back injuries. While he recovered, he bought a Bass boat and began fishing in tournaments, planning his next act as a professional fisherman and guide. But the unresolved investigation nagged at him. He spent nearly every day on the water, as though each day of freedom would be his last.

Jeremy Ridgeway and Donald Ball returned home: Ridgeway to California, where he would draw disability payments for post-traumatic stress disorder, and Ball to Utah.

The story of Raven 23 got curiouser and curiouser the more I looked into it—especially from the perspective of the media coverage. It looked to me as though the federal agencies involved in the case—the State, Defense, and Justice Departments and the FBI—had taken a gun battle in the world's most dangerous city and spun it to suit their competing messages to the American public. As it dawned on the Blackwater team that the repeated questioning by different government agencies was something other than an after-action report, some of the men—mainly those in the first two trucks, which had been farthest from the action—began publicly questioning the battlefield conduct of their comrades in the command and follow vehicles.

The media glare fractured the team, with those in the front trucks—away from the action—beginning to separate themselves from those who had fired their weapons. Many of the team were passing around news articles about the incident, and accusations were beginning to fly.

In a September 16, 2007, email addressed to Team 23 TST, Ridgeway wrote, "I, Jeremy Ridgeway, was given a document provided by [Blackwater Deputy Detail Leader] Jeffery Gooch written by the press. In the document it stipulates that member/s of Raven 23 Tactical Support Team ordered other members of our team to cease fire while under hostile enemy engagement and pointed his/their weapon/s at other team members. This acquisition [*sic*] is FALSE and highly offensive, each member of our team is a professional and conducts themselves as such. As we are held accountable for our actions, those who make false acquisitions [sic] that could discredit a professional organization such as our [sic] should be held equally accountable for such damaging commentary."[3]

It appeared to me, as I looked through the 2007–2008 news coverage, that the State Department had leaked the men's protected statements to assure the public that the shoot had been clean and that Blackwater personnel had, in fact, come under fire. But as pressure to shift the blame for the Iraqi government's anger mounted, stories detailing Blackwater's past misdeeds began to appear, as well as allegations—anonymously sourced, of course—that the State Department was trying to cover up more bad behavior by its highly paid security force.

The team came undone under the pressure, with some occupants of the lead vehicle and ERV criticizing shooters in the command and follow vehicles for the volume of fire they had expended. Nick Slatten, who had fired two shots from inside the command vehicle, confronted Adam Frost for calling their battlefield actions into question during conversations in the Blackwater camp. Nick pointed out to Frost that the only occupant of the first two vehicles who had been facing the action—turret gunner Donald Ball—had joined in the firing along with the command and follow vehicle gunners. He also pointed out that Frost himself had begged the team "Don't let me get shot" as he exited the ERV to hook up the tow strap to the disabled command vehicle.

Frost, who testified against his teammates under a grant of immunity from the government, admitted under oath that the only Raven 23 member he had seen shooting wildly was the government's star witness, Jeremy Ridgeway, who had fired his assault rifle on automatic into a tanker truck and two vehicles as the convoy exited the square.

Frost also testified that the mood in the Blackwater camp had become increasingly divisive as word of an impending FBI investigation into the Nisour Square incident began circulating. He testified that he, Mealy, and Murphy met with Blackwater brass to complain about the incident. The three would become key government witnesses, with Frost and Mealy testifying under immunity grants.

Those developments should be considered in the context of US foreign policy. A history lesson is helpful here. After Republicans lost control of the House of Representatives and Senate in the 2006 midterm elections, President Bush admitted that his policy in Iraq was failing and the country was slipping into civil war. American voters expected the Democrats they elected to end the war, stop the massive defense spending, and bring the troops home. The administration debated whether sending more troops to Iraq to tamp down the burgeoning civil war would make Iraqis' hatred of Americans worse or generate gratitude for stability.

In the end, President Bush sent a "surge" of twenty thousand more troops to Iraq in a last-ditch bid to get the country under control. He called it "The New Way Forward in Iraq." The policy was supposed to result in a "unified, democratic federal Iraq that can govern itself, defend itself, and sustain itself, and is an ally in the War on Terror," and the strategy shifted from fighting the insurgency to helping Iraqis "clear and secure neighborhoods, [protecting] the local population, and [ensuring] that the Iraqi forces left behind are capable of providing security," Bush said in an address to the nation on January 10, 2007.

Sending five additional brigades into Iraq—most of them into Baghdad—required Bush to extend the tours of most of the US Army and Marines troops already in Iraq to counteract record low recruitment. That "press ganging" of US troops fostered an understandable resentment of military contractors, who were better paid and better equipped and got to go home every three months.

The Intercept's Jeremy Scahill noted in his 2007 book *Blackwater: The Rise of the World's Most Powerful Mercenary Army* that Secretary of Defense Robert Gates had worried about the pay disparity and sought a legal opinion about whether he could "put a noncompete clause into security contracts" to bar US troops from joining Blackwater or other private forces. "I worry that sometimes the salaries they are able to pay in fact lures some of our soldiers out of the service to go to work for them," the book quoted Gates as saying. Apparently, Gates was looking into adding a "'noncompete' clause . . . into security contracts." Scahill wrote that "[Erik] Prince said it would be 'fine' with him but asserted that 'it would be upsetting to a lot of soldiers if they didn't have the ability to use the skills they learned in the military in the private sector.'"[4]

The New York Times had reported extensively about the failure of efforts led by General David Petraeus to stand up the Iraqi Army and Iraqi National Police, which simply used the training and weaponry given them by US troops to escalate their civil war. A May 22, 2006, *Times* report said that attempts by US civilian advisers to reconstitute the police and give the Iraqi citizenry any semblance of security had "become overwhelmed by corruption, political vengeance and lawlessness unleashed by the toppling of Saddam Hussein." The job had been handed over to the US military, the *Times* reported, but "the military's plan for police units that could help restore order in Iraq would be no match for the forces tearing at the country in places like Basra and Baghdad." Background checks conducted by police investigators "found more than 5,000 police officers with arrest records for crimes that included attacks on American troops."

By September 16, 2007, the military was looking for a scapegoat. It needed an explanation for why Iraq was still a boiling cauldron of hatred and mayhem, and in Nisour Square they found one.

CHAPTER FIVE

✦✦✦

THE GOVERNMENT IS (ALMOST ALWAYS) OUT TO GET YOU

God, why is betrayal the only truth that sticks?
—ARTHUR MILLER, *AFTER THE FALL*

EVERYBODY CAN DO BAD things, even your own "side."

My journalistic mentors, mainly politically incorrect old guys who chain-smoked and hid liquor bottles in their desk drawers, taught me to be unsparing in my coverage no matter the politics of the people involved. Coming of age in the 1960s, they distrusted power of every stripe and showed a misanthropic streak that I find abides in the best editors.

As I reviewed the media coverage of the Raven 23 case, I remembered a case I had covered in 2001 that had taught me not to make heroes of people with whom I sympathize.

Sara Jane Olson, née Kathleen Ann Soliah, was a soccer mom from Minnesota and the respected wife of an emergency room physician. She raised three kids, acted in community theater, supported liberal causes, and enjoyed all the activities and amenities available to an upper-middle-class midwestern woman.

The first time she appeared in Los Angeles Superior Court, she reminded me of an older alumna from my all-girls Catholic high school in St. Louis—privileged, educated, and wholesome—and not at all of the domestic terrorist that the district attorney said she was.

Soliah was on trial for participating as a member of the Symbionese Liberation Army (SLA) in a 1975 bank robbery in Carmichael, California, in which a forty-two-year-old bank customer and mother of four named Myrna Opsahl, at the bank to deposit church collections, had been shot dead. Soliah had spent more than two decades on the lam before her case was featured on *America's Most Wanted* and somebody turned her in. She was charged with killing Opsahl, planting bombs beneath two LAPD patrol cars, and falsifying government documents to create her alias. Yet some influential people in Los Angeles County opined that her conduct since leaving the SLA proved that she was a productive member of society and should not be prosecuted.

When that argument did not convince District Attorney Steve Cooley, Soliah was allowed, despite her relatively elevated economic status, to draw from a public fund known as the Professional Appointee Court Expenditure (PACE) to pay her defense costs. PACE had been established to help poor people defend themselves in California's death penalty and "three strikes" cases carrying mandatory life sentences. Allowing Soliah to use six figures' worth of public funds to pay her private attorneys when death penalty defendants were limited to an average of $6,000 seemed questionable to me. So I wrote a story. Soliah was quickly cut off from PACE.

A day or so after the story appeared (and was picked up by the *Los Angeles Times*), I attended a press conference about Soliah's case at the Los Angeles offices of the American Civil Liberties Union, an organization whose work I generally admire and support. As soon as the ACLU members realized who I was, they actually hissed and asked how I could do such a story. How could I not? I asked. But I felt ashamed—like a traitor.

I thought about that incident as I reviewed the media coverage and dug deeper into the case files of the Raven 23 case throughout 2017. I was in a holding pattern most of that year, waiting for the Washington, DC, appeals court to rule on whether the convictions should be thrown out because of the misconduct and vindictiveness delineated in the NACDL amicus brief and the technical arguments made by defense lawyers at the January 19, 2017, oral arguments.

A year after taking the case on, I still had not been able to interest any publisher or news outlet in taking a closer look at the government's conduct or analyzing whether the underlying facts of the case supported the men's convictions. An agent who represented military books told me to come back after the story had "an ending." Former colleagues at Reuters and other major outlets listened to my pitch but, after learning who the defendants were, regarded me in the same way as the ACLU members defending Kathleen Soliah had. Again I felt a little ashamed for asking.

In the Raven 23 case, the Washington, DC–based press contorted itself to find ways to exonerate the FBI and DOJ for, at best, a biased and shoddy investigation and prosecution and, at worst, clear violations of the Raven 23 defendants' constitutional protections.

It had taken the DOJ three tries to indict the Raven 23 men, and each visit to the grand jury had involved the same constitutional rights violations. Prosecutors tried in 2007, 2008, and 2013 before they could get indictments to stick. Had I been covering the case for *The New York Times* or *The Washington Post*, I would have asked the prosecutors why, if the case was so strong, they had had to violate their professional ethics to bring it to trial. That's what US District Court Judge Ricardo Urbina believed happened, as he explained when he threw the case out. He wrote "the way the prosecution conducted itself throughout the grand jury process" was "reckless" and that this resulted in "a clear violation of the defendants' constitutional rights."[1]

In a *Washington Post* story that appeared after Urbina threw the Raven 23 case out in 2009, journalist Del Quentin Wilber wondered how the DOJ had found itself defending the conduct of "a seasoned and well-respected prosecutor" such as Assistant US Attorney Kenneth Kohl. "How could such a high-profile case, one that generated international headlines and roiled U.S.-Iraq relations, implode so badly?" the article asked while noting that the DOJ's reputation had "already been marred by prosecutorial misconduct" in the 2008 corruption case of then senator Ted Stevens, a debacle that had cost Stevens his Senate seat. Wilber noted that Urbina's accusations of government misconduct could be lethal to Kohl's Raven 23 case, because another federal judge had been investigating Kohl's colleagues in the Stevens case.

Prosecutorial misconduct doesn't have to imply that defendants are innocent, but journalists should ask why well-respected professionals need to bend the rules. A plausible explanation is that the case is weak. Yet rather than question whether Stevens and the Raven 23 defendants were innocent and had been railroaded by unethical prosecutors, Wilber, like many in the DC press corps, seemed more concerned with whether these allegations of prosecutorial misconduct would prevent DOJ from winning.

"Legal experts have said the Justice Department faces a difficult task in winning a reversal, pointing to what they consider a detailed and well-reasoned opinion by . . . Urbina," he wrote.

The government's evidence underpinning the manslaughter and murder charges was laughable. The case would not have made it past a preliminary hearing in the Los Angeles criminal courtrooms I had sat in for nearly two decades.

But more damning to the case was the evidence that hadn't

been collected. No autopsies or bullet trajectory analyses had been conducted to match bullets to victims. There were no photographs of the bodies or body parts of the fourteen dead (except for those of two victims inside a burned-out car). The one bullet fragment that the investigators had recovered from one of the seventeen wounded civilians was a match not for the Blackwater weapons but for the AK-47s carried by the Iraqi insurgency. The vehicles that supposedly had been blown to hell by the Blackwater machine guns and grenades had been moved immediately after the incident and stored for almost a decade in an open, uncovered parking lot before the case made it to trial. Neither Iraqi nor American investigators had shut down the crime scene where the supposed worst massacre of the Iraq War had taken place; State Department investigators had waited two days to search for evidence in Nisour Square, and the FBI showed up three weeks later.

I once saw a Los Angeles Superior Court judge throw out a case because the police investigator had left bagged evidence in his patrol car while he went to eat lunch. In another, a judge disallowed charges when police left evidence unattended outside an evidence locker in a secured area of a police station. If both of those cases had been thrown out because cops had failed to ensure the chain of evidence, how had the Nisour Square case been allowed to continue to trial?

The first attempt to prosecute the men took place in late 2007. The State Department's initial finding that Nisour Square had been "a good shoot" did not stick. In late November 2007, a grand jury convened in Washington, DC. Frost, Murphy, and Mealy testified, along with other members of the Raven 23 convoy. All admitted to having read the protected statements of the men who had fired their weapons, as well as the media coverage about the Nisour Square incident.

The government later concluded that the witnesses had not confined their testimony to only their personal experiences in

Nisour Square but had embroidered their accounts with parts of the protected statements—a violation of the men's Fifth Amendment guarantee against self-incrimination. The DOJ decided to withdraw the tainted case from the grand jury and start over.

Later, I would realize that part of that dysfunction was due to interagency battles. Emails leaked to *The New York Times* on April 12, 2015, the day before the Raven 23 men were sentenced, showed that a political rift had developed between the prosecutors and the investigators—that is to say, DOJ prosecutors, on the one hand, and FBI and State Department investigators, on the other—as they worked up the case in 2008 for a second grand jury. In the emails, FBI agents pressed the prosecutors to charge the men with using assault weapons to commit a felony—that curious charge that carried a mandatory minimum thirty-year prison sentence. Congress had designed the charge to enhance the sentences of drug dealers during Reagan's "war on drugs" in the 1980s, but it had never been applied in a war zone. The FBI's push to use it was especially bizarre and cruel, considering that the weapons had been issued to Blackwater by the US government to defend the lives of other Americans. That lack of precedent, in fact, was probably why the DOJ initially resisted using the gun charge. "We are getting some serious resistance from our office to charging the defendants with mandatory minimum time," Kohl wrote to lead FBI agent John Patarini in an email shortly before Kohl appeared before the grand jury in December 2008.

Why, then, did Kohl and the FBI feel confident in insisting on that inappropriate charge? In internal emails published by the *Times*, FBI investigators expressed optimism that the incoming Obama administration would be more willing to include the gun charge against the Raven 23 men. They'd turn out to be right. During his presidential campaign, Barack Obama had pledged to end the wars in Iraq and Afghanistan, and he and his main opponent, New York senator Hillary Clinton, had seemed to battle each other over who hated military contractors more. Obama later chose Clinton as his secretary of state, and the two would spend more federal tax dollars on private military contractors to fight foreign wars than any other US administration in history. By 2017, as I sat reviewing the Raven 23 case, Obama was drawing fierce criticism both in the world press and at home for his use of drone strikes to "surgically" kill insurgent leaders across the Middle East.

The Bureau of Investigative Journalism found that Obama had authorized 563 strikes, largely by drones, that had "targeted Pakistan, Somalia and Yemen during [his] two terms, compared to 57 strikes under Bush. Between 384 and 807 civilians were killed in those countries, according to reports logged by the Bureau."

I did not see that coming when I voted for Obama in 2008 (and again in 2012) with the hope that he would shut down the inexorable screw-up that was the Iraq War. Yet the *Times* story showed that those FBI investigators had somehow known that the new administration would allow the questionable charges to proceed against men and women on the front lines.

"I would rather wait for a new administration than go forward without those charges," FBI agent Carolyn Murphy wrote in a 2008 email leaked to the *Times*. Michael Posillico, a State Department investigator assigned to the case, responded, "It's hard for me to say we should wait for the Democrats, but this is one such time I have to." The emails also revealed that some FBI agents wanted prosecutors to charge the Blackwater contractors with second-degree murder, as well as lying to investigators for discrepancies about how much ordnance they had used during the firefight. As for the obstruction allegations, both Paul and Dustin voluntarily followed up their initial RSS interviews with additional statements made within two days to reflect that they had fired grenades during the battle. That was apparently what the FBI investigators referred to as "lying."

But no matter how prosecutors charged the case, it was weak, and they must have known it. As they worked up a second attempt at indictments, the FBI leaned hard on the five men to try to extract plea agreements.

In July 2008, Kohl approached Dustin's attorney to discuss whether he would cooperate with the government's investigation. "They were doing everything they could to try to get us to turn on each other," Dustin told me during one of our prison phone calls. "We were still contacting each other via email. Whenever they kept coming and asking me if I wanted to take a deal, I wouldn't do it. The other guys—they were trying to get me to turn on them, on my brothers. There was no way. Why would you admit to doing something you didn't do? There's no logic in that. I'm not going to lie just to save my own ass. That's just not who I am or what I am."

I asked him why he had omitted the M203 grenade from his ordnance tally. In the heat of battle, he had simply forgotten, he said. As soon as he had remembered it, he had gone in person to amend the report.

Likewise, Evan rejected a plea offer made around the same time through his attorney. "I was appalled by it," he told me. "I would never accept guilt for something I didn't do."

The government soon ratcheted up the pressure. FBI agents showed up at Dustin's home in Maryville, Tennessee, where he lived with Kelli and their two young children. The agents approached him as he stood in his driveway to ask if some random person lived at the address. Dustin told them, "You know who lives at this address. If you need something, call my attorney."

The worst story I heard about that in-between time came from Nick, who had FBI agents from Washington, DC, following him and his family—not subtly—in Sparta, Tennessee, population

5,009. "It was just obvious that we were being surveilled . . . they were driving around the community and asking people questions about me . . . trying to dig up dirt on me because they didn't have anything because I'm innocent," Nick told me. "So that's what they try to do when they don't have any evidence—try to make you look like a bad guy."

As they had done with Dustin, the agents followed Nick to his home and asked to question him. "They were following me around, but when they came to my house, they came with a lot of people, so I just gave them my lawyer's card," Nick told me. "They said, 'We can't talk to you because you have an attorney,' and I said, 'All right.' Then one of them who was from the local office . . . he stuck out his hand to shake my hand and I shook his hand and he said, 'I just want you to know this is BS.'"

The government also leaned hard on Ridgeway, and in late 2008, he cracked. Ridgeway kept his November 18, 2008, plea agreement secret from the rest of the Blackwater men and continued to communicate with them under the prosecutors' watchful eye.

In a 302 memo dated December 1, 2008, FBI agent Ryan Sparacino advised Ridgeway to use his MySpace account "as a way to access the pages of other individuals" and that Ridgeway recalled that "Liberty, Heard, Vargas and Watson all maintained MySpace accounts."[2]

Critics of the US criminal justice system explain that the practice of pushing plea bargains—supposedly to free up crowded court dockets—strongly incentivizes the government to coerce innocent people into confessing to crimes they didn't commit. An underappreciated corollary of this, however, is that in a "prisoner's dilemma" situation where a group of defendants contains only one actually guilty member, the guilty member is strongly incentivized to take a deal and get innocent people into trouble. Plea bargains are good for tired governments and guilty people, bad for wrongly charged citizens.

I learned from conversations with Joseph Low, the chief instructor of the Trial Lawyers College, that it was not illegal for prosecutors to threaten to charge them with murder to scare them into taking a plea deal. "It's not illegal in any way for them to do that," he said. "When they wouldn't play ball, [the prosecutors] decided to do what they always do, which is to use their leverage to force people to do what they want. One of the great powers that the government has, that prosecutors have, is this: They have the most viable commodity to trade that is available to anyone, and that is their freedom."

Low was not surprised at my description of the pretrial harassment by the FBI and the DOJ against the Raven 23 men; he had seen it many times in his defense career, along with unlawful arrests meant to inflict "mental torture [and] painful, shameful torture to your emotional well-being."

The government's playbook never varied in high-profile cases, he said. "And then the government comes and says, 'Well, had enough? We'll give you your freedom back if we get what we want.' Now, they don't say it like that, but the implication . . . is 'We need someone who can testify that they saw them do it. Now, if you've got something to trade, we can give you your freedom back. But you may not have anything to trade.'" He continued, "Now you're a witness, and you're sitting there thinking 'Let me see if I heard that right: they need someone to say "This person over here shot that thing over there." I need my freedom, and they need someone to say that? What do I gotta say?'" Low said, laughing ruefully.

The NACDL noted in a 2018 report that only 3 percent of federal criminal cases go to trial, with 97 percent of defendants pleading to crimes as prosecutors ratchet up the pressure to plead rather than face an escalating number of charges of greater severity. The NACDL called it "the trial penalty" and saw it play out in the 2014 trial documents, the 2017 appeal, and the two trials that followed in 2018.

"Trial by jury has been replaced by a 'system of [guilty] pleas which diminishes, to the point of obscurity, the role that the Framers envisioned for jury trials as the primary protection for individual liberties and the principal mechanism for public participation in the criminal justice system," the NACDL report said. ". . . The virtual elimination of the option of taking a case to trial has so thoroughly tipped the scales of justice against the accused that the danger of government overreach is ever-present. And on a human level, for the defense attorney there is no more heart-wrenching task that [sic] explaining to [a] client who very likely may be innocent that they must seriously consider pleading guilty or risk the utter devastation of the remainder of their life with incalculable impacts on family."

The National Registry of Exonerations concluded that government misconduct was "a major cause of convictions of innocent defendants" and estimated that between 1989 and 2019, as many as 20 percent of defendants pleaded guilty to crimes they did not commit to avoid being victimized by corrupt cops, prosecutors, and judges.

A by-product of this corrupt "system" was the false testimony that those unfortunate defendants make against codefendants who had refused to admit guilt for crimes they did not commit. In the case of Jeremy Ridgeway, however, prosecutors found a pliable if not particularly trustworthy witness to carry their story. The court documents I obtained, including FBI interview notes, correspondence between his attorney and the DOJ, and the transcript from his plea hearing, showed an interesting "shaping" of the story Ridgeway would tell at trial.

As I reviewed his testimony and sworn statements, it seemed that Ridgeway had had a hard time finding his footing in life. He had graduated from high school in Port Jefferson, a wealthy waterfront suburb on Long Island, and followed in the footsteps of his father, a US marine, by enlisting in the army in 1989. He had received a general discharge from the army eighteen months later for repeated misconduct. That included "missing formation, leaving post without permission while stationed in Korea." "I was very young; very immature; made bad decisions," he later testified.

He then moved to San Diego, where he enrolled at the police academy but never worked as a cop. For the next fifteen years, he wandered from dead-end job to dead-end job: delivering pizzas, working part-time at a deli, doing shifts as a security guard. Along the way, he appealed his general discharge from the army and received an honorable discharge. In 2002, he joined the National Guard to fulfill his army contract and, the next year, deployed to Iraq with Operation Iraqi Freedom. He returned home with a case of post-traumatic stress disorder so severe that he was fired from his security job for taking leave to get treatment.

Ridgeway, with two young children and a wife to support, filled out a Blackwater application online. He sailed through it until he arrived at the section asking about his mental health history. Ridgeway knew that if he disclosed his PTSD diagnosis, he would probably be declared ineligible. So he lied about it. He lied about his combat experience, about the weapons he had qualified on, and inflated his responsibilities for the National Guard.[3]

He had been extremely fortunate in that a few years after the wars began, the US military had had to lower its recruiting requirements and raise its maximum recruitment age to keep boots on the ground in Iraq and Afghanistan. Erik Prince also broadened Blackwater's hiring criteria to service the fifty-plus contracts he had won from the US government. Whereas he had previously required Special Forces training, he began accepting veterans with special operations training and clean records as the number of private military contractors in Iraq and Afghanistan quickly surpassed the number of US soldiers. He told me that "Sixty-six percent of the military-age population [eighteen-to-twenty-four-year-olds] [was] not able to serve in the military—not even able to apply to serve in the military because . . . they're too heavy, they're too unfit, they're too medicated, they have criminal records, or they have too many tattoos." Blackwater's required skill set was even more niche, making it difficult to find recruits.

By December 31, 2006, Ridgeway again found himself in Baghdad, assigned to the Raven 23 TST team and still suffering from undisclosed PTSD. His teammates described Ridgeway to me as a talented marksman.

In his first sworn statement to State Department investigators on September 18, 2007, he described his actions in Nisour Square as consistent with those of the other turret gunners in the rear two trucks. "As we entered the traffic circle near the area of [Nisour Square], I heard the sound of gunfire and observed a white sedan entering the traffic circle from the south and heading directly towards our convoy. . . . I perceived this to be an immediate threat upon my life and the lives of those in my convoy . . . I observed muzzle flashes and the sound of automatic gunfire coming from the southwest approximately 200 meters from my position . . . I continued to hear automatic gunfire however I could no longer determine where the fire was coming from."

In an email written less than twenty-four hours after the Nisour Square gunfight, he defiantly told his father, "The Department of State may choose to get rid of us however we did nothing wrong so I assume this will blow over."

But it didn't blow over—and almost a year later, in August 2008, he received a target letter from the Justice Department and began negotiating. His attorney sent a letter on October 31, 2008, reiterating Ridgeway's claims that he had behaved "honorably, courageously and responsibly at every point during the incident."

It is impossible to tell what exactly caused Ridgeway to change his version of events so radically over the following nineteen days; neither he nor his attorney responded to several attempts to connect over the years. Ridgeway testified at the men's 2014 trial that he had "changed as a person" and felt a need to "tell his story" about his crimes to a jury.[4] On November 18, 2008, he told the government that he would testify against his Raven 23 teammates in exchange for reduced legal exposure for his actions in Nisour Square.

Now that they had Ridgeway on board, the prosecutors made a second attempt at getting indictments against Dustin Heard, Evan Liberty, Paul Slough, Nick Slatten, and Donald Ball by making Ridgeway the star of the second grand jury proceeding. Rather than calling other witnesses to testify and again "taint" the evidence with the men's protected statements, prosecutors chose to "summarize" the statements they had made to the first grand jury. The government said it also "redacted" the testimony—supposedly to remove references to the protected statements. Rather than have live witnesses testify, an FBI agent read it to the grand jurors.[5]

Those efforts, supposedly to avoid using the men's statements against them, provided the Justice Department with a powerful opportunity to shape the narrative of what had happened at Nisour Square. And the prosecutors took full advantage of that opportunity in a way that strikes me as breathtakingly unethical.

The second grand jury convened in late November 2008. Besides Ridgeway, FBI agent Robyn Powell was the sole live witness who presented the summarized evidence. Unsurprisingly, on December 4, 2008, it returned indictments against Nick, Paul, Evan, Dustin, and Donald. Each was charged with fourteen counts of voluntary manslaughter, twenty counts of attempt to commit manslaughter, and one count of using and discharging a firearm during and in relation to a crime of violence. Paul, then twenty-nine years old; Nick, twenty-four; Evan, twenty-six; Dustin, twenty-six; and Donald, twenty-six, faced potential maximum sentences of ten years in prison for each manslaughter charge and seven years for each attempted manslaughter charge, plus a mandatory minimum thirty-year sentence for the firearms charge that FBI investigators had demanded.

At a press conference announcing the indictments and Ridgeway's guilty plea on December 8, 2008, Patrick Rowan, assistant attorney general for the National Security Division of the DOJ, noted that the case represented the first use of the Military Extraterritorial Jurisdiction Act (MEJA) to be filed against non–Defense Department private contractors. MEJA had been amended in 2004 to allow the government to prosecute contractors who provide services "in support of the mission of the Department of Defense overseas." That last statement was a head-scratcher. Blackwater had certainly been called on to rescue US troops in Baghdad and vice versa, but there was absolutely no evidence that the company had been consulted or included in planning or supporting DOD missions.

Rowan went on to say that the government "alleges today that at least 34 unarmed Iraqi civilians, including women and children, were killed or injured without justification or provocation by these security guards in the shooting at Nisour Square. Today's indictment and guilty plea should serve as a reminder that those who engaged in unprovoked and illegal attacks on civilians, whether during times of conflict or times of peace, will be held accountable."

Rowan also lauded the FBI for its "dedication to respond to any crime scene; be it in the United States or on foreign soil." But there was no mention of the fact that FBI agents had shown up three weeks after the incident, examined a contaminated crime scene, and turned up a wealth of information showing that US military contractors had been attacked by enemy insurgents.

The same day that the government announced the indictments, the five Raven 23 defendants surrendered at the federal courthouse in Salt Lake City, nearest Donald's hometown, and entered not-guilty pleas. They were released on their own recognizance later the same day with a list of bond conditions, including a ban on possessing firearms that rendered their main job skill moot. It was the first time they had faced news cameras outside the courthouse. There were a handful of shouting protestors as well, in stark contrast to the US marshals, who handled their formal arrests and booking inside the building with kindness and respect.

The DOJ also announced that day that Ridgeway, thirty-five, had taken a plea deal in exchange for testifying against his former teammates. What no one knew until much later was that Ridgeway's cooperation agreement included "providing email exchanges and statements made among the proposed defendants" as well as monitoring their MySpace pages for prosecutors.[6]

For his actions in Nisour Square on September 16, 2007, Ridgeway pleaded guilty to killing one Iraqi civilian and attempting to kill a second.

CHAPTER SIX

ALLIES IN UNLIKELY PLACES

And where we had thought to be alone, we shall be with all the world.

—JOSEPH CAMPBELL, *THE HERO'S JOURNEY*

IT WAS NOW LATE 2017—two years since I had heard about the case and a year since I had met the Raven 23 men—and I was having to face the fact that I'd gotten into a situation that was far bigger than I knew how to handle. I needed allies.

Oral arguments in the men's appeal of their convictions took place in Washington, DC, on January 17, 2017. The families asked me to attend with them, but I had just begun classes for my master's degree in writing at Lindenwood University in St. Charles. Joe Bob surprised me by quitting his job, selling his house in Taft, and joining me in my hometown to finish his undergraduate degree.

The appellate court's answer finally came on August 4, 2017: The three-judge panel upheld the 2014 convictions of Dustin, Paul, and Evan and ordered Chief US District Judge Royce Lamberth to conduct a new trial for Nick on the dubious murder charge.

The court did, however, rule that the gun charge against Dustin, Paul, and Evan and its mandatory minimum sentence of thirty years constituted cruel and unusual punishment and ordered Judge Lamberth to resentence them. It was a small and hollow victory, but it brought us to a standstill. I worried that it would take months, if not years, for a result that would put the case before the public and make it newsworthy again. I did not know it at the time, but forces were gathering to change that impossible situation.

In the spring of 2018, my agent called to say that a movie studio executive named Micheal Flaherty wanted to contact me to talk about a podcast series based on my book *Netflixed: The Epic Battle for America's Eyeballs* that I had released a few weeks earlier via the podcast company Wondery. I had met Flaherty once at a 2005 media event at the Mandarin Oriental hotel in New York promoting the release of the Walden Media–Walt Disney film *The Chronicles of Narnia: The Lion, the Witch, and the Wardrobe*, based on the C. S. Lewis book of the same title. I doubted that Flaherty would remember me from that crowded press junket thirteen years earlier. I wondered why a studio executive who produced multimillion-dollar movies was calling me and suspected some kind of trick. I told my agent to give him my phone number, and a few days later, he called me.

Micheal Flaherty had an interesting professional life, and he exuded a playful obsession in everything he did. He had listened to my Wondery podcast and wanted to turn my Netflix book into a feature film or streaming series. We had several discussions about how to tell the story and about whether any studio would want to make a movie or series about its biggest rival.

Mike's peripatetic journey to Walden had brought him into contact with the world of Boston politics—a contact sport he never tired of and a city he often visited to help out old friends. After college at Tufts University, he had become a research assistant for *National Review*. He had survived less than a year before quitting and going to work as a camp counselor.

His father had intervened and gotten him a job as a page in the Massachusetts Senate. It involved running errands, changing water bottles, and vacuuming offices. One day he left a copy of an article he had written that had been published in the most recent issue of *National Review* on the desk of William M. Bulger, the legendary president of the Massachusetts Senate. With it he left a note: "Thought you might enjoy this. Mike (I am the page that vacuums your office in the mornings)."

Bulger had a soft spot for underdogs, and the thought of hiring the guy who cleaned his office over one of the hundreds of Ivy League graduates who had applied to work at the Senate appealed to his radical egalitarian view that everybody should get an opportunity. The famously private Bulger invited Mike to his office and offered him a job—first answering his correspondence and then helping write his speeches. After Mike had written a speech on school choice, Bulger assigned him to work on education reform legislation as well.

Bulger had an unwavering belief in the transformational power of education that was infectious. He had attended Catholic schools in South Boston before becoming a "Triple Eagle"—a graduate of Boston College High School, Boston College, and Boston College Law School. His brother James was a different story. He did not have the same educational opportunities and pursued a completely different path. Better known by his nom de guerre, "Whitey," James had served time in a number of prisons for organized crime and eventually found himself number one on the FBI's Most Wanted List. It amazed Mike that two brothers who had grown up in the same family, same house, and even same bedroom had chosen paths that could not be more starkly different.

Mike formed Walden Media with his college roommate, Cary Granat, and his brother, Francis X. "Chip" Flaherty, in 1999, hoping to create quality children's films and teaching materials based on the books his wife, Kelly, an elementary school teacher, was assigning her classes.

They found a backer in the Denver billionaire Philip Anschutz, a conservative Christian investor who had made his money in oil, gas, and railroad businesses and was expanding into the entertainment industry. At the time, Anschutz owned the Staples Center in Los Angeles, the Los Angeles Kings hockey team, and a minority interest in the Los Angeles Lakers. He eventually bought United Artists and controlled Regal Entertainment Group, a Dothan, Alabama–based movie theater chain I had covered as an entertainment reporter at Reuters. The purchase of Regal put him in control of one of every four movie screens in the United States.

Although Granat had had success making the *Scream* horror movie franchise, Anschutz, a grandfather, wanted to make movies that families would watch together. He laid down the rules for Walden before investing: no R-rated movies, always follow your mission statement, and hire only people who follow the mission statement to appeal to people's better angels. I did not know it at the time, but I could not have found a better connected, fiercer advocate or more talented communicator for the men of Raven 23.

Mike was a conservative at heart and had friendships with conservatives of many stripes. William J. Bennett, the Reagan administration secretary of education, served as chairman of Walden's educational advisory board. Democratic Congressman Michael Bennet from Colorado, who had voluntarily left to be the deputy mayor of Denver and then the head of Denver Public Schools, oversaw theater. William McGurn, *The Wall Street Journal*'s editorial page editor, allowed Mike to write editorials to scratch his itch for politics. He knew the Fox News personality Laura Ingraham and the political commentator David French and his wife, Nancy French, an author, through Grace Chapel in Lexington, the largest evangelical church in New England. His best friend from Grace Chapel was Chai Ling, one of the student leaders of the 1989 Tiananmen Square protests. In life and in politics, he embraced the nineteenth-century British politician William Wilberforce's concept of cobelligerents: people who fight for a common cause while disagreeing on everything else.

Ultimately Mike and I decided that no studio was going to buy a series about its biggest competitor, so we shelved the idea of a Netflix movie. One day he asked me, "Do you have anything else you're working on?"

I took a deep breath. I knew immediately what I wanted to tell him about, but I was sure that he would think I was crazy. The arguments I had been writing for my master's degree work came flooding out in an emotional tumble. He let me go on and then kindly asked if I had written a treatment. I emailed him the query letters I had been sending around, and not a day later, he called to say he was all in.

Later, he confided that he had had a "visceral negative reaction" to hearing that the men had been Blackwater guards. Erik Prince had made the rounds of Hollywood, trying to turn his 2013 memoir *Civilian Warriors: The Inside Story of Blackwater and the Unsung Heroes of the War on Terror* into a movie. Walden had been among the first studios Prince had pitched. The movie had never been made, and although Mike had been a supporter of the Iraq War, he had changed his opinion by the time Prince and his agent had shown up.

After reading my summary of the case, Mike told me that he could hardly believe the "cartoonish villainy" of the government. "It seems like a bad script," he told me. If that was true, the government, if it wants to, can set its sights on anyone and destroy them, he said. His friendship with Bill Bulger had shown him that. When "Whitey" Bulger was being pursued as a federal fugitive, politicians had raked his brother over the coals for not reporting one anodyne conversation he'd had with his brother years before, Mike told me. Ultimately, Bill Bulger's career had been ended due to the incident. "I thought the Bulger case was a Boston thing—people settling old scores," he said, adding that this could not be happening on an international level. After years of rejections, I felt a rush of gratitude toward him for picking up the burden of bringing the case to light.

As he watched old news stories on YouTube and dug deeper into the politics of the war, the existence of what he described as "a military-media industrial complex" became clear to both of us. Every cable news network had high-level ex-military officers employed to deliver the Pentagon's talking points, and the journalists apparently had no interest in exposing the nation's misadventures in Iraq and Afghanistan. "There is one party, and the press has abandoned its role as an adversary—it's more of a cheerleader," he told me. "The only way we get the truth out is through social media."

Mike saw a solution in a fusion of movie marketing and a political campaign. We had to devise a way to grab people's attention and get them rooting for the Raven 23 men. We had no major media platform—other than the huge number of people he knew in the conservative media—and no money to bring the scheme to life.

Then there was the problem of the huge and growing case files. I had read most of the trial transcripts, but there were thousands of pages of supporting evidence, depositions, pretrial motions, and other esoterica that I had had neither the stomach nor the time to tackle. Somehow, I had found the one person who could help me tease out the narrative. Over the next few months, Mike and I read over the case files and pieced together the story of what was, at best, a flawed prosecution by ambitious people and, at worst, a public perversion of justice by one of the nation's most prominent courts.

I'd solved one mystery: what had happened in Nisour Square. Michael and I were going to have to tackle a far bigger one: What was the reason for the cover-up? And how far up the ladder of the US government did the corruption go? Answering those questions meant looking back at the machinations of a judge who just wouldn't stay in line.

CHAPTER SEVEN

─────── ★★★ ───────

JUDGES MAKE ALL THE DIFFERENCE

Four things belong to a judge: To hear courteously; to answer wisely; to consider soberly; and to decide impartially.

—SOCRATES

AS WE REVIEWED THE government's ever-changing theory of the Raven 23 case, Mike and I realized that the DOJ had learned from its failed grand jury appearance in 2007 that it needed more than a new narrative, it needed a different set of facts—"Facts" that would show that there had been no gunmen in Nisour Square, nor even any threats to make the Blackwater team fear for their lives.

But they would run up against an obstacle: a government-skeptical judge named Ricardo Urbina. The case was set for trial on February 2, 2010, but the thirty-five-count indictment against the Blackwater men did not survive that long.

As Kohl and Malis constructed their Blackwater case in late 2008, Judge Urbina rendered a decision in another questionable DOJ case involving seventeen Chinese Muslims, known as Uighurs, who had been detained without trial as potential terrorists for seven years in the US detention camp for "high-value prisoners" at

Guantánamo Bay, Cuba. The DOJ had called the Uighurs a security threat and wanted them held indefinitely. Urbina had ordered their release and denied the government's motion demanding that the Uighurs remain imprisoned pending an appeal. "Because the Constitution prohibits indefinite detentions without cause, the continued detention is unlawful," he ruled.

Human rights advocates stood in the courtroom and cheered. But the prosecutor, John O'Quinn, then made a curious argument—one that was bone chilling in light of what would later happen in the Raven 23 case: "[The Courts] have to be particularly circumspect because of the potential for interference with foreign relations and with diplomacy."

P. Sabin Willett, a Boston attorney representing the Uighurs, countered, "I'd never heard before that our relationships with other nations are a lawful basis to hold somebody in a prison."

A little over a year after he freed the Uighurs, Urbina again clashed with the Justice Department in the Raven 23 case—this time over the Fifth Amendment's protection against self-incrimination.

About a month before the case was set for trial, he handed down a ninety-page decision throwing out the indictment on the grounds of prosecutorial misconduct and a lack of evidence against the Raven 23 defendants. In his December 31, 2009, ruling, he pointed out that the DOJ's entire case rested on the protected admissions by the five Raven 23 team members who had fired their weapons. The statements did not reveal any illegal or criminal activity, but the men's admissions that they had fired their weapons and killed people during the gun battle had been crucial to the government's case, the judge said, because forensic scientists had been unable to match bullets from the scene to any specific weapon. In other words, if it had not been for those statements, the government would have faced a difficult—if not impossible— task of identifying the shooters on the Raven 23 team because there was no other direct evidence to prove that they had fired their weapons.

Urbina also noted that Blackwater's State Department contract specified that the men's statements could not be used against them in a criminal case and that prosecutors had wrongly insinuated to grand jurors that the defendants had been operating under some shady immunity deal rather than an employment agreement commonly used in US police departments. Similar agreements allow internal investigators to gather information about officer-involved shootings.

Urbina criticized Kohl for "purposefully flout[ing] the advice" of senior Justice Department advisers against using the statements to guide the investigation. Prosecutors relied upon the men's protected statements to apply for search warrants and to question witnesses, among other things, he said. He slammed the prosecutors for presenting the tainted case to a grand jury, citing "reckless behavior [that] was in keeping with the way the prosecution conducted itself throughout the grand jury process."

He pasted the DOJ for withholding "testimony of numerous percipient witnesses who had provided substantial exculpatory evidence to the first grand jury, present[ing] the second grand jury with distorted and self-serving 'summaries' of the accounts of other witnesses and impl[ying] to the second grand jury that the defendants had given inculpatory statements to State Department investigators which the government could not disclose to the grand jury because they were given 'in exchange for immunity.'"

He also criticized the FBI for the shortcomings of its investigation, concluding that US law does not support charges based on tainted or, in this case, nonexistent evidence. "The court notes that Nisour Square was not sealed as a closed crime scene between the shooting on September 16, 2007, and the arrival of FBI investigators several weeks later," he wrote. "Agent Scollan testified that when he visited the scene shortly after the incident, he noticed an Iraqi man, possibly a police officer, who appeared to be walking through the scene and picking up objects that may have been evidence. Agent Scollan testified that the scene 'was extremely clean—picked clean as if it was being groomed for a garden.'"

Last, the judge dismissed the government's contention that its use of the compelled statements, "far from being unimportant and insubstantial . . . pervaded nearly every aspect of the government's investigation and prosecution . . . the government's use of those statements appears to have played a critical role in the indictment against each of the defendants. Accordingly, the court declines to excuse the government's reckless violation of the defendants' constitutional rights as harmless error."

He concluded that "When a judge, upon close examination of the procedures" that had brought the Raven 23 case to his courtroom showed that "the process aimed at bringing the accused to trial has compromised the constitutional rights of the accused, it behooves the court to grant relief in the fashion prescribed by law. Such is the case here."

Mike and I were intrigued by Judge Urbina's finding that the DOJ had withheld what he called "substantial exculpatory evidence" that would have exonerated the men from the second grand jury because the department would turn around and do it again with a third grand jury on October 17, 2013. A question that we got a lot from skeptics was "How did they get indicted in the first place?" along with "Why did the judge and the appellate court let it happen?"

Grand jury proceedings are secret, so I thought that there was no way to see the evidence that had led the grand jurors to conclude that the indictments were in any way appropriate, even by the low bar the prosecutors had to overcome—that is, until I came across a twelve-page letter written earlier in 2013 to the DOJ prosecutors by Donald Ball's attorney, Steven McCool, and posted on the website The BLT: The Blog of Legal Times. It commented on the inside baseball of all the big cases underway in the nation's capital. That particular item noted that McCool, a former assistant US attorney, had won a dismissal of all charges against Donald Ball.

In his scathing letter to the DOJ, McCool cited the grand jury transcripts in great detail. He described a litany of vindictiveness—same song, new verse—that matched Judge Urbina's complaints about the DOJ and involved some of the same prosecutors.[1] For example, Kohl had "purposefully manipulated the Iraqi witness accounts so the grand jurors would not learn that some of these witnesses reported seeing gunfire from helicopters or airplanes, or from Vehicle 2 where Messrs. Murphy and Frost occupied turret positions. Mr. Kohl did this because he did not want to undercut his theory of the case; that is, no shots were fired from the air or by Messrs. Murphy or Frost." Further, he noted, "For some reason, Mr. Malis decided not to present . . . statements from other witnesses not connected with Blackwater, who reported that they heard AK-47 gunfire. Instead of presenting this exculpatory evidence, Mr. Kohl worked hard to keep evidence of incoming gunfire from the grand jurors." The letter concluded, "Finally, Mr. Kohl stunningly failed to tell the second grand jury that Mr. Ball was briefed on a 'Be On the Look Out' Report to look for a white sedan, as it could be carrying a vehicle-borne improvised explosive device [car bomb]."

McCool ominously referred to the prosecutors' code of ethics and to potential disciplinary action that could be taken against them as a result of the grand jury boondoggle: "DOJ policy makes clear that impeachment evidence is exculpatory and must be disclosed . . . any evidence that is inconsistent with any element of any crime charged against the defendant, turn it over; any information that casts doubt upon the accuracy of any evidence, including but not limited to witnesses' testimony, turn it over; . . . err on the side of disclosure."

Not surprisingly, prosecutors dismissed Ball from the case, saying that the government "has exercised its prosecutorial discretion . . . based on its assessment of the admissible evidence against him."

In a normal situation, that might have been that for the other men as well. But far higher stakes were at play. The government clearly understood that it needed to get around Urbina. In a write-up of the ruling four days later, *New York Times* reporter Matt Apuzzo noted that the case was "steeped in international politics" and "inflamed anti-American sentiment abroad. . . . The Iraqi government wanted the guards to face trial in Iraq and officials there said they would closely watch how the U.S. judicial system handled the case."

Apuzzo noted that the fate of Ridgeway, "who turned on his former colleagues and pleaded guilty to killing one Iraqi and wounding another" was unclear. "Had he gone to trial, the case against him would likely have fallen apart, but it is unclear whether Urbina will let him out of his plea deal." I thought it was an odd detail in a story that focused more on the international optics of the ruling rather than the fact that the judge had just served up a flaming dish of prosecutorial misbehavior that exactly tracked that in the Senator Ted Stevens case in 2008.

As I reviewed the media coverage of Urbina's ruling, I wondered why the beat reporters had failed to ask Kohl, Malis, and Attorney General Eric Holder to account for the agency's conduct toward the US citizens whose constitutional guarantees they had continued to violate. Instead, they let it roll on.

The symbolism of the New Year's Eve ruling was appropriate, I thought as I read Urbina's scorching opinion. The curtain had been rung down on what should have been the last act of a farce written and performed by the Department of Justice. It would rise again on a bizarre second act almost four years later. The prosecutors took a while to assemble their next effort, but they realized that the incoming Obama administration—and a new judge who would take the case from the retiring Urbina—would be more supportive of their attempts to use the Department of Justice to carry out foreign policy at the expense of the constitutional rights of US citizens. As for Dustin, Evan, Paul, and Nick, they were free for the first time in two years to make New Year's resolutions that were not shadowed by the threat of prison.

Paul and Christin Slough were at her parents' home in Sanger, Texas, for a New Year's Eve party when they heard that the case had been dismissed. "All of us, of course, were thrilled, but in a sense, it was bittersweet because we never got to tell our side of the story, and frankly, we haven't had that chance to this point," Paul told me from prison. "After Judge Urbina had thrown out the case, we felt a tremendous amount of relief that we were out from under the burden of that leviathan. Even with the threat of them bringing it back, there still was just this feeling of freedom. We wanted to continue living our lives."

Evan and his then fiancée, Paola, were in Boston, driving back to New Hampshire to visit his parents when he heard the news. "It was snowing, and I got a call from my lawyer [Bill Coffield]," he told me. "I answered the phone call, and he had my dad on the line, but he was required to tell me first that all charges against all of us had been thrown out. I started to cry. I was so emotional."

The couple drove to the restaurant in Rochester where his mother, Deb, worked, and celebrated with his parents and best friend, Chris Buslovich. "I was so happy I could go on with my life. Normally I am not a drinker, I don't like to drink beer but on that day my best friend, Chris, told me that it was a special occasion and I had to have a beer. That may have been the last beer I drank," Evan told me in a phone call from prison.

Coffield warned the family that the government would probably appeal and that they should "not get too excited," Brian Liberty said. They had less than a month to enjoy that sense of possibility.

Secretary of State Condoleezza Rice managed to keep Blackwater security in Iraq until Bush left office in January 2009. When Hillary Clinton took over that month, the State Department "fired" Blackwater "from its job protecting U.S. diplomats in Iraq," ABC News reported. The firing came after the Iraqi government had followed through on its threats to suspend Blackwater's license to operate in the country and cited "lingering outrage" over the Nisour Square shootings, ABC reported.

Iraqi Prime Minister Nouri al-Maliki had been under "intense pressure from Iraqis, with leading political and resistance figures demanding that Blackwater leave immediately" after the Nisour Square shootings, the activist Jeremy Scahill reported in his 2008 book *Blackwater: The Rise of the World's Most Powerful Mercenary Army*. That pressure had only intensified in the ensuing three years, especially after Iraqis had discovered that the Blackwater operatives could not be tried in Iraqi courts under Coalition Provisional Authority Order 17, which exempted US military forces and military contractors from Iraqi law.

In his book, Scahill parroted the prevailing opinion among Iraqis in 2008 that "if the United States took contractor crimes seriously, it would have pursued avenues of alternative prosecution or sanction of alleged killers—if for no other reason than to show the Iraqis that the United States would not simply shrug off their concern and outrage."[2] The goal of such a proceeding, it seemed, was not to find out the truth but to reassure Iraqis. The distinction was an important one.

The Obama administration had picked a side in the Iraqi elections that came just weeks after Urbina made international headlines for dismissing the Raven 23 case. Obama was already facing outrage from Sunnis in Iraq and throughout the region at the United States' continuing support for al-Maliki's Shi'a government. The US president seemed intent on ensuring al-Maliki's return to power following the national elections set for March 7, 2010. Given the controversy about that support, the last thing Obama needed was more bad press in Iraq.

When Urbina threw the Blackwater case out just two months before the Iraqi election, he added more pressure to an explosive situation. A *New York Times* editorial published on January 10, 2010, agreed that Urbina had correctly killed the indictment over prosecutorial misconduct but criticized the Justice Department for failing to police military contractors and described the Iraqi government as "furious" at the case's dismissal.

On January 23, 2010, Vice President Joseph Biden suddenly popped up in Baghdad at a joint press conference with Iraqi President Jalal Talabani to express "my personal regret for the violence in Kisoor [*sic*; should be Nisour] involving Blackwater employees in 2007" and to announce that the Justice Department would appeal Urbina's decision. He said that the Obama administration was "disappointed by the judge's decision to dismiss the indictment, which was based on the way in which some evidence was acquired." He assured the Iraqis that "a dismissal is not an acquittal."

When Christin Slough saw Biden's mangled statement on the news, she was shocked to hear the second most powerful person in the world condemn her husband and his colleagues before they had a chance to put on a case. "I was kind of in denial," she told me. "I just couldn't believe it. I had read Judge Urbina's opinion and I [thought] there is no way this [appeal] is going to happen. He's just grandstanding. This is all political. He's just saying what these people need to hear right now, and there is no way he is going to succeed because our justice system works." Although the defense attorneys had warned that the government could choose to refile the case, she said she had chosen "to believe it wasn't coming back, that it was going to die quietly."

Paul was riding his favorite gray mare, rounding up stray cattle outside Stephenville, Texas, when his attorney called him to say that the government was appealing Urbina's ruling. "I was crushed. I didn't know heads from tails for a minute, and I literally thought about loading up my mare and grabbing Christin and taking off," he told me during a call from FCI El Reno. "I didn't take off because frankly, we'd done nothing wrong. We'd done our job. Our principal got home safe; we had done what we were told to do. There was nothing to run from." Underlining that optimistic belief, Paul and Christin decided to go ahead with plans to start a family. Lily Slough was born in 2013.

Coming down off the "running and gunning" of years in combat had been a tough transition for Dustin Heard. He spent his days going back and forth to physical therapy for his broken back and Veterans Administration psychologists for post-traumatic stress disorder. "I went from high tempo to nothing. I had no drive, no nothing. And so I started fishing . . . that's always been a passion of mine, but I used it to fill the void of 'What am I doing?'" he told me later. Dustin and Kelli also decided to expand their family after the indictments were dismissed.

"Let's put it this way," Dustin said on a call from FCI Memphis. "When I got home [in 2007], we wanted to have another child. But it's difficult to even talk about this because when you're in a circumstance when you're facing all of these charges, it's a difficult choice to bring another life in the world because of all the uncertainty." Nevertheless, Dustin and Kelli welcomed their son, Quinn, in the summer of 2011.

With his plan to join the SEALs indefinitely on hold, Evan returned to Colombia with Paola. Before the Nisour Square incident, he had worked between Blackwater contracts as a personal trainer by day and enjoyed Cali's nightlife with Paola and their friends. As a third grand jury proceeding loomed, he became obsessive about his diet and workouts. "My way to deal with the stress of all this stuff, the legal things and what happened in Iraq, was controlling my workouts and diet because it was the only thing I had control over," he said. "I was dealing with a lot of things, and I just didn't want to go out. I didn't want to eat at a restaurant. I wanted to go to the gym . . . and eat my own stuff." His and Paola's relationship suffered, and they separated and divorced before the 2014 trial but remained close.

The news that the government would reinstate the case heightened the sense of unreality that had permeated Nick Slatten's life since he had returned from Baghdad. About six weeks before Urbina threw out the indictments, prosecutors had dismissed Nick from the case for lack of evidence. That decision had come on the heels of a three-week court proceeding called a *Kastigar* hearing that Urbina had held to determine whether the government had allowed the protected statements to taint the evidence. The hearing had made clear that the only evidence against Nick, who had been inside the command vehicle looking out the porthole, had come from Frost and Mealy, who had changed their initial accounts of the events of September 16, 2007, after reading the protected statements of their teammates. Perhaps fearing that the clear evidence of taint would doom the entire case, prosecutors had removed him as a defendant.

Even so, Nick felt himself floating, detached from his loved ones in Sparta, and robbed of his dream of joining the Central Intelligence Agency as a sniper. "They put my face in the paper, and now I'm not marketable anymore," he told me. "I'm blown—I can't ever do what I wanted to do." He was angry and bitter and finding it hard to turn off his battlefield setting. "You go from an environment where you're a killer or you'll be killed," he said. "Especially as a sniper . . . you've almost got to shut off any kind of emotion . . . and it messes up your relationships with normal humans. When you come back, it's almost like, is war reality or is this place reality? It takes your mind a long time to catch up with the fact that they both are reality."

Of course, what can make the world feel even *less* real is the disorienting sensation of being persecuted by one's own government. Years after Nisour Square, powerful figures were going to move heaven and earth to replace Urbina with a judge and a venue of their choosing.

CHAPTER EIGHT

★★★

HOW WIKILEAKS REVEALED THAT HILLARY CLINTON MADE THE RAVEN 23 MEN POLITICAL PRISONERS IN THEIR OWN COUNTRY

Power concedes nothing without a demand. It never did, and it never will.

—FREDERICK DOUGLASS, LETTER TO
GERRIT SMITH, MARCH 30, 1849

IN MY EXPERIENCE, the stupidest ideas come from people with unchecked power and runaway egos, and a lot of those types touched the Raven 23 case throughout the three presidential administrations it survived. The higher-ups in the Bush administration had not seemed particularly interested in the case; that much was clear from the emails published by *The New York Times* in which FBI agents had expressed frustration at the administration's reluctance to pursue the gun charges.

During the Obama administration, things had changed. The same agents' hope that the Democrats would be far more willing to pursue the case had been proven correct. While I could understand why Obama had not wanted to create diplomatic problems with the Iraqis out of the gate, it still seemed unusual that he would prosecute the Raven 23 case so vigorously considering that he had a mounting number of civilian casualties of his own to explain by the time the third round of indictments was handed up in 2013. I just could not figure out what had been in it for Obama, Joe Biden, and especially Secretary of State Hillary Clinton, who had had nothing to do with Nisour Square or the hiring of Blackwater.

Two days after he took office in 2009, Obama ordered a drone strike that killed one militant and ten civilians—including four or five children, according to *The New York Times*.[1] Obama vastly expanded the drone assassination program after inheriting it from President George W. Bush.[2] In 2014, the Bureau of Investigative Journalism wrote that "the Obama administration has launched more than 390 drone strikes in the five years since the first attack that injured Qureshi—eight times as many as were launched in the entire Bush presidency. These strikes have killed more than 2,400 people, at least 273 of them reportedly civilians"—including 12 wedding guests in Yemen and 60 people attending a funeral in Pakistan.[3] But the Centre for Investigative Journalism in London puts that number at as many as 535 civilian deaths from the Obama drone war—including at least 60 children—in just the first three years of his presidency.

Certainly, needing a scapegoat for the government's actions during the "surge" explained why the Bush administration didn't just drop the case after the men's protected statements became public and hopelessly tainted it—or when State Department and US Army investigators found AK-47 shell casings and witnesses who had seen enemy gunmen.

Ultimately, however, both administrations seemed more than willing to sacrifice US citizens and Iraqi civilians for their desired

PR outcomes. To fully explain how easily the government sacrificed the liberty of innocent American citizens to meet nebulous policy goals would require access to classified information.

When the Obama drone program came to light, *Washington Post* columnist James Downie said in an opinion piece on May 5, 2016, that The Intercept's analysis of the leaked documents showed "the disturbing ease with which an innocent civilian—American or not—can be added to the U.S. government's main terrorist database, such as on the basis of a single 'uncorroborated' Facebook or Twitter post. In a 2014 court filing, the government admitted that 469,000 people had been nominated in 2013 for inclusion in an additional government database of 'known or suspected terrorists.' Only 4,900 were rejected. Presumption of innocence this is not. And although Osama bin Laden's name was in a terrorist database long before he was killed, so too was the name Abdulrahman al-Awlaki—innocent, 16 years old, an American citizen and killed by a U.S. drone strike."

It chilled me to think that Obama, a man who had taught constitutional law, had had no better solution to quelling sectarian violence than to kill innocent people who happened to be in the wrong place at the wrong time and blaming the mess on a politically convenient target. I flashed back to one of the first discussions about the Iraq War that I'd had with Joe Bob, in which he had—surprisingly—told me that we should "leave those people alone." Had anybody else thought of that?

Obama wasn't the only high-profile figure who had been bullish on the Raven 23 case. Why had Hillary Clinton, a lawyer herself, helped to resurrect a Bush administration case that was declared dead on arrival by a judge elevated to the federal bench by her husband, President Bill Clinton? Those were smart people—and they had to have known that the case was a dog.

That political gamesmanship was not in my wheelhouse, but Mike loved it and created a database of articles and passages from books about the Iraq War to try to understand the machinations. He reached out to people he knew in Congress and the agencies involved in the case to uncover the prevailing opinion about the case and what it represented to those people.

President Clinton appointed Urbina to the US District Court in 1994, about a year into his presidency. A great deal had changed since Urbina had taken the bench. Hillary Clinton had gone from first lady to US senator. She had lost the 2008 Democratic presidential primary to Obama and was now biding her time at the State Department, hoping to follow him as president. Her fellow cabinet member Attorney General Eric Holder also owed his position to Bill Clinton. The president had elevated Holder from the DC Superior Court bench to deputy US attorney under Attorney General Janet Reno. Under Obama, Holder became the first black attorney general.

Reviving the case meant more than just contradicting a judge appointed by a Democratic president. To do so, Clinton would have to cooperate with both Holder and Vice President Joe Biden.

Holder had sat on Obama's vice presidential search committee and passed over Hillary despite her strong showing in the 2008 primary. Instead, he and the other two search committee members had chosen Joe Biden, despite the fact that Biden had torpedoed his own run for president with a number of racially insensitive comments.

Hillary absolutely destroyed Biden in a head-to-head matchup in the 2008 Democratic primary. She won over 17 million votes, a fraction of a percentage point less than Obama. Biden withdrew from the race after a disastrous showing in Iowa. He was roundly rejected by the voters and managed to attract only a single percentage point at the caucus. By the time Hillary conceded to Obama months later, she had beaten Biden by a margin of 250 to 1 in votes. Yet Biden would probably be Clinton's adversary in the 2016 Democratic presidential primary, and he had the world stage as the vice president.

Mike and I wondered if there was any love lost between Clinton and the two men and, if so, why she would have cooperated to revive the Raven 23 case. We just could not find the upside. Then we considered their political regrets. Like Biden, Hillary had voted to authorize the Iraq War in 2002. Mike joked that those "yes" votes had "haunted all Democrats like Banquo's ghost" as things in Iraq had gone from bad to worse.

Anger at the Great Recession and bank bailouts was rising and would soon lead to the Occupy Wall Street movement. The last thing Obama needed was more anger—at home or abroad. During a National Security Council meeting in June 2009, Obama had turned to Biden and said, "Joe, you take Iraq." That was predicated on Biden's supposed expertise in foreign policy. Biden had been the chair of the Senate Foreign Relations Committee when the war had been authorized. Any screwups in the already shaky situation in Iraq's march toward democracy would land on his doorstep. Also, he had been one of the leading proponents of invading Iraq and using service contractors such as the Blackwater men. Nobody, by the way, supported reinstating a national draft to supply the manpower needed to bring stability to the war-torn country. Biden certainly was not in any position to advocate for a draft; he had received five deferments during the war in Vietnam.

But Biden wasn't the only politician second-guessing how Bush conducted the war in Iraq. When Holder became attorney general, he did not hide his interest in using the power of his office to expiate the sins of the Iraq War. In a speech before the American Constitution Society in November 2008, he had some choice words for the Bush administration. "Other steps taken in the aftermath of the attacks were both excessive and unlawful," he opined. "Although we did not respond to 9/11 by imprisoning Muslim Americans, our government authorized the use of torture, approved of secret electronic surveillance of American citizens, secretly detained American citizens without due process of law, denied the writ of habeas corpus to hundreds of accused enemy combatants, and authorized the use of procedures that violate international law and the United States Constitution. . . . We owe the American people a reckoning."

He wasted no time following up. In 2009, he asked a special prosecutor to investigate the CIA's handling of about a hundred high-value terrorists captured by US forces on the battlefield. They were being held in the Detention and Interrogation Program—loathed by liberals and progressives alike.

The move met with objections from both sides of the aisle. For starters, a task force under the Bush administration had already conducted an investigation that had absolved the CIA. Now a bipartisan group of seven former CIA directors voiced their displeasure. The group complained to Obama that Holder's political point scoring had exposed CIA employees to "an atmosphere of continuous jeopardy" that would "seriously damage the willingness of many other intelligence officers to take risks to protect the country."[4]

CIA Director Leon Panetta made his anger at Holder's actions clear in a profanity-laced screaming match with the attorney general. Later, Holder admitted that he hadn't read the lengthy memos that his own prosecutors had prepared, spelling out the reasons for not charging the agents with crimes.[5] It was clear that Holder was out for blood.

Holder, Clinton, and Biden may have recognized the weakness of the Raven 23 case, but they were also ambitious people who seemed to want to ride the coattails of the politically incendiary Nisour Square incident. Doing so would bring the promise of a better job, enhanced political popularity, and a shot at redemption for previous political sins.

That apparently was the modus operandi of the Obama White

House, according to President-elect Obama's chief of staff, Rahm Emanuel, who told the Wall Street Journal CEO Council in November 2008, "You never want a serious crisis to go to waste. And what I mean by that [is] an opportunity to do things you think you could not do before."[6]

As I recalled the lessons of the Rampart scandal and the O'Melveny PR blitz in LA, I realized that all of those people had had reasons for colluding to achieve one result, even if it hadn't made sense at first glance.

In the shark-infested waters of Washington, DC, prosecuting four nobodies from Red State Flyoverland probably seemed like a way to get retroactive forgiveness for the lousy decisions that had placed those men—and the tens of thousands of other US war fighters and Iraqis—in harm's way to begin with. In practice, it seemed that even people who contended with one another as fiercely as Biden, Clinton, and Holder did were willing to cooperate to smear heroic war fighters if it furthered their political ends and eased their guilty consciences. The problem was this: We had a hunch about why the government was doing it, but how could we hope to prove it?

WikiLeaks would provide the answer. In 2016, the nonprofit media organization had launched a searchable archive of leaked government documents, including more than thirty thousand emails sent to and from Secretary of State Clinton. Clinton had not been in office a year when the Obama administration had doubled down on prosecuting the Raven 23 men after Judge Urbina had thrown the case out.

The initial cache of documents spanned June 30, 2010, to August 12, 2014, but on February 2, 2018, WikiLeaks uploaded an additional thousand or so emails. In trying to understand why the flawed case was so important to the State and Justice Departments, one of Paul Slough's lawyers, Eric Jaso, scoured the WikiLeaks database and found startling evidence that the pressure to prosecute Dustin Heard, Evan Liberty, Paul Slough, and Nick Slatten was coming from Iraqi politicians.[7]

Jaso unearthed a series of diplomatic cables that had begun the day after Judge Urbina had dismissed the case on December 31, 2009, and gone on for about a month afterward, showing that the mounting pressure the State Department was putting on the Department of Justice to prosecute the case was calculated to help Clinton and Obama attain their foreign policy goals.

Once Jaso and his partner David Harrison pieced together the emails and cables, they saw that news of the dismissal of the case had spread rapidly in Iraq and must have provoked terrible unease in Clinton's office.

On Saturday, January 2, 2010, at 8:53 a.m., Secretary Clinton fired off an email to Harold Koh, the legal adviser of the State Department:

> Harold—
>
> First, Happy New Year to you and your family and thank you for all your great work this past year. I am looking forward to the year ahead.
>
> Second, what can we do about Judge Urbina's ruling? . . . Can the US file a civil action against the company? Pay compensation to the victims? What other options do we have?
>
> All the best, H.[8]

Koh responded that he had "already put these very questions" to his team and noted that the press had reported that "State Department lawyers appropriately warned the DOJ prosecutors, but that the DOJ lawyers chose to take a different route."

Presumably, the buck-passing between the two agencies sprang from the warning that the case would be tainted by the men's leaked statements—a violation of their Fifth Amendment protection against self-incrimination, as well as the fact that there simply was no evidence to support the theory that they shot without provocation.

The diplomatic cables from the US Embassy in Baghdad painted a picture of the chaos that had followed Urbina's ruling, fed by the Iraqi government and its imams. The series of cables began with a January 4, 2010, missive from Chargé d'Affaires Robert Ford, whose subject line read "Public outrage over Blackwater decision generating heavy fallout."

"Public outrage has erupted within Iraq over the decision of U.S. District Judge Ricardo Urbina to dismiss the charges brought against Blackwater employees for their role in the deaths of 17 Iraqis on September 16, 2007. GOI [Government of Iraq] spokesman Ali al-Dabbagh condemned the decision on January 1 and called on the U.S. Department of Justice to appeal the decision. . . . He also indicated that the GOI might expel former Blackwater employees out of Iraq, potentially complicating security services for the Embassy. . . . Members of the Iraqi Parliament have even raised holding a referendum on the Security Agreement (SA)," the cable, marked "Confidential," read. It had been sent to the Department of Justice, the National Security Council, and the secretary of state.

The Security Agreement, also known as the Status of Forces Agreement (SOFA), was a big problem for Obama and Biden. Before making good on their campaign promise to pull troops out of Iraq, they had had to ensure that the upcoming election in March 2010 happened without controversy or violence and that the winner was Nouri al-Maliki. Then there was the small task of stabilizing the new government, something that had quickly proven to be much harder to achieve in reality than to promise on the campaign stump. That meant keeping troops and contractors in Iraq past the 2011 expiration date of the current SOFA.

The Iraqis were now threatening to hold SOFA hostage unless

the Obama administration "did something" about Nisour Square. Rather than treating the threat as a game of brinksmanship by al-Maliki, who had allowed Iranian terrorists to overrun significant elements of both the Iraqi police and military, the Obama administration quickly caved in to the political pressure.

"Other Iraqi politicians, religious leaders, and journalists have expressed strong outrage at the judicial decision and called for extraditing the Blackwater employees to Iraq, taking the case to an international court, or for additional legal action to be taken in the U.S. So far our security contractors' operations have not been affected, but they both need license renewals from the Ministry of Interior," the cable said. Ford then observed that Iraqi politicians and imams were calling for the expulsion of anyone who had worked for Blackwater, which included a substantial number of people now working for other companies, such as DynCorp International and Triple Canopy.

Last, he advised the Obama administration to "publicly acknowledge the suffering of the victims' families. (Many of them have received small compensation payments from the Embassy, but we should not mention this, obviously.) . . . The fact that Iraqi lawmakers and other[s] might exploit the judge's decision to revive calls for a referendum on the Security Agreement shows we need to address in some fashion Iraqis' perception that justice has not been served."

In the next cable, dated January 5, 2010, al-Maliki and Vice President Adil Abd al-Mahdi urged the US government in a meeting with Senator John McCain to appeal Urbina's ruling "to give the right impression" to Iraqi citizens. "Iraqi officials whom we met with today clearly do not want the Blackwater issue to further cloud our bilateral relationship, and strongly implied that a USG [US government] appeal would help them to assuage public outrage over the issue, and make the GOI less vulnerable to criticism for letting private security contractors in the country," Ford wrote.

Furthermore, prosecuting the Blackwater guards was "a political necessity" to make al-Maliki, the Obama administration's choice for prime minister, "look tough" against the occupying US government in the upcoming March 7, 2010, elections.

Ford said that rhetoric was coming from all over Iraq. An influential Shi'a imam who was also the head of Iraq's Human Rights Committee asked during prayers if "the killing of innocents is considered a defense of US National Security?" Another Human Rights Committee member said that Urbina's decision had shown "disdain for the blood of innocent Iraqis by the US Judiciary." The Iraqi Lawyers Union agreed.

Another imam, on the same day, said during prayers that the Blackwater decision "shows that Iraqi blood has no value to the Americans."

"Most Iraqis do not intuit the concept of an independent judiciary and therefore suspect that the U.S. executive branch orchestrated the dismissal of the case," Ford wrote after conferring with a prominent Iraqi attorney who said he had difficulty comprehending Urbina's ruling.

Ford also reported that Iraqi Vice President al-Mahdi was planning to use an upcoming visit to Washington, DC, to press for action against the Blackwater guards. He said that the matter was "especially sensitive" to al-Mahdi because a Blackwater guard had gotten away with killing his bodyguard in 2006. Erik Prince had immediately fired the man but had had no authority to prosecute him, nor had the Bush administration prosecuted him after he had returned to US soil.

In a cable dated January 8, 2010, Ford said that Ambassador Christopher Hill had explained to Attorney General Holder the problems that Judge Urbina's decision was causing in Iraq. Hill said that he had assured al-Maliki that the US government took Iraqis' feelings very seriously and would continue to take an active interest in the case.

On January 11, 2010, the Iraqi vice president brought up the case in a meeting with Senators Joseph Lieberman, John Barrasso, John Thune, and John McCain. He again stressed the importance of an appeal and again mentioned that a Blackwater employee had killed his bodyguard. Ford's cables warned that the Iraqi politicians were looking for political cover and believed that Judge Urbina's decision would inevitably harm US-Iraqi relations.

I tracked down Ford, now a professor at Yale University, to find out more about his assertion in those cables that he had doled out money to victims of US-caused violence. I wanted to know more about that. I emailed him, and we set up a time to talk. He was refreshingly frank, immediately recognized the cables, and said he had not personally written them but had approved and sent them.

He told me that he had first gone to Iraq in 2003, after the Bush administration had invaded. He had gone to Najaf, a holy city for Shi'a pilgrims in Iraq, with the Coalition Provisional Authority and "quit in disgust in December."

"The CPA was the most pathetic thing I ever saw," he said. "I got called back to Iraq by Colin Powell. I didn't want to go, but I got called back." He had worked with Director of National Intelligence John Negroponte and Zalmay Khalilzad in 2004 and then become ambassador to Algeria. He had not been in Iraq for the Nisour Square incident, but he had returned to take the number two position at the embassy in Baghdad in 2008, this time at the request of Secretary of State Condoleezza Rice.

In 2009, he had worked for Christopher Hill as deputy ambassador at the embassy. The job, he told me, had been "day-to-day management—budgets, security, consular affairs, visas, passports." The reporting back to Washington, DC, had also gone through his office, which was how he had come to sign those cables in 2010. "I sent out of Iraq hundreds of cables over my time. So I looked at them. I didn't write any of them, but I approved them," he said.

I asked him about the condolence payments. "I was the one who gave the families the money that was referred to in those cables," he said. "That was my job . . . the compensation money that we offered." He figured that that had occurred in the first half of 2009. "We didn't do it that often because we didn't have that many people killed by our security people," he said in total contradiction to media reports about Blackwater. "I'd be hard pressed to think of another incident like that. Where Blackwater security killed people like that."

He also described the resentment that the State Department had created for itself, especially among Iraqi civilians, with its stubborn adherence to CPA-era policies—policies for which Blackwater had been unfairly blamed. "You have these huge American vehicles, these Humvees and these mine-resistant vehicles, MRVs, and they were just gigantic," he told me. "They had right-of-way, and when you saw them coming down the street, they were extremely intimidating, I think partly by intent for security reasons. So it just added an air of abnormality to the traffic and then the standard procedure—this is not Blackwater, I'm not blaming them at all—this is what the State Department diplomatic security wanted, and I could never get it changed. They wanted us to go in these very visible convoys, and they would beep and honk and they would literally jam people in the roads and get them out of the way."[9]

The protocols "would just make life miserable for the regular Iraqi driver," who would have to pull over and try to get out of the way while the diplomatic convoy zoomed past, he told me. "So it was exceptionally disruptive, and that had been going on long before this Nisour Square incident, so I cannot say that we were particularly popular with our military forces and our Blackwater and all, and we knew that."

For all his candor about the mess that US diplomatic and military leaders had created for the people who had carried out their orders, he was surprisingly insistent that the US government had rooted out anti-American insurgents from the Iraqi government by 2008 or 2009. While acknowledging that Iraqi police and military uniforms were available on the black market and that insurgents had often dressed as police, he was "not aware of any instance in 2007, '08, '09 where Iraqi police operated as insurgents against the U.S. In 2004-5, absolutely yes," he said. "But the relationship between Americans and these insurgent types evolved, and there came to be a certain 'live and let live.' So I would be uncomfortable with you suggesting that people in the Iraqi security forces were attacking Americans. There were undoubtedly skirmishes . . . we did not view Iraqi forces as hostile to Americans. We were doing training missions with them."

The embassy may not have viewed them as hostile to Americans, but the Americans on the ground told a different story, I told him. They were well aware that the Mahdi Army and Badr Organization had infiltrated every organ of the Iraqi government and were planning organized attacks against US forces daily.

"There were undoubtedly a lot of Badr people brought into the Interior Ministry," he acknowledged. "Frankly, we warned President Bush about it and were told to live with it."

He agreed that "in 2004, 2005, absolutely yes . . . the Iraqi police operated as insurgents against the US" and that "anyone in the Iraqi government connected to the JAM [the Mahdi Army] or to Muqtada al-Sadr's political block was anti-American, and certainly we would have to be concerned about their willingness to look at the evidence in an impartial way."

That double-speak was confusing—had the Iraqi government been infiltrated with terrorists or not? Or had the US diplomatic leadership simply been intent on creating a story in which Iraqi militants had somehow suddenly laid down their weapons and sung "Kumbaya" with US forces on the ground? In that case, incidents such as the one at Nisour Square showing the brutal reality that nothing had really changed on the ground in Iraq after the "surge"—and that we were losing—had to be blamed on somebody else.

Ford then cautioned me to "beware of applying American judicial standards to what foreign countries do. I wouldn't blame the Justice Department for Iraqi failings [because] you have to deal with the government you are dealing with. The Justice Department wouldn't have been in a position to pick who on the Iraqi side would do the investigation. So in a sense I mean anybody in the US government operating in Iraq had these kinds of issues."

Well, I said, when you promise to deliver "American justice" and try Americans in a US court, don't you have to adhere to US legal standards? If justice isn't the goal, what kind of "democracy" are we creating in Iraq?

Mike and I were starting to get a picture of what had really been going on in Baghdad—and it was a lot different from what Americans had been told by their government and the media. That information would not come to light until many years after the 2014 trial and long after the men and their families learned that their government was going to appeal Urbina's dismissal of the case.

While Harrison and Jaso, whom Christin Slough hired in 2018 to pursue presidential pardons for her husband and his three comrades, were thrilled to see their argument that the Raven 23 men were political prisoners substantiated, they were also disappointed to be correct. "You expect everything to work the way it should work," Harrison said later.

Yet the DOJ felt confident enough to refile the case because things in Washington, DC, were, in fact, working as they usually did. An ally had appeared in the person of a judge named Royce Lamberth.

CHAPTER NINE

★★★

THE GUILTY CONSCIENCE OF AMERICAN WARMONGERS

Judges are the weakest link in our system of justice, and they are also the most protected.

—ALAN DERSHOWITZ

BEFORE HE WAS ASSIGNED to the Raven 23 case, Judge Royce Lamberth had left a long, slippery trail through the Washington, DC, legal system, but when Mike and I tried to interview people who had written books and academic papers about him, no one would talk to us. That was remarkable because there was a lot to say about him, starting with the September 11, 2001, attacks on the World Trade Center and Pentagon.

After reading several accounts of Lamberth's dealings with the US intelligence communities, we believed that as he had sat in his town car watching the Pentagon smolder, as described by former National Intelligence Agency general counsel Stewart Baker in his book *Skating on Stilts: Why We Aren't Stopping Tomorrow's Terrorism*, Lamberth could have traced the failure to prevent the attack to the chilling effect of an official letter he wrote in 2001.[1]

At the time, Lamberth was the chief judge of the Foreign Intelligence Surveillance Court (FISC), which meant that he was the judge who decided whether to let intelligence agencies conduct secret surveillance—wiretaps and the like—on terror suspects. The court also controls how much of that information the spy agencies can share with law enforcement agencies such as the FBI.

One case in particular illustrated how FISA—and Lamberth, in particular—created red tape that tied the hands of intelligence agencies in the lead-up to 9/11. Seemingly incensed by what he perceived to be a problem, Lamberth's fix overcorrected the issue by creating an unworkable solution. Six months before the September 11 attacks, Judge Lamberth accused an FBI agent of lying on a wiretap application—a felony and career-ending accusation. An investigation later found that the agent had inadvertently made a paperwork error, but Lamberth would not let up. Attorney General John Ashcroft and FBI Director Louis Freeh begged him to back off. In response, Lamberth barred the agent from his courtroom and demanded an internal investigation.

Baker recounted the gravity of this incident in his book. "For the first and only time in its history, the FISA court was disciplining an FBI agent, singling him out by name, and barring him from any appearance before the court," he wrote. "Why? Because the court no longer trusted his assurances that the FBI was observing the elaborate set of rules that the court had erected to protect the civil liberties of terrorist suspects."[2] There was a significant chilling effect sent through the FBI by Lamberth's censure of the agent. Lamberth was well aware of and proud of the effect, telling Baker in an interview for the latter's book, "We never rescinded it. We enforced it. And we sent a message to the FBI."

Next, the FISA court, led by Lamberth, upped the ante by requiring every supervisory agent (again according to Baker's book) "to sign the FISA applications filed by their offices. They had to confirm all of the facts that the application set forth. Assistant US attorneys were required to do the same. . . . The new requirement forced every agent and every Justice official to double- and triple-check their compliance with the wall. Any error, any misstep could lead to sanctions. . . . The government began to miss deadlines for submitting wiretap applications."

Government sources confirm this: "While the Department attempted to correct the process that had led to erroneous filings, a large number of FISA surveillances, including many related to international terrorism, expired in the spring and summer of 2001."[3]

Baker went on to say that Lamberth's wrath had had grave consequences. When FBI agents learned from the National Security Agency that a high-level al-Qaeda terrorist named Khalid al-Mihdhar had entered the United States in August 2001, they refused to open a criminal investigation into him because they probably anticipated FISA pushback.

"FBI Headquarters refused to accede to the New York field office recommendation that a criminal investigation be opened . . . based on Headquarters' reluctance to utilize intelligence information to draw the connections between al-Mihdhar and the USS *Cole* bombing necessary to open a criminal investigation," explained one later-declassified Joint Intelligence Committee report examining the lead-up to the disaster.

Describing the atmosphere in the intelligence world at this point, the report's author points directly to Lamberth's court. "The consequences of the FISA Court's approach to the Wall between intelligence gathering and law enforcement before September 11 were extensive. FBI personnel involved in FISA matters feared the fate of the agent who had been barred and began to avoid even the most pedestrian contact with personnel in criminal components of the Bureau or DOJ because it could result in intensive scrutiny by OIPR and the FISA Court."[4]

Nobody wanted to risk crossing Judge Lamberth, Baker wrote.

Less than a month later, al-Mihdhar helped pilot American Airlines Flight 77 into the west wall of the Pentagon. Not surprisingly, Judge Lamberth changed his tune on allowing agencies to swap information on terrorists—but not until after the hijack attacks killed 2,996 people and destroyed the World Trade Center and part of the Pentagon. As he sat in his car near the Pentagon, he began approving wiretaps by phone.[5]

He told National Public Radio in a 2013 interview about the FISA meetings he had attended after the planes had hit the World Trade Center. "In the days following 9/11, I went to some of the most bloodcurdling meetings and briefings in my lifetime, to hear some of the things that were being told might be the next follow-up," he recalled.[6]

In its report, the 9/11 Commission did not address Lamberth by name but had plenty to say about his order. "Action officers should have been able to draw on all available knowledge about al Qaeda in the government," the report said. "Management should have ensured that information was shared and duties were clearly assigned across agencies, and across the foreign-domestic divide."[7]

Next, as we worked to get a clearer picture of Lamberth's reputation and influence, I found an academic article by George Washington University Law School professor Richard J. Pierce, Jr., that gave us some hints about why people were so scared of Lamberth. In the 2004 article titled "Judge Lamberth's Reign of Terror at the Department of Interior," Pierce described Judge Lamberth as the poster child for judicial reform. Pierce illustrated Lamberth's courtroom tyranny by enumerating the threats the judge had made against whichever side he apparently chose to be the loser. Lamberth, he said, "routinely uses threats . . . to induce lawyers, witnesses, and other government employees to take positions he favors and to refrain from taking positions he disfavors."[8]

In a case involving the US Department of the Interior, Lamberth sanctioned more than eighty government employees, including two secretaries of the Interior, a treasury secretary, two assistant secretaries of the Interior and lower-level DOJ employees who never even appeared in his courtroom, Pierce said.

The judge also shut down the DOI's website more than once, leaving the public "unable to access information about popular national parks and monuments and [making] it difficult for Interior agencies to communicate with one another," NBC News wrote in a March 15, 2004, story on its website.[9]

"The disconnections at the DOI lasted from one month to two years," Pierce wrote, adding that the outages and Judge Lamberth's sanctions—for which the targets of his ire had to retain attorneys—cost the US government more than $3.7 million. "People did not want to do any work on the project without first consulting an attorney," Pierce wrote. "Some employees were even prepared to resign rather than expose themselves to the stress and risk of working on a project that had already produced five contempt citations against Cabinet Secretaries and Assistant Cabinet Secretaries and threats of contempt to seventy-five lower-level government employees."

Two years after Pierce wrote his article about a lawsuit between the Department of the Interior and a Native American tribe, the DC Court of Appeals took the rare step of throwing Lamberth off the case for bias. That had happened only three times since 1893.

I emailed Professor Pierce and explained that we, too, had a case that illustrated why Lamberth needed to be removed from the federal bench. "I am afraid I can't be of help. Everything I know about Judge Lamberth was in the article you reference," Pierce wrote back.

"Wimp," Mike wrote to me when I forwarded the email to him.

There seemed no rhyme or reason in how Lamberth picked the winners in his courtroom, but once he decided, no evidence seemed to get into the way of his decision. After going all out for the Native American tribe against the federal government in the Department of the Interior case, the judge had seemed to switch sides to favor local government officials in a 2016 case involving the San Antonio Police Department. In 2016, he ruled that the family of a schizophrenic man who had died in police custody could not sue the city of San Antonio for civil rights violations. San Antonio police officers had beaten, repeatedly tased, and sicced a police dog on thirty-year-old Pierre Abernathy in his family's front yard. His family had tried desperately to tell the seven officers about his mental illness but had been ignored. Pierre's neighbor testified that Abernathy, who was African American, had curled up into a ball and cried out for his mother as the officers had beaten him for fifteen minutes straight. Abernathy's brother had heard the officers shout: "Yeah! Get some!" Abernathy died before he got to the hospital. But Lamberth had dismissed the case, citing Abernathy's "near superhuman ability to resist" the horde of police officers attacking him.

"In light of the context in which the officers found themselves in their attempts to apprehend and detain Abernathy, the Court concludes that the defendants deployed force that was neither clearly excessive nor clearly unreasonable," the judge wrote.[10]

We needed some context for Lamberth's behavior, but we could not get anyone who had actually practiced before him to talk to us. We kept on digging, never expecting the spectacular hypocrisy we stumbled upon next.

Lamberth was born in Texas but spent his entire career in Washington, DC, melding his two personas by showing up at political functions in a cowboy hat and boots. He started his long civil service career as a federal prosecutor in 1974. President Ronald Reagan appointed him to the bench in 1987 after reading a news article about how Washington civil rights lawyers hated him. Before starting his government job, Lamberth had spent a few years in the army's Judge Advocate General's Corps defending US soldiers in Vietnam against war crimes charges.

In a striking parallel to the Raven 23 case, Lamberth flew into a remote Vietnamese village in 1969 to defend six Army Rangers accused of killing North Vietnamese soldiers, slitting them open, and stuffing their bodies with rice. The soldiers were heard bragging about the mutilation and were reported to army investigators.[11]

Lamberth recounted in a news article that while flying into the combat zone near the village where the men's bodies lay—where presumably women and children also lived—the helicopter carrying Lamberth had lost an engine. Mistakenly thinking he was under fire, Lamberth said, he had grabbed an assault rifle and begun "firing like hell" into a tree line.

When Lamberth arrived at the village, he was taken to a shed where blood and rice were spilled on the floor, but there were no bodies. He described how proud he was to get the war crimes charges against the Rangers dropped because the army investigators could never find the bodies—thus no autopsy, no forensic evidence, no crime. He described in both accounts how his reputation had grown among soldiers as the man to turn to if they were accused of a crime.

He might have been talking about himself—or the government's star witness, Ridgeway—when he later concluded during the Raven 23 men's sentencing that "it's clear these fine young men just panicked," I thought. Lamberth's final pronouncement to the packed courtroom would be even weirder, in light of the Vietnam episode: "The overall wild thing that went on here just cannot ever be condoned by a court. . . . The message here about deterrence for future cases is one that the Court needs to send to people who are entrusted with automatic weapons, that they have to be careful and have due regard for the consequences of firing automatic weapons."

But the case wasn't really about warning people to be careful around firearms; it was about furthering opaque foreign policy objectives.

In April 2011, the Court of Appeals for the District of Columbia found that Judge Urbina had rejected too much evidence as tainted by the protected statements and sent the case back to him with instructions to review the evidence against each defendant individually. "We find that the district court's findings depend on 'an erroneous view of the law,'" the appellate panel wrote. The justices instructed Urbina "to determine, as to each defendant, what evidence—if any—the government presented against him that was tainted as to him," to determine whether the tainted evidence justified dismissing the case. But Urbina had retired that January, and the case was reassigned to Lamberth, chief judge of the District Court for the District of Columbia.

But the reassignment wasn't random. During a conversation with one of the defense attorneys much later, we discovered something interesting about how Judge Lamberth had come to preside over the case. I wondered aloud how he had been assigned to the case after Urbina had retired in 2012. In 2014, he had been three years older than Urbina and had reached the age at which federal judges generally take "senior status"—basically retire—when the Raven 23 case began.

One of the defense attorneys suggested that Lamberth had been assigned the case because he had taken Ridgeway's plea in 2008. While I was researching the case, I found two interesting documents in the PACER federal court filing system, dated June 8, 2012. The first was a document showing that the Raven 23 case had been randomly reassigned from Judge Urbina, who had retired, to Judge Richard Leon by the chair of the court's calendar and case management committee.[12]

The second document, dated the same day, showed a reassignment of the same case from Judge Leon to Judge Lamberth, citing "case incorrectly assigned" as the reason for the switch. I called and left messages for Judges Leon and Urbina, but no one ever returned my call to explain why Lamberth had snatched it. Leon, a George W. Bush appointee, was nearly a decade younger than Lamberth and, like Urbina, had sided with Guantánamo Bay detainees over the DOJ in a slew of wrongful detention cases. How very convenient for prosecutors that the case had not landed with Leon, I thought.

Later, an anonymous tipster would send us an email that illustrated the gulf between the powerful and the inconsequential in Washington, DC, and that underlined how easily Lamberth and other powerful figures could move the levers of justice. The group email, dated January 2019 and addressed to Judge Lamberth, DC Chief Appellate Judge David Sentelle, and Supreme Court Justices John Roberts and Brett Kavanaugh, confirmed Judge Lamberth's attendance at a monthly poker night. The poker game was held at the homes of the nation's most powerful lawyers and judges—and Judge Lamberth has had a place at the table for at least twenty years.

Richard Pierce, the George Washington University professor who wrote about Lamberth, called it "the Judges' Club." Combine those deep connections with Lamberth's longtime access to the nation's secrets via the FISC, and you have a recipe for power run amuck. It is no wonder that people are afraid to report Judge Lamberth's egregious conduct. "For a government lawyer, filing a complaint against a member of the District Court for the District of Columbia is a lot like attempting regicide. . . . Even in the unlikely event that the complaint yields the ultimate 'success' of impeachment, the lawyer still would have to fear reprisals by other members of the 'Judges' Club.'"[13] "Government agencies and their lawyers dare not complain about the members of the 'Judges' Club' before whom they know they will have to appear again and again," Pierce wrote. It was hard to have faith, in light of evidence that the government had manufactured charges and upheld them with perjured testimony, that anything would be different at the appellate level.

The DOJ also brought in a new team—Assistant US Attorneys Anthony Asuncion, John Han, and T. Patrick Martin—to rid the case of everyone who had been exposed to the protected statements. The DOJ created a "filter team" or "taint team" to review each piece of evidence and witness statements before Asuncion, Han, and Martin saw it.

The prosecution team, including FBI and State Department investigators, returned to the scene in Iraq—now five years after the fact—to reinterview witnesses and look at "evidence," including the vehicles stored in a parking lot with no cover from the heat or elements. Defense attorneys asked to be included on the trip but were denied; it was too dangerous, the government told them.[14]

The new prosecution team declined to reindict Donald Ball—for reasons that they did not elaborate on—but moved forward with a superseding indictment against Dustin, Evan, Paul, and, controversially, Nick, whom the previous team had dismissed from the case three years earlier for lack of evidence.

The third grand jury returned indictments on October 17, 2013, just days before the deadline that Lamberth had set for the government to decide whether to refile the case. Interestingly, the government had somehow decided as a result of its "reinvestigation" that only thirty-two people had been killed or injured during the Nisour Square incident rather than the thirty-four stated in the previous indictments.

The new indictment charged Nick with fourteen counts of voluntary manslaughter and sixteen counts of attempted manslaughter—despite the fact that his statement and an accounting of ordnance showed that he had fired two shots. Evan and Dustin were charged with thirteen counts of voluntary manslaughter and sixteen counts of attempted manslaughter, and Paul was charged with thirteen counts of voluntary manslaughter and eighteen counts of attempted manslaughter. The prosecutors also threw in the controversial gun charge, which raised their minimum sentences to thirty years—the charge of "using and discharging a firearm . . . during and in relation to a crime of violence" that FBI investigators had demanded.

The new prosecution team had a problem: They had allowed the statute of limitations on manslaughter and attempted manslaughter charges against Nick to expire after the previous team had dismissed him from the case. Although they had no new evidence to warrant changing their position on whether there was sufficient evidence to charge him, they went ahead and did so. Nick's attorneys argued fervently to the appeals court that allowing the government "to change its position now [to reindict him] would pave the way for egregious manipulation of the judicial system." They were not wrong.

The appeals court ruled in 2014—just weeks before the trial was set to begin—that the statute of limitations prevented the government from reindicting Nick on the same charges.[15] Incredibly, the government demanded that Nick waive the statute of limitations so it could charge him again with manslaughter and attempted manslaughter. If he refused, the prosecutors threatened to charge him with murder, which carries a mandatory life sentence and has no statute of limitations.[16]

When he declined their offer, prosecutors charged him with a single count of murder. Even more ridiculous, the government was now accusing him of the premeditated killing of Ahmed Haithem Al Rubia'y, the driver of the white Kia—a shot that Paul Slough said had been his in at least four sworn statements and one that Nick could not have taken from his position inside the command vehicle.

There were no witness statements or forensic evidence to support the charge, and a ballistics analysis showed that it was not even possible at the angle in which the command vehicle was facing. "A more textbook case of vindictive prosecution can scarcely be imagined, and to countenance this result will ensure that defendants think twice before validly exercising their legal rights," the National Association of Criminal Defense Lawyers wrote about the murder charge in its 2016 amicus curiae brief.

Even more incredibly, seventy-one-year-old Judge Lamberth—true to his word that the case would "end on my level while I'm still alive"—allowed the spurious charge to proceed to trial a month later.

CHAPTER TEN

──── ★★★ ────

JUDGE LAMBERTH TIGHTENS THE KNOT

Never attempt to win by force what can be won by deception.
　　　　　　　　—NICCOLÒ MACHIAVELLI, *THE PRINCE*

A FEW WEEKS BEFORE Paul Slough and his wife and daughter left for Washington, DC, for his trial in 2014, the family made a pilgrimage of sorts to a peaceful spot they called "God's Green Acre" overlooking a canyon on Rick and Vivian West's ranch near Dickens, Texas.

They often went on drives in the evenings when they stayed at the ranch, and loved to stop at that particular vantage point and look across the canyon over a land so vast that "you can watch your dog run away for two days," Paul told me later. A constant West Texas breeze cleansed the spring air, the year's first birds and buds were emerging, and Paul felt he could almost see the curvature of the earth. Lily had just turned a year old and was cooing and trying to string together her first sentences.

The couple would go back in their minds to that still, golden moment often, in the years that followed, as their anchor point.

The Raven 23 families steeled themselves to attend the trial at the E. Barrett Prettyman U.S. Courthouse in Washington, DC, in what they believed would be the final stop on a long road to redemption—until, that is, the trial began on June 11, 2014.

Christin Slough rented a home in Falls Church, Virginia, for the duration of the trial and Paul, Lily, Dustin, and Nick moved in with her to give themselves some small sense of normality. Evan stayed at his brother Aaron's home in Arlington.

Nick's mother, Reba, made the nine-hour drive from Sparta to sit in the cool, marble-walled federal courtroom for the surreal experience of watching her son go on trial for murder and his friends, young men she now knew well, for a massacre. Other family members occasionally joined her when they could leave work for a few days and could afford flights and hotel rooms.

"We just thought the system was going to work for Nick and he was going to be freed," she told me. But from my reading of the trial transcript, the system had been stacked against the Raven 23 men long before they arrived in court. First of all, venue rules dictate that trials "shall be in the district in which the offender, or any one of two or more joint offenders, is arrested." That meant that the Raven 23 trial should have been held in Utah, the home state of Donald Ball, where the men had first surrendered and entered their plea. Or in Texas, where Paul lived, or Tennessee, where Nick and Dustin resided. Even New Hampshire, Evan's home state, would have been acceptable.

In allowing the trial to go forward in Washington, DC, Judge Lamberth ignored a long-standing legal precedent stretching back to colonial times that protects US citizens from being tried far from home. In the Declaration of Independence, the nation's founders condemned King George III for "for transporting Us beyond the Seas to be tried for pretended offenses"—namely for treason.

But Lamberth had sided with prosecutors who had gamed the system by "choreographing the voluntary surrender of a cooperating witness [Ridgeway] in the District of Columbia and labeling that surrender an 'arrest,'" the National Association of Criminal Defense Lawyers had argued in their amicus brief.

In fact, Ridgeway had flown from California to Washington, DC, on his own and met FBI agents at the airport. He testified that he had never been handcuffed or read his Miranda rights. An FBI agent had "dangled his handcuffs in front of me and said, 'If you can behave yourself, I will not put these on you,'" he said. He had never been put into a jail cell and after entering his guilty plea was allowed to return home.[1]

"If this construction stands, the district court will have effectively construed [the venue law] to mean that the venue shall be proper in 'whatever district the government prefers'—as that will be the practical result of such a ruling," the NACDL wrote to the appellate court. "The Constitution cannot tolerate such a result and this Court should not either."

Lamberth allowed it, I think, because no jury anywhere but in Washington, DC, would convict decorated veterans for defending themselves and their comrades in a firefight. And the prospect of the international media coverage that was sure to follow the case was simply too irresistible to pass up.

Lamberth also tore down another roadblock that should have prevented any trial from being held by declaring that he did not "believe" in the Military Extraterritorial Jurisdiction Act (MEJA), the federal law that directs the way in which US courts prosecute military contractors for crimes committed overseas and that would, if respected, have stopped the case before it reached trial. MEJA applies only to contractors who accompany the US military or have a mission supporting the Department of Defense, meaning that Blackwater's contract with the State Department should have shielded the Raven 23 men from prosecution under MEJA.

The matter was so clear that Gordon England, the deputy secretary of defense, had written about it in a 2007 letter to then Senator

Barack Obama and then testified at trial that the Raven 23 men had not worked for or supported the mission of the DOD. ". . . it wasn't our incident. I mean, we were—this was not a Department of Defense issue. . . . I mean, this was a State Department issue, not a DOD issue," England testified at the men's trial. In response, Lamberth stubbornly declared, "If I believe this, I would dismiss the case right now for lack of jurisdiction. I don't believe this."

During jury selection, the judge snapped at a potential juror who said she could not serve on the jury for the five months that the trial would last because she had to pick her child up at daycare an hour before the court planned to adjourn each day. "What a poor excuse for a citizen you are," he told her.[2]

He warned prosecutors and defense attorneys not to try the case in the media, Jessica Slatten, then a staff attorney for the Florida Supreme Court, recalled. But stories continued to appear throughout the proceedings, citing information that could only have come from the prosecution team. From the first day of trial to the last, Lamberth expressed his bias by consistently favoring prosecutors and disfavoring the defense: He allowed the government to show the jury several photos of the children and families of the alleged Iraqi victims, over the objections of defense attorneys, but barred Dustin Heard's lawyer, David Schertler, from showing the jury a photograph of Dustin, his wife, Kelli, and their two young children as part of his opening statement and closing argument.[3] Prosecutors were allowed to display numerous photos of the alleged Iraqi victims, including a child who had died at a different location and whose parents claimed he had been killed in Nisour Square only after seeing a television advertisement about the case. Throughout the trial, Lamberth would indulge the prosecution in rambling, pointless questioning to elicit graphic, emotional testimony from Iraqi witnesses that had no probative value. The defense objected constantly to those prejudicial displays, but Lamberth overruled their objections.

For all the machinations of the "taint team" and the costly three-year "reinvestigation," the new prosecution team's case theory looked in most respects like the narrative that Urbina had thrown out four years earlier—except for the government's bizarre new theory that Nick Slatten, an evil racist, had set off the Nisour Square shootings as part of his plan to kill as many Iraqis as possible as retribution for 9/11.

The government's three-hour opening statement read like a dime-store version of a Tom Clancy novel. Assistant US Attorney T. Patrick Martin described to the jury how Slatten had crouched in the belly of the BearCat, peering through the scope of his sniper rifle "with hatred in his heart, an intense dislike and hatred for the Iraqi people.

"In his mind, they were responsible for 9/11, not just Iraq, a country, but the Iraqi people were responsible for 9/11, one of the worst days in our history," Martin told the jury. "In his mind, ladies and gentlemen, he was there in Iraq to get payback. In his mind, the Iraqi people were that opportunity. He would tell his teammates when he would kill Iraqis, got another kill on my weapon. . . . I'm getting closer and closer to evening the score. And, ladies and gentlemen, he thought they were animals, he thought they were subhuman, and that made it easier for him to do exactly that." He went on to say that Slatten had confided in Jeremy Ridgeway after the Nisour Square incident that he had "popped a man's grape; his head, and the man slumped forward."

The FBI's interview notes, called 302s, had been included in the documents I had received and reviewed along with witness statements, pretrial hearings, and pretrial motions. Nowhere had I seen any statement from any witnesses describing such conversations between Nick and anyone else. I went back to the 302s and discovered the phrase "popped his head like a grape" in handwritten FBI notes and ascribed to Evan Liberty, who had been talking about a completely different event.

Nick's attorney, Tom Connolly, moved for a mistrial after the government's opening statement. Judge Lamberth turned him down flat. I also noticed that the prosecutors and the FBI agents had taken to identifying the defendants by their battlefield nicknames in their handwritten notes, which seemed odd and disrespectful.

Martin went on in his opening statement to describe how the Kia had begun moving forward only after the driver had died because "he does not have the ability to apply pressure to the brakes, the most basic of functions. As it rolls forward, Defendant Paul Slough . . . sees it coming. He shoots into the windshield of that car a series of shots from his rifle. And by shooting, ladies and gentlemen, he draws the attention of the other members in the convoy. Others join in, they see this crawling vehicle coming towards the convoy and they join in." It was a neat theory, but it contradicted the testimony of about a dozen witnesses, including Army Captain Peter Decareau, who testified at trial that he had interviewed several Iraqi bystanders who had seen the white Kia "punch forward," drive around the vehicles in front of it, and behave like "a car bomb" before the Raven 23 convoy had begun shooting.

Martin spent the balance of his opening statement either mischaracterizing the evidence—the victims "were looking around and they didn't see anybody that was shooting at the defendants"—or pumping up the government's star witnesses (by that time, Ridgeway had been joined by others): Jimmy Watson, Adam Frost, Mark Mealy, Matthew Murphy, and two army officers, Colonel David Boslego and General Michael Tarsa, some of whom would contradict themselves by the end of the case.

Almost every Monday, the trial began with defense attorneys complaining to Lamberth in sidebar conferences that prosecutors had dumped hundreds of pages of new evidence—some of it exculpatory evidence the defense had not ever seen—and now the government wanted to show it to the jury. "The Government received these e-mails, as we understand it, a year ago," defense attorney Brian Heberlig told Lamberth on the morning of Monday, July 28, 2014. "This is now becoming a pattern . . . I mean, we keep getting on the Friday night before the next week or sometimes the Sunday night, a dump of hundreds of documents . . . this is becoming gross incompetence and it's prejudicing us to a significant degree."

The trial transcripts showed that the government had suffered absolutely no consequences for continually violating the rules of criminal procedure right in front of the judge's nose. In fact, Lamberth often had allowed the disputed evidence to come in.

It was so fantastical, I wanted to laugh. That this farcical theory of the Nisour Square case had resulted in lifelong prison sentences for four decent young men who honorably served their country—my country—made me weep instead.

Frost essentially complained repeatedly about his discomfort with Ridgeway and Evan, and occasionally Nick, having thrown frozen water bottles at Iraqi civilian vehicles when Frost believed there had been no threat.

Frost, who arrived in Baghdad on his first Blackwater contract in April 2007, testified that he had had a "man-to-man" talk with Nick, then completing his second year with Blackwater in Baghdad, about the use of water bottles. Under questioning by prosecutors, Frost said he did not agree with Nick's supposed statement that "anything on two legs [in the Red Zone] was a threat." Under cross-examination, he admitted that "our views are the same, just expressed differently."

Although testifying that he had seen no threats in Nisour Square, Frost said he was "not happy" about getting out of the truck to hook up a tow strap to the disabled command vehicle. "I turned around, and I looked at Jeremy, and I looked at Doc and said, 'Don't let me get shot,'" he testified. "I think I hooked up that truck faster than I had ever done in training and then yelled at them, 'Get back in the vehicle.'"

Why, I wondered, if there were no gunmen and no threats and no one was shooting, would Frost be "anxious" about getting shot?

Prosecutors next asked Lamberth to allow them to introduce newly discovered "crucial" evidence related to them by Mealy the previous evening. That evidence, which the defense team had not been able to research or verify, involved a gun battle at Amanat (the city hall) in Baghdad that had occurred four months before the Nisour Square shootings. Mealy had mentioned "seeing some person on a rooftop unarmed just pushing a broom or something to that effect," Martin, the prosecutor, said. "He mentioned it to Mr. Slatten who was outside of the vehicle, and Mr. Slatten said, 'Shoot the motherfucker.'"

Martin argued that the government should be allowed to question Mealy about the incident—despite the fact that it had nothing to do with Nisour Square or the killing of the Kia driver, not to mention the defense's inability to review it—because "it fits within our general notice as to evidence of intent and evidence of willingness to shoot unprovoked and also unarmed citizens." The defense objected, but Lamberth allowed the jury to hear it.

Mealy, who had been granted immunity in exchange for his testimony, testified under cross-examination that Nick had had the opportunity to shoot the man himself and had not done so, nor had Mealy ever seen him shoot any unarmed civilians.

As I read through Mealy's testimony, it was clear that his job as a witness was to flesh out the concept of Nick as a race warrior. He testified, rather monosyllabically, that upon returning from the hour-long firefight at Amanat in May 2007, Nick had bragged about the number of Iraqis he had killed. Mealy also said that he had "heard some comments . . . derogatory comments toward Iraqi people in general," adding that he found the battlefield pejorative "Haji," which was used by several members of the team, offensive.

"Do you recall his saying or describing Iraqis as not being worth anything?" Martin asked.

"I don't recall that off the top of my head, no," Mealy said.

Assistant US Attorney Anthony Asuncion asked Ridgeway to describe not the actions of the defendants in Nisour Square but incidents that had nothing to do with whether they had killed anyone. He elicited an admission from Ridgeway that he and his friends had "called [Iraqis] 'Hajis,'" then asked "whether anyone . . . struck you as someone who had even more feelings about Iraqis in a derogatory way." Ridgeway immediately pointed out Nick in the courtroom, saying "Mr. Slatten made several, more than several comments that he was getting payback for 9/11, and he was well on his way."

He and Asuncion then went through a lengthy examination of Evan's "inappropriate use of water bottles" to clear roadways and launch at civilians before Ridgeway admitted under cross-examination that he, too, had thrown frozen water bottles at people he believed were no threat to the convoy and had broken one vehicle's windshield.

At another point in Ridgeway's testimony, Asuncion showed the jury a photo of Ridgeway holding out his middle finger to the camera while several Raven 23 members mugged in the background. The defense objected to the photo as "unflattering" and to the extended and pointless character assassination that had nothing to do with the charges.

"Overruled," Lamberth said.

Asuncion capped off his examination of Ridgeway with this masterpiece: "All right, Mr. Ridgeway, I just want to make sure we understand what you testified about today. You didn't see any insurgents that day at all?"

"No sir, I did not," Ridgeway said.

"And you didn't see anyone at all firing at your convoy that day?"

"No sir, I did not."

"And you didn't see anyone or anything that you perceived to be an imminent threat to you that day?"

"No sir, I did not."

"But you nonetheless decided to shoot?"

"Yes sir, I did."

"And do you understand that you were shooting at unarmed people?"

"I do understand that, sir."

On cross-examination, defense attorney Brian Heberlig asked Ridgeway exactly when his "guilt" and "regret" about his actions in Nisour Square had caught up with him, causing him to disavow his earlier insistence that he had "acted honorably at all times."

"It was after the period in which you had been threatened with a thirty-year mandatory minimum criminal charge, correct?" Heberlig asked him.

"Yes, sir," Ridgeway said.

The government, after destroying the credibility of its own key witness, kept Ridgeway on the stand for three days.

During pretrial hearings, Donald Ball, Paul and Christin Slough, Evan Liberty and his wife, Paola, and Dustin Heard were having a drink at a bar near the courthouse when Ridgeway and his attorney walked in. Ridgeway and the attorney sat down at a table nearby, not noticing his former teammates, who had shaved off the beards they had worn in Baghdad for the trial. Dustin called the waitress over, slipped her a sizable tip, and gestured toward the table. "Send him a beer and tell him it's from Raven 23," he said.

They watched as the waitress conveyed their message. Ridgeway turned to look at them, his face white, and he and his attorney got up and left. He told prosecutors the next day that he had felt threatened.

The testimony of the government's star witnesses—Ridgeway,

Mealy, Murphy, and Frost—left much to be desired in confirming the prosecutors' theory of a murderous melee, and its expert witnesses actually contradicted the charges by testifying that the only forensic evidence taken from the scene was a bullet in the Kia's headrest matching Ridgeway's weapon and AK-47 shrapnel taken from a wounded man's leg.

The defense called a former Green Beret named Brett Fishback to testify that he had witnessed—and almost been struck by—AK-47 rounds that had been fired from south of Nisour Square toward his position, four hundred meters north of the traffic circle.

Fishback was a Green Beret weapons sergeant or specialist, and his specialty was Russian-made weapons—particularly "AK-47 of different country types." He trained other special operations personnel or other armies and individuals on the operation and maintenance of everything from pistols to rocket launchers, he said. During his 2005–2006 Iraq deployment, he had also instructed Iraqi commandos how to operate weapon systems, including AK-47s and pistols, and trained them in urban combat, he said. He did not know any of the defendants, and although he had subsequently worked for a private military contractor, it was not Blackwater.

Fishback then torpedoed the prosecution's theory that any AK-47 shell casings recovered from Nisour Square after the September 16, 2007, incident were "old" and had probably been fired during previous gun battles. The AK-47 ammunition issued to Iraqi troops was "surplus ammo" sold to the Iraqi government by other nations after it "reached a certain age," he testified. That ammo appeared to have a "greenish lacquer" or a "reddish copper tint to it," he said. "And then you had other ammunition that looks similar to how Americans would make it, with brass, but it's not the shiny brass that you would see, it's a very dull, dingy kind of tannish look."

More important, Fishback testified that he had been patrolling with a security detail in the Red Zone north of Nisour Square at around noon when he had heard and felt a massive explosion. The explosion had been followed a few minutes later by "an eruption of just gunfire," he said. "You could hear AKs, you could hear M-4s, you could hear a belt-fed weapon system going off, as well as four or five grenades." It had most definitely been a two-way gun battle, he testified. At one point in the incident, about twenty rounds had landed near him and his team, causing them to take cover, he said. One of the rounds had pierced a steel awning covering their vehicle and dented it, he said. The rounds were coming from the south to the north—opposite to the direction in which the Raven 23 convoy was firing.

He had picked up one of the rounds, examined it, and found that "it was very consistent with AK rounds. It looked like a 7.63 by 39 round just because of the coloring. It was a reddish tinge that is consistent with surplus ammunition that's used."

Though the government had nothing in the way of proof, its case was riding on the emotional testimony of the forty-six Iraqis flown to the United States for the trial, the largest number of foreign witnesses ever to testify in a US trial. Their testimony was heartbreaking to hear—and highly prejudicial to the defendants—and it went on and on. One witness testified to having lost a family member whose remains had never been found. She knew that Blackwater personnel had killed him, she said, because he had driven through Nisour Square every day and had not come home after September 16, 2007. The family member of another alleged victim testified that he had been shot under a bridge near Baghdad International Airport, more than a mile from Nisour Square.

Hospital records for one of the injured, Hassan Jaber Salman, indicated that he had been treated in 2005 for the bullet wound to the chest he claimed had occurred in Nisour Square. At least four victims who claimed they had been shot had no record of being injured by shrapnel or a bullet, and one injured man had no hospital record at all.[4]

After watching their testimony go unchallenged, Nick confronted the defense team one day in their "war room." "You have to challenge the bodies," he told them.

His lawyers did not want to bring up victims who had nothing to do with his murder charge, but the other attorneys said they worried that either they or Dustin, Paul, and Evan would look "callous" if they challenged the victims. Each of the men weighed in, urging the attorneys to challenge the victim list, to no avail. "That is a dumb strategy. Fourteen dead and twenty wounded looks callous," Nick argued angrily. "There are maybe four or five that they can prove."

When they returned to Falls Church that evening, Christin confronted Nick about his abrasive behavior, which had been escalating as the trial went on. "I don't think it's beneficial for you to talk to our lawyers that way," she said.

"You just tell me that when you come visit me in prison," he said. "You realize we are all going to prison, right?"

The one person whose testimony was missing from the roster of Iraqi witnesses was the lead investigator, Colonel Faris Karim of the Iraqi National Police (INP).

That was a first: I had never covered a criminal trial in which the lead investigator had not testified. Why, I wondered, if prosecutors had gone to the expense and trouble of bringing over nearly four dozen witnesses from Iraq, had Colonel Karim not been among them?

Karim had an ally and a mouthpiece in Colonel David Boslego, whom Martin, the prosecutor, billed as one of "two veteran army officers who knew this space like the back of their hand" and who "found nothing to support the notion that this was a two-way battle."[5]

Boslego, whose main mission was liaising with the INP, testified that he knew Colonel Karim quite well but initially denied that he had told FBI investigators in 2007 that Karim was untrustworthy because he and his men had been "shaking people down" at security checkpoints. Boslego testified under cross-examination that he was unfamiliar with two reports by US military authorities that had recommended disbanding the INP because it had been irredeemably infiltrated with Iran-backed militants who were spreading sectarian violence instead of keeping the peace. In fact, Boslego testified, he had supported handing over the Nisour Square investigation to Colonel Karim, the INP's head of intelligence, because he viewed the State Department as "the enemy." Astonishingly, he also described Nisour Square as a safe place, mainly because it was located in a richer area of Baghdad with well-controlled checkpoints. He said that on September 16, 2007, he had been meeting with INP General Hussein al-Awadi at the INP headquarters adjacent to Nisour Square when they had heard over al-Awadi's radio about an incident involving "South African" soldiers. After returning to Forward Operating Base Prosperity to don his body armor, Boslego said, he had returned to help al-Awadi stand down about a hundred Iraqi Army troops who were holding Raven 22 in Nisour Square. He said that he and al-Awadi had then walked around the traffic circle, checking for evidence of a two-way gun battle, and that he had seen no sign of enemy gunfire. "Sir, it appeared to be a one-way gunfight," he told jurors. He based his conclusion on the fact that he had found no "larger weapons such as a rocket-propelled grenade launcher" at the scene and his feeling that it would be "generally suicidal for any insurgent to attack a U.S. convoy with small arms alone."

Under cross-examination, he admitted that al-Awadi had ordered him to stay on the roadway and that the Iraqi general's large contingent of bodyguards had had control of the scene and had joined Iraqi troops in picking up shell casings and other items and stuffing them into bags. He was not sure whether the items had ever been turned over to US authorities. He said that when he had accompanied State Department investigators back to Nisour Square on September 20, 2007, he had seen them collect evidence at "a few specific points" where the Raven 23 men had reported receiving gunfire. He also testified at length about a return trip he had made to Nisour Square on September 22, 2007, to search the traffic circle and surrounding areas for "expended ammunition, specifically the brass cartridges that are used with small arms ammunition." He said he had decided to conduct his own investigation "based on the lack of thoroughness of the State Department effort." He described a meticulous search of Nisour Square and its environs conducted by himself and his team and concluded that their failure to discover AK-47 rounds proved that there had been no gunfight. He also downplayed the threat to the Blackwater convoy from the white Kia, testifying that vehicle-borne improvised explosive devices (VBIEDs) "have to be almost touching an armored vehicle in order to have—be a significant threat to them, depending on how much explosives they contained."

Though physically absent, Colonel Karim was an omnipresent figure at the trial, if only in the testimony of others. Mohammed Kinani told the jury that Karim had found him and other Nisour Square victims by advertising on television and had coached them in their statements to US investigators. He also testified that Karim had boasted that "if he told the witnesses to go left, they'd go left. If he told them to go right, they'd go right." In the criminal trials I had covered in California state and federal courts, that admission would likely have resulted in a mistrial for witness tampering.

However, Lamberth overlooked that and several Brady violations, instances in which prosecutors had hidden or failed to turn over exculpatory evidence. Two months into the trial, prosecutors "discovered" photographs of AK-47 shell casings in Nisour Square taken seven years earlier by US Army Captain Peter Decareau. That crucial piece of evidence had not been turned over to the defense attorneys—a clear violation of the Brady rule, which requires prosecutors to hand over evidence favorable to the defense. In a normal case, a violation of this rule can and often does result in a mistrial.

The situation was so egregious that it was apparently the talk of the Washington, DC, judicial community. US Appellate Court Justice David Sentelle told an interviewer from the Historical Society of the District of Columbia Circuit the same week, on August 7, 2014, that he "would like to see prosecutors quit getting themselves and the country in these *Brady* violation problems when they do not turn over evidence that is favorable to the defense. . . . I don't know if you are familiar with the trial Royce has going on now but there was some dramatic exculpatory evidence for the Blackwater defendants that was not turned over. . . . Royce had to stop the trial to instruct the jury and even have some witnesses recalled that the prosecution should have turned this evidence over and didn't. . . . The defendant has a right to know what the evidence is even if . . . [prosecutors] don't want him to."[6]

The photographs of the AK-47 shell casings—the caliber used by Iraqi insurgents—again contradicted the government's theory that no enemy gunmen had shot at the Raven 23 convoy in Nisour Square. Despite the stunning blow to the government's case, Lamberth dismissed the defense team's motion for a new trial.

Nor did the judge react much when prosecutors allowed a former Blackwater contractor to testify that Evan Liberty had fired excessively during a January 23, 2007, rescue of a downed helicopter—only to be confronted on cross-examination with the fact that Evan was not even in Iraq at that time.

Prosecutors also were allowed to mislead the jury about the death of a nine-year-old boy who was shot by a black-tipped M-993 bullet. "Defendants did not understand why the government failed to elicit any evidence regarding this black-tipped ammunition, but presumed it was a judgment call to avoid presenting the jury with irrelevant, inflammatory evidence given that black-tipped rounds were not issued to Blackwater contractors," the defense wrote in a motion for new trial on April 27, 2015.[7]

But during their rebuttal argument at the end of the trial—when it was impossible for the defense to respond—the government argued that the black-tipped round came from Paul Slough's M-240 machine gun—even though its own expert had testified that Paul could not have fired the round that killed the child.

"The prosecution could get away with anything," Reba Slatten told me. "Our attorneys were very smart. Very intelligent. They did a wonderful job, but the judge would shut them down. He wouldn't let them put on a case, really."

The pervasive bias was not lost on the Raven 23 families, nor was the fact that for much of the trial, Lamberth was visibly ill. More than once, his courtroom staff had to wake him up in the middle of testimony. It got so bad that the families nicknamed him "Sleepy."

During our first interview on May 22, 2019, Reba Slatten, a nurse, told me that Lamberth "was emotional" during all three of her son's trials and "would sleep a lot too."

"I think he's sick. Well, actually I know he's sick," she said. "They had to take some time off [from the trial] because he was sick . . . to have some procedures done."

To me, the strangest aspect of the trial was the prosecutors' new explanation of how Nick had murdered the Kia driver. During pretrial hearings, Lamberth had told Nick's attorneys that he would not grant a separate trial for their client, even though the murder charge required Nick's attorneys to defend him by incriminating his codefendant Paul Slough.

Defense attorney Tom Connolly pointed out to the jury that not one of the government's seventy-odd witnesses had seen Nick Slatten shoot the Kia driver, that the government had failed to prove that he had deliberately killed Ahmed Haithem Al Rubia'y with premeditation. The government's own FBI ballistics experts testified that no bullet fragment or shell casing taken from the interior of the Kia matched Slatten's weapon. Nor was there any possible trajectory from Slatten's position inside the command vehicle to any shot at the Kia. In fact, the analysis of bullet fragments taken from the Kia's steering wheel matched the type of machine gun wielded by Ridgeway, who had testified that upon hearing Slough shoot at the vehicle, he "turned and fired" at the driver's head. "So again, we have a first-degree murder case with no eyewitnesses, no forensics," Connolly told the jury. Every prosecutorial malfeasance that Judge Urbina had cataloged in his dismissal of the 2009 indictments had manifested itself in this debacle of a case, just as he had predicted.

Jessica Slatten, who is an attorney, laid it out for me when I asked what she thought had gone wrong. "Numerous erroneous legal rulings by the trial court plus misconduct by the prosecutors involved in this case denied Nick a fair trial," she said. "In a complicated war zone incident like this one, these errors and this misconduct [were] the difference between an innocent man going free versus dying in prison for shots that were not his."

CHAPTER ELEVEN

──── ★★★ ────

VERDICT

If we are mark'd to die, we are enough
To do our country loss; and if to live,
The fewer men, the greater share of honour.

—WILLIAM SHAKESPEARE, *HENRY V*

THE CASE WENT TO the jury on August 28, 2014. Almost two months later, on October 22, the jury rendered its verdict.

Kelli Heard was in her classroom in Maryville, Tennessee, when Dustin called to say that the jury had reached a decision. He was about to step into the courtroom but said he would call her the minute the hearing was over. "I was like 'Yes, here it goes,'" she told me, barely able to speak at the memory. "It was more nervous butterflies, like—this is over. There's going to be media; they'd been at our house before. It was finally going to be over. And they weren't allowed to have their cell phones, so I knew it would hit the news before I got a phone call. I told my coworkers, and my coworkers prayed with me. Prayed for strength. Prayed that the right decision would be turned over and he would be coming home safe."

As she waited, she kept refreshing the news page on her phone until a story appeared. "It says 'Guilty.' And I just stared at it. And

I refreshed the page again. And it says 'Guilty.' This isn't right. And I refreshed the page again. 'Guilty,'" she said. She staggered to the classroom next door and barely got out the words "It says they're guilty." The teachers swung into action. "They said, 'What can we do?' I said, 'There are kids in my room. I can't let them see me like this.'"

Every day of jury deliberations, Brian Liberty walked around the National Mall, carrying his suit and waiting for Evan's lawyer, Bill Coffield, to call him to say that the verdict was in. After nearly two months of deliberations, Evan and Aaron told him to go home to their mom, Deb. The next day, the jury came back with a verdict. Aaron called his father after the hearing, disturbed, to describe what had happened to Evan. "They cuffed him immediately, all four of them, and led them out of the courtroom. And they stripped them and put them in their [prison] uniforms. My son Aaron tried to ask [the US marshals] if he could talk to Evan for a few minutes. They denied him, which very much upset Aaron."

Aaron tried to retrieve Evan's suit, but it had disappeared, Brian said. "When they came down [from the jail], they were hustled right out with the marshals. And the marshals weren't happy with the verdict. The marshals sat behind them for the whole trial. They could be interchanged with these guys."

Six months later, on April 13, 2015, the four men were sentenced.

It seemed as though the defense had finally caught a break. During the sentencing hearing, one of the main prosecution witnesses, an Iraqi police officer named Sarhan Dheyab Abdul Monem, radically changed his testimony. He testified for three days in a row and said he had been the Iraqi police officer closest to the convoy.

During trial, Officer Monem testified that he had approached the white Kia after the first shots were fired and found the driver dead. But after the verdict, he wrote in a victim impact statement that he had never left his police kiosk because he had been paralyzed with fear. He wrote that he could hear the Kia driver pleading with his mother to get out of the vehicle. Prosecutors turned over that statement to the defense three weeks after Monem made it—and five days before the sentencing hearing—buried at the bottom of a stack of similar statements.

Monem first testified that he had seen bullets from the Raven 23 convoy hit the Kia driver and his mother. In the victim impact statement, he disclosed that he had seen nothing. In fact, he said, he had been able to hear the woman and her son debating about whether to get out of the car *after* Nick Slatten, who had supposedly shot them, had fired the only two rounds he discharged during the entire incident.

The law requires the government to immediately disclose material changes in witness testimony to the defense, in this case because Monem could not have seen what he testified to at trial—that Nick had fired unprovoked shots that had killed Ahmed Haithem Al Rubia'y and his mother. The stunning revelation cut the government's theory of the case dead. Defense attorneys immediately called for a mistrial. Judge Lamberth held a closed-door hearing with just the prosecutors and Monem.

This ex-parte communication was so unbelievable that I had to check with the defense attorneys, who confirmed that they had not been allowed to attend the hearing and question Monem.[1]

In an April 27, 2015, motion for a new trial, the defense argued that Monem was "the sole witness the government relied on" to tie Nick's two shots to the death of the Kia driver.

"Without Mr. Monem, the government could not support its theory of the case," the defense wrote, adding that the extraordinary circumstances obliged the court to hold an evidentiary hearing.

Lamberth then concluded that the radical change in Monem's testimony was not important and could not have affected the trial's outcome. "The court finds that Monem did not provide perjurious testimony at the trial of this matter," he said. "The court further finds that in any new trial, Monem's Victim Impact Statement could be used as merely impeaching material, and further finds that in any new trial, the introduction or use of Monem's Victim Impact Statement would probably not produce an acquittal."

The National Association of Criminal Defense Lawyers would later write to the DC appeals court on the Raven 23 men's behalf about that stunning violation of the Constitution committed by a sitting federal judge, "Although the statement submitted to the court itself triggered a host of questions, the district court refused to inquire further, denying the Appellants' new trial motion without holding a hearing, and without even directing further inquiry into the witness's contradictory and incongruous statements. That cannot possibly be the proper way for a district court to respond."

The sentencing hearing proceeded with Martin and his colleagues pushing for sentences of fifty-plus years in prison for Dustin, Evan, and Paul and life for Nick. "Now, as Your Honor knows, Mr. Slatten himself was found guilty of murdering Mr. Ahmed Al Rubia'y. Mr. Heard was found guilty of killing six individuals and attempting to kill another eleven. Mr. Liberty was found guilty of killing eight individuals and attempting to kill another twelve. And Mr. Slough was found guilty of killing thirteen individuals and attempting to kill another seventeen. All told, fourteen deceased victims, seventeen injured, many severely."

Those body counts seemed completely random to me. There had been no autopsies. The only bullet fragment taken from a wounded man had come from an AK-47, according to the testimony of the government's ballistics expert. So how had the government assigned blame for the shootings with such precision? It was a complete fantasy and one that Judge Lamberth apparently had no problem accepting.

Why? I wondered again as I read the transcript of the sentencing hearing.

Apparently because the government's key witness, Jeremy Ridgeway, said so. At the sentencing hearing, Dustin Heard's attorney, David Schertler, accused the government of trying to hang the Raven 23 men for Ridgeway's deeds while at the same time calling Ridgeway a liar and criminal: "He admitted pleading guilty to avoid a 30-year mandatory charge in exchange for what he believes—his lawyers are going to come in and ask you for probation. That's why he pled guilty. And when he pled guilty, he continued to lie to the Government about what he did and tried to put the blame on others for a full year before the Government finally pressured him into admitting what supposedly he truly had done. And then when we see what he truly had done, it was far more egregious, far worse than anyone else in this case did."

The effect of this argument was nil. Lamberth sentenced Nick Slatten to a mandatory term of life in prison. He sentenced Dustin Heard, Evan Liberty, and Paul Slough to thirty years and a day in prison, saying he had been moved by the hundred or so family members and friends who filled the courtroom that day. "There's no witness that an AK-47 was ever fired at them," he said, apparently forgetting that several witnesses had testified to just that. "It's clear that these fine young men just panicked. And it's not just a matter of panic, because they were issued these deadly weapons and entrusted with them with training and guidelines that should have told them that when you fire a weapon like that you only fire it when necessary and with due regard to the consequences of your firing it."

Despite being thrown under the bus by prosecutors who called him a liar, Ridgeway found favor with Lamberth, who sentenced him to one year in prison and continued to defend that sentence for years. "You can't compare cooperators who fully come forward and agree that they did wrong, who have changed their lives, you can't compare how a Court sentences them to how a Court sentences your client," Lamberth told the defense at the men's resentencing in 2019.

Another striking aspect of the sentencing hearing was the number of times the names Erik Prince and Blackwater came up. Erik Prince was not on trial, yet Judge Lamberth allowed the witnesses to go on and on about Prince and his political influence, his wealth and power, and his misguided attempts at checkbook diplomacy with the victims. But those men were not Erik Prince, and they were not Blackwater. Like every other American, they deserved to be judged for their own actions, not on the reputation of their employer.

The New York Times described the sentences as "a long-fought diplomatic victory for the United States, which asked a skeptical Iraqi government and its people to be patient and trust the American criminal justice system. That faith was tested many times over the past eight years as the case suffered several setbacks of the government's own making," the newspaper continued, completely missing the point that those "setbacks" had been violations of the constitutional protections of US citizens.

The next day, as Dustin, Evan, Paul, and Nick sat stunned in the DC Jail, I read their names for the first time at the breakfast table, thanks to Jessica Simpson and a stolen newspaper.

CHAPTER TWELVE

———— ★★★ ————

HOW TO GET A PARDON

Let your plans be dark and impenetrable as night, and when you move, fall like a thunderbolt.

—SUN TZU, *THE ART OF WAR*

IN MID-2018, I INTRODUCED Mike to Jessica Slatten and Christin Slough, whose missions were now diverging as they focused on what would come next for Nick and Paul. With her brother facing life in prison for a killing that Paul—and the laws of physics—said that Nick had not committed, Jessica was absorbed in rectifying the mistakes of the 2014 trial.

Nick's trial attorney, Tom Connolly of Harris Wiltshire & Grannis, took the case to Dane Butswinkas, then the cochair of commercial litigation at the storied criminal defense firm Williams & Connolly. Jessica consulted constantly with the new team and with Nick, and she kept Mike and me supplied with pretrial motions and news about his upcoming retrial. Nick was in very good hands.

In 1967, Edward Bennett Williams founded the firm that would become Williams & Connolly and seemed to relish taking—and winning—cases involving both the famous and the infamous. He owned the Washington Redskins football team and the Baltimore

Orioles baseball team and served as the treasurer of the Democratic National Committee, but he took clients of every political stripe. The Georgetown Law Library is named after him. His client roster included Teamsters boss Jimmy Hoffa; Senator Joseph McCarthy, the proponent of the anti-Communist "Red Scare" in the 1950s; and Texas governor and US Treasury Secretary John Connolly.

The firm would go on to represent would-be presidential assassin John Hinckley, Iran-contra figure Oliver North, and President Bill Clinton and consult with President George W. Bush in the disputed 2000 election. Williams "was vilified either as a Communist or as a right wing reactionary" depending on the case, *The New York Times* wrote in his August 14, 1988, obituary.

Interestingly, Williams & Connolly was hard at work on another high-profile case when the Raven 23 men's legal odyssey began: the government's botched prosecution of Alaska Senator Ted Stevens, who in 2008 was charged with and found guilty of supposedly failing to report that he had taken gifts from an oil field services company that had paid to renovate his home. The prosecutors had achieved the victory, however, by concealing the fact that a key witness had contradicted his own testimony. In one interview, the oil field services company executive Bill Allen had said that Stevens had accepted a renovation worth $80,000 (Stevens himself said he had paid $160,000 for the work), but later in court, Allen alleged that it had been worth $250,000.

The DOJ had allowed Allen to inflate his earlier estimate. Notably, he ended up serving only two years in prison for admitting to bribing other officials. It later emerged that several women had accused Allen of assaulting them when they were underage, raising the question of whether the DOJ had offered to look the other way about the allegations if he gave it the answers it wanted about Stevens. Prosecutors denied that, but "all the decisions on whether to prosecute Allen on federal sex charges were made in Washington, and the Anchorage office wasn't involved," the *Anchorage*

Daily News reported in 2010, citing an interview with US Attorney Karen Loeffler.

In any case, Williams & Connolly convinced Attorney General Eric Holder to drop the case against Stevens in 2009 after uncovering the discrepancies in the Allen interviews. The pattern of prosecutorial misconduct was quite similar to the behavior that Kohl and Malis exhibited in the Raven 23 case at exactly the same time.

Holder's agency ended up paying Stevens's legal bills. The federal judge presiding over Stevens's trial, Emmet Sullivan, said he had "never seen mishandling and misconduct like what I have seen [in this case]." It was, though, too late for Stevens, who'd lost his election and been thrown under the bus by major politicians and media figures. "Their conduct had consequences for me that they will never realize and can never be reversed," he said. Sullivan laid out the full political implications of DOJ's corruption when he wrote, "The government's ill-gotten verdict in the case not only cost that public official his bid for re-election, [but] the results of that election tipped the balance of power in the United States Senate."

After being publicly excoriated by both the judge and the defense team, the Justice Department "investigated" the prosecutors in the Stevens case, but the latter ended up with slap-on-the-wrist suspensions that an administrative law judge later rescinded. The Williams & Connolly attorneys did not hesitate to take a public swipe at the DOJ in 2010 after Stevens died in a plane crash. "Senator Stevens was innocent, and insisted on fighting the charges," they said in a statement. "Even after the case against him was dismissed, he remained profoundly affected by the government's misconduct and its implications for others. His fervent hope was that meaningful change would be brought to the criminal justice system so that others would not be mistreated as he was by the very officials whose duty it is to represent the United States justly and fairly."

"Until recently, my faith in the criminal system, particularly the judicial system, was unwavering," Stevens had told the court. "But what some members of the prosecution team did nearly destroyed my faith."

In other words, the firm and its newest client, Nick Slatten, and his lawyer sister were well matched. As an attorney, Jessica Slatten found the hardest thing to swallow about how the Department of Justice had conducted her brother's case was its pursuit of a conviction at the expense of his civil rights. She had been an attorney for a little over a year when the Nisour Square incident occurred. "In the beginning, I was really idealistic," she told me. "I believed that a full and fair review of Nick's conduct in the square—which was not shooting or killing the Kia driver—would result in no criminal charges against him."

Even though her brother had been indicted in 2008, she believed that justice had prevailed when the government had voluntarily dismissed the indictment, taken him out of the case, and publicly acknowledged that the evidence against him was hopelessly tainted. But she lost all illusion that the government's purpose was justice when prosecutors charged Nick with first-degree, premeditated murder of the Kia driver a month before the 2014 trial began. "Knowing that the truth does not actually matter in this case, knowing that Nick's actual innocence doesn't matter is an impossible pill for me to swallow as an attorney," she told me. She also believed that it was "misguided" to believe that a civilian justice system could fairly judge a military engagement and was "deeply afraid" as she approached Nick's first solo trial that her brother was going to die in prison for something he had not done.

Despite the failures in the trial, she still held the US justice system to be the best in the world, she told me; not perfect, but she hoped that a jury would see that overwhelming evidence showed that Paul Slough, not Nick, had killed the Kia driver and that the two bullets Nick had fired had been justified. "At this point, I'm just grateful for post-verdict and appellate processes that give the justice system a chance to finally get it right," she said.

When she talked to Nick in prison, he was always upbeat. Every time she asked how he was doing, he'd tell her he was "blessed."

Her younger brother was the strongest person she knew; that had been true of the eighteen-year-old kid who had joined the army right after high school in wartime, and it was true of the thirty-five-year-old veteran who had been discarded by the government he had spent his life serving. Every moment she could spare from her work at the Florida Supreme Court, she filled with helping his new legal team.

By that time, the funds provided by Blackwater for the Raven 23 legal defense were long spent; the four trial teams, plus Ridgeway's attorney, had each taken a lump sum to defend the men, and that money had barely stretched to the appeal. Evan's attorney, Bill Coffield, remained on the case, unpaid, as an adviser.

When Connolly described the case to him, Dane Butswinkas could hardly believe what he was hearing. He had never served in the armed forces but held a deep respect for the military rank and file because his father, a Vietnam veteran, had proudly served and retired from a decorated career in the US Navy at the rank of warrant officer, the highest rank attainable for an enlisted serviceman. His father had died in 2016, about a year before the Raven 23 case landed on his desk.

Butswinkas quickly assembled a defense team consisting of litigators Barry Simon, Tobin Romero, Simon Latcovich, Amy Mason Saharia, and Krystal Commons to dissect the first trial and find a new direction. They took the case in December 2017, about three months after the appellate court ruled. Lamberth had set Nick's trial for June 2018.

* * *

CHRISTIN SLOUGH WAS ALSO in the market for a new attorney following the disappointing appeals court ruling that had failed to set her husband free and now pitted Nick Slatten against him over the Kia driver's shooting. She spent several months after the appellate ruling trying to get her bearings. "We had at that point exhausted all of our judicial options, and I was trying to figure out, where do we go from here?" she told me. "I thought, we're going to have to get a presidential pardon to get this done, so how do you navigate that? There's absolutely no road map for this because it is not a common thing."

She started googling "pardon attorneys" but found that no such specialization existed. She looked up lawyers who had represented other pardoned defendants and still got nowhere, so she just started talking to anyone who could lead her to the White House. "You're just going to have to find people that are connected to the president who are credible to take this information to him," she thought.

Her search led to David Harrison and his partner Eric Jaso of Spiro Harrison & Nelson of Montclair, New Jersey. Jaso was a member of the Federalist Society, a hugely powerful nationwide organization of conservative lawyers that was instrumental in helping President Donald J. Trump decide on Supreme Court nominees. Another advantage was that the firm was located in New Jersey. The DC-based trial lawyers had been unwilling to confront Judge Lamberth about his intemperate behavior and bad rulings because they'd had other cases in front of him. After talking to Harrison, she said she thought, "He does not give a flip about Lamberth or what he thought."

Harrison spoke with her on the telephone several times before deciding whether to take the case. The notoriety of the case and the politics of trying to get an unlikely pardon from a Republican administration didn't bother Harrison, who had grown up in a liberal household in Nutley, New Jersey, and maintained those political leanings. Christin, he thought, seemed to feel hopeless.

"This is someone that needed our help, and she was genuine," he told me. "After the appeal, they didn't know where to turn. You felt her desperation."

After their initial discussions he wanted to help, but he and Jaso dug into the case files first to make sure they understood it and that they could do something about it. The first thing that piqued their interest was Judge Urbina's catalog of prosecutorial misconduct and "the shenanigans that went on with the grand jury." "Our initial sense from just reading the reports was that it just didn't all add up," Harrison said. "This narrative that these guys went into that square and just decided to kill a bunch of innocent people. It didn't make sense. Certainly terrible things like that do happen, but the evidence told a very different story."

After he reviewed the trial transcript and appellate decisions, Harrison told Christin he would take the case. He was honest about their chance of success. "This is a long shot, and we've never gotten anyone pardoned before," he told her. "But Eric and I will use whatever resources we have to tell their story."

Next it was Christin's turn to be honest. "We don't have a lot of funds, but I can go out and raise funds if I have a goal," she said.

Harrison cautioned her not to fundraise or even publicly discuss the possibility of a pardon. "If we are too public about this, we run the risk of inviting a counter-campaign from those that may be opposed to a pardon, including the DOJ. We first should try to reach the president through nonpublic channels," he warned.

They negotiated a capped contract, a sum that represented Christin's entire retirement account and some of her father's retirement funds. But a few months into the case, Harrison stopped sending her bills. "I can tell that my bills are making your family struggle financially, and I'm not sending any more," he said. "I'll just send you bills for expenses that we incur." Christin never again received a bill from Harrison. The firm handled the rest of the case pro bono.

After the appellate court's ruling made it clear that Paul would stay in prison, possibly for years, Christin began suffering from anxiety and panic attacks so severe that she worried that her heart might stop, that she would die from the stress of her predicament. She felt the tight unity with the other Raven 23 families slipping away and found herself in a prison of the mind. "There's nothing we can do here. There were no more letters to be written, there were no more campaign rallies to attend because we were all attending campaign events trying to figure out who was going to be the president that was going to pardon these people," she later told me. "We had been doing all of those things, and I think that when we hit post-conviction, in my estimation, they checked out of the fight because they didn't think there was any fight left."

She did not want to burden Paul or anybody else with her struggles. "We literally had ten minutes a day to administer our entire life. So when is that going to come up?" she asked. "When are you going to have a deeply revealing, soul-level conversation about the fact that your cheese is sliding off your cracker in your ten minutes a day that you get to talk?"

It was a lipstick that set her on a path to sanity and gave her time and resources to pursue the pardon. Paul's sister Robin had given her a lipstick from a line she was selling at her medical spa. Christin liked it and wanted to buy more, but the price was prohibitive. If Christin wanted to earn some free products and extra money, she could sell them online, Robin said.

Christin initially rejected the idea of getting involved in a network marketing operation. "I had a really great job at a bank—I wasn't going to sell these. But I didn't want to pay twenty-five dollars for lip color, and if I sold them for a few weeks . . . I'm going to get a bunch of free stuff."

It turned into a side hustle, and she discovered that she had a knack for sales. The intense emphasis on personal development and networking skills transformed her life. She realized that she needed to have something to focus on and to be with people who did not know her as "a single mom with a husband in prison."

"I went from laying in bed at night, doom scrolling and looking at everybody's highlight reel . . . to ending up in all these groups with these girls that are sharing trainings and sharing mindset stuff," she said. "It's superfun, and nobody had any idea who I was."

Inadvertently, she created an army of women who, upon learning of Paul's plight and the pardon effort, would go to battle for her. Joni Rogers-Kante, the California-based founder of the company SeneGence, a skin care and cosmetics firm, got Christin an appointment with House Speaker Kevin McCarthy and handed a pardon packet to a White House staffer on a golf course.

The years since Paul had been incarcerated had seemed "like being in a warehouse in the dark and every door is dark and you just have to go bang on each door and figure out what's behind it," Christin said. Her mindset became a constant process of refining her message to journalists and any other contacts who could help Paul and the other Raven 23 men. She educated herself about news cycles: who to approach to get onto news shows and what three bullet points executive producers needed to hear to give her airtime.

She also began recruiting people to her cause. She started with her local congressman, Michael Burgess, a Republican from Lewisville, Texas. "I was so overwhelmed at the time," Christin told me. "He literally sat there and explained the three branches of government to me and what he could do as a legislator, what he couldn't do, at what point [Congress] could get involved."

Burgess focused on the prosecutors' misuse of the weapons charge and suggested that he would author a bill to prevent the law from being used in combat settings. Lobbying for that legislation would give Burgess and Christin an excuse to visit members of Congress to talk about the case "in a way that is relevant to them because it's a legislative issue," she said.

If and when a pardon was considered, "there's people with

knowledge and people with background and people who understand it from a legal point of view," they reasoned. Despite the astronomical odds against obtaining four pardons, the Sloughs never considered going it on their own, and they instructed Dave Harrison to write the pardon materials with the aim of freeing all four men. "There was no point presenting a pardon packet for Paul and having all of that work done and not Dustin, Nick, and Evan," Christin said.

As Nick's trial got underway in June 2018, Harrison and Jaso began pulling together the pardon packet and deciding where to send it. Harrison also tried to get in touch with Erik Prince. Although the Blackwater chief had been "supportive" in the limited interaction they'd had, the two men had very little contact over the coming months.

Many of Judge Lamberth's rulings had bothered Harrison: the manufactured jurisdiction in Washington, DC, the way prosecutors had leaned on Ridgeway to testify, the government's clumsy threats to force the others to take plea deals, the weapons offense, and, of course, prosecuting Nick for first-degree murder to save the government from its own incompetence.

He and Jaso spent the rest of 2018 formulating their argument and developing a working document that they revised as they learned new information about the case. They also spoke with the other Raven 23 families to get input and to explain their strategy. He and Jaso knew that the pardon was not their typical case; they were not going to make any money from it, and that gave them the freedom to try whatever strategy might get results.

It was clear to Harrison and Jaso that in the Raven 23 prosecution, the Bush and Obama administrations had found a breathtakingly simple way to advance their shifting goals in Iraq. For the price of a criminal trial or three, they could keep US troops and corporations in Iraq, soothe the justifiable rage of the Iraqi people at the civil war they had unleashed, and elect their chosen candidate, Nouri al-Malaki, as Iraqi prime minister. Biden in particular had placed the men atop a pyre of media outrage, and the DOJ and FBI had taken turns feeding it with specious accounts of a civilian massacre.

They knew they would have to bypass the normal path for presidential pardons, which ran through the Department of Justice, because the basis for the pardon was, at least in part, based on the misconduct alleged against the prosecutors. The DOJ acted as the gatekeepers for cases that were presented to the White House Counsel's Office, and Harrison did not think that approach would be fruitful. Also, there were the complications that Nick Slatten's case was still winding through the courts and the other men had not been resentenced. A pardon is typically considered a strategy of last resort, when all other judicial remedies have been exhausted.

With a little digging, they learned the name of the person who was handling pardon requests in the office of White House Counsel Pat Cipollone. They had some conversations with that person and submitted the pardon packet in late 2018.

They knew it would be a slow path, and they wondered whether submitting it so far ahead of the traditional pardon season—the end of a presidential administration—would be positive or negative.

CHAPTER THIRTEEN

★★★

THE PERSECUTION OF NICK SLATTEN

The greatest glory in living lies not in never falling, but in rising every time we fall.

—NELSON MANDELA, MAY 10, 1994, INAUGURATION ADDRESS AS PRESIDENT OF SOUTH AFRICA

WHEN THE WILLIAMS & Connolly lawyers looked at Nick's case, their strategy was blindingly obvious: They would declare that Nick Slatten was innocent. Period.

They knew that the odds were long that a Washington, DC, jury would sympathize with their client; only 6 percent of Washington, DC, voters are registered Republicans. They also knew that the Iraq War was unpopular among Democrats and liberals, and one of the reasons it was unpopular was the Nisour Square incident.

But at the trial, they could finally tell the jury that Paul Slough had killed the Kia driver and dismantle the government's race-baiting theory, because Paul was no longer Nick's codefendant. Paul had recounted in statements made on September 16, 2007, September 18, 2007, September 20, 2007, and September 23, 2007, that he had fired two rounds from his M4 rifle at the white

Kia and hit the driver. Investigators had found a bullet fragment from Ridgeway's weapon in the Kia's headrest—and none from Nick's sniper rifle.

As if that were not enough, the Williams & Connolly team would show that it had not been possible for Nick to hit the Kia through the porthole inside the command vehicle. The position of the vehicle was easy enough to confirm; the puddle of radiator fluid was visible in both the remaining drone footage and video shot from the Green Zone tower. They divided up the thirty or forty witnesses among the team members and got to work, reviewing everything each witness had said in court or to the government in interviews over the previous decade and preparing to vigorously cross-examine them at trial. This time, there would be no holding back to avoid looking callous.

With three grand jury proceedings, the trial, and the *Kastigar* hearings (in which prosecutors had to prove that they had evidence other than the men's protected statements), not to mention the government interviews, the lawyers had a lot more material than normal from each witness, and they planned to use it to gain every advantage possible. When they received the government's witness list, it became apparent that the DOJ had been just as motivated to convict Nick Slatten the second time. The government had flown a number of the Iraqi witnesses from the 2014 trial to Washington, DC, for the second go-round, at a significant cost to taxpayers, even though their testimony had not been relevant to the single murder charge against Nick and should not have been admitted.

But the DOJ was again going to put on the same dog-and-pony show—halfway into a third presidential administration and seven years after US troops had left Iraq. The case no longer had any political value, so at that point, I thought, the prosecutors must be blinded by vengeance. Nothing else explains why the government believed it could prove, as Judge Lamberth explained to the jury, that Nick Slatten had "caused the death of Mr. Al Rubia'y . . . did so with malice aforethought . . . did so after premeditation . . . there were no mitigating circumstances . . . and . . . at the time of the charged conduct, Mr. Slatten was employed by the armed forces outside the United States." In the absence of evidence, the prosecutors' main strategy, it seemed, was again to blacken Nick's character by any means to prove that he had premeditated the killing of the Kia driver with malice aforethought.

Pulling from its 2014 playbook, the DOJ opened its case on June 28, 2018, by again claiming that Nick had made derogatory comments about Iraqis that it appeared were actually said by someone else—that was clear from the handwritten FBI 302s taken down during the agents' interviews with other witnesses.

"Liberty 'popped his grape.' . . . This is what Liberty said," according to Ridgeway's 302 in notes taken by FBI Agent Thomas F. O'Connor on July 22, 2009, in the presence of AUSAs Kenneth Kohl, John Malis, and Steven Ponticiello.[1]

Assistant US Attorney T. Patrick Martin set the tone for the trial with the first words of his opening statement: "His words about the Iraqi people: 'Their lives are not worth anything. They're not human. They're animals.'"

When I read the transcript later, I wondered whether Martin or anyone else on the prosecution team knew how normal Americans—not even combat veterans—talk about our enemies. The term "Ali Baba"—a generic term for a bad guy—has been circulating in American slang since at least the first Gulf War, and I felt pretty sure that everyone in that courtroom was aware of and had probably laughed at World War II–era cartoons such as "Bugs Bunny Nips the Nips," featuring pejoratives such as "Monkey Face" and "Slant Eyes." By that measure, I guess we all have murder in our hearts.

A quick search of "Military jargon in Iraq and Afghanistan" on Military.com turns up the following list of names for Iraqis and their accoutrements: Haji, Haji armor, Haji mart, Haji patrol.

So it's pretty clear that Nick Slatten, if in fact he did make those statements, was in good company—and not just with his comrades in arms.

Joseph Low IV, the former judge advocate general and defense attorney, told me that the tactic is common when evidence is thin. "Every time I get a case where the government goes hard on his character, it tells me right away that they have no evidence," he said. "Prosecutors are trained in prosecutor school how to manipulate juries by name calling . . . so that the juries hate [the defendant] and do whatever they want to them." Puritans had used the same tactics in colonial witch hunts, he said. "The evolutionary trait known as tribalism is switched on in the reptile part of their brain and they do what you want them to do. It's as manipulative as hell."

But the Williams & Connolly attorneys had prepared a counterattack, and they dropped their first bombshell on the government's first witness, Colonel David Boslego. Boslego, who in 2007 had been tasked with liaising with the Iraqi National Police, had testified at the 2014 trial that he had conducted his own investigation six days after the Nisour Square incident, believing that the State Department investigators who had combed the traffic circle on September 20, 2007, had done a shoddy job. He had testified that he had found no evidence that a two-way gunfight had occurred.

During his initial examination, Assistant Attorney General Fernando Campoamor-Sanchez led Boslego on an extended description of the damage caused by American-made bullets and grenades all around Nisour Square and on a Nantucket sleigh ride of a story about grenade damage to the wall surrounding a nearby girls' school. None of it had anything to do with the shots that Nick Slatten had fired, nor with the shooting of the driver of the white Kia. Boslego went on for more than twenty minutes, talking about each location where he had stood and photographed damage or minutely scrutinized buildings and other structures for damage.

When Simon Latcovich stood to cross-examine Boslego, he was nervous. His questioning of Boslego, a West Point graduate and retired army colonel and now a police detective, would set the defense's tone for the trial. If he was not polite and respectful, Latcovich was sure that the jury would hate him just as he was trying to build credibility with them.

"You talked a lot about the patrol that you did on Sept. 22, correct?" he asked Boslego. "And all the places that you went during that patrol. . . . And you went into some detail about. In fact, I think by my count, sir, you testified for twenty minutes about that Sept. 22 search."

"Yes, sir," Boslego said.

"You actually weren't on that search; true?" Latcovich said.

"Yes, sir. True," Boslego admitted.

"You were not on the patrol that you testified at length about that you said went out and collected evidence, correct?"

"Yes, sir," Boslego said.[2]

No one was more surprised than Latcovich at that scene, which could have been ripped from a *Law & Order* script. The implications were broad—not just for Nick but for Paul, Dustin, and Evan, who had been convicted in 2014 in part by Boslego's support of the claim that there had been no insurgent gunmen in the square.

Under questioning by Campoamor-Sanchez, Boslego admitted that the Iraqi National Police had been considered corrupt and partisan and had had no experience with democracy, and that many had committed terrible atrocities. "While they were good at fighting, they were not necessarily good at being unbiased policemen," he testified. "So there was also a huge corruption problem based on the activities of the senior commander at the time prior to General Hussein Alawadi."

Though Boslego claimed that al-Awadi had cleaned up much of the problem after taking over about a year before September 16, 2007, corruption problems had still existed in the INP. Interestingly, he testified that al-Awadi's deputies had been chosen for him by Iraq's Ministry of Interior. "There were a lot of people that wore National Police uniforms or were assigned to the National Police that were actually like bodyguards of the elected officials. And these elected officials and their bodyguards were documented having done some terrible atrocities. And of course, the National Police . . . were attributed with these activities. . . . There were still problems, individual policemen within his organization, but they received—if they were caught doing something sectarian or providing intelligence to the militias, they were very severely handled, to include death penalty for policemen caught doing that type of activity."

Under cross-examination, Boslego tried to dance away from Latcovich's questioning about an Iraqi Army soldier who had been killed south of Nisour Square that day. He then professed to have no knowledge of 2007 findings by General Peter Pace, the chairman of the Joint Chiefs of Staff, and the Independent Commission on the Security Forces in Iraq concluding that the Iraqi National Police should be disbanded and reorganized because of the INP's deep involvement in sectarian violence. But then, nonsensically, Boslego admitted to Latcovich that he had met with members of the Independent Commission on the Security Forces in Iraq in 2007 during their visit to the Iraqi National Police headquarters.

Boslego went on to testify about Colonel Karim, the lead Iraqi investigator for the Raven 23 case: "He's a former Iraqi Special Forces Officer, had experience going deep into Iran during the Saddam regime. And he was entrusted with the security of the facility of the National Police Headquarters," he told Campoamor-Sanchez. As he had in the 2014 trial, he again admitted under cross-examination that Karim had been known for shaking down people at the checkpoints surrounding the National Police headquarters. The prosecutor quickly appealed to Lamberth to shut down Latcovich's damaging line of questions, and the judge complied.

Latcovich then fired a series of questions at Boslego, citing statistics gathered by the US Central Command (CENTCOM) about attacks that had occurred while Boslego was in Iraq—questions that reminded the jury that in 2007, Baghdad had been the most dangerous city on Earth.

"Colonel, isn't it true that on Sept. 9, 2007, insurgents in multiple buildings shot machine guns at an armored Blackwater convoy at Gray 55 [the Amadat city hall building] in Baghdad?"

"Sir, isn't it also true that on Sept. 10, 2007, insurgents fired at both Blackwater and Army units during a mission to recover a downed Blackwater helicopter—downed by insurgent fire?"

"Sir, isn't it also true that on Sept. 12, 2007, insurgents used an explosively formed penetrator bomb to attack an armored Blackwater vehicle and injure two people, and then followed up with a secondary attack using machine guns?"

"Sir, isn't it true that on Sept. 16, 2007, insurgents detonated a vehicle-borne IED . . . near the Izdihar compound in Iraq, requiring the evacuation of Rodeina Fattah, a USAID employee under Blackwater protection?"

"Isn't it true that on Aug. 1, just weeks before Nisour Square, there was . . . a car bomb attack at a gas station in the Mansour neighborhood that killed more than five people?"

"Isn't it true that there were intelligence reports in August 2007 that Al-Qaida was attempting to recruit an ambulance driver to attack the hospital with a VBIED?"

"Sir, isn't it also true that on July 5, 2007, insurgents using belt-fed machine guns attacked checkpoint 12 at the Green Zone, which is very close to Nisour Square?"

"Colonel, isn't it true that in the 15 days leading up to Sept. 16, 2007, there were more than 45 IED or VBIED attacks in Baghdad alone?"

"Colonel, isn't it also true that in the 15 days leading up to Sept. 16, 2007, there were more than one hundred small arms attacks in Baghdad . . . small arms includes machine guns, right?"

"You would agree, sir, that in August of 2007, 293 coalition soldiers were wounded in Baghdad alone?"

"You would agree that 34 coalition soldiers were killed in August 2007 in just Baghdad?"

"And so in the first nine months of 2007, more than 2,500 coalition soldiers were wounded in Baghdad alone. True, sir?"

"So you do know, sir, whether 350 coalition soldiers were killed just in Baghdad in the first nine months of 2007?"

Then Latcovich deftly impeached Boslego's 2014 testimony that suicide VBIED attacks had been "extremely rare," which had undercut the Raven 23 turret gunners' reasons for shooting at the white Kia: "Sir, isn't it true, from Jan. 1, 2007, to July 16, 2007, there were more than forty suicide VBIED attacks just against coalition forces in Iraq?"

Again, Campoamor-Sanchez tried to interrupt the relentless attack on his first witness. "The fact that Central Command may have information doesn't mean he does or his unit does," the prosecutor complained.

"Your Honor, they've sponsored this witness to come in and say that there were no suicide VBIED attacks. It is important that during his command, people who he worked for didn't agree with that," Latcovich argued.

Again Lamberth sided with the prosecutors. "The objection is sustained," he said.

At a pretrial hearing in February 2018, Nick's lawyers had asked the government to disclose whether they had any confidential information tying any Iraqi police or military officers in Nisour Square to terrorist groups. Despite numerous follow-ups by the defense attorneys, the prosecutors had not "discovered" any relevant information until about two weeks before the trial was set to begin.

The government had initially refused to give the report to the defense, saying it was classified. That gambit had failed because three of the defense team had top secret clearance to view classified documents. Lamberth had ordered the prosecutors to hand it over. What they discovered was incendiary: Two of the "civilian" victims had ties to insurgent groups, and the third person had the same name, age, appearance, and résumé as the lead investigator in the case, Colonel Faris Saai Abdul Karim. The same Colonel Karim who had allowed his men to shake down cars at checkpoints "may have ties to insurgent groups," the defense wrote in a motion to compel the intelligence report underlying those allegations. "The government's contention that there were no insurgent 'victims' in the square depends almost entirely on Colonel Karim's identification of the victims. If Colonel Karim himself had ties to insurgent groups, there is good reason to conclude that his 'investigation' was biased."

Furthermore, the defense team accused the government of casting "serious doubt" on the Nisour Square investigation by failing to follow up on US intelligence reports that Karim had ties to insurgent groups. Instead of handing over the underlying intelligence reports, the government had again "summarized" the now eleven-year-old reports.

The defense asked Lamberth to either force the prosecutors to turn over the reports or dismiss the case. The judge did neither. The defense would have to content itself with the summaries, he ruled.

Karim's influence over the government's case against Raven 23 was profound. He had told the FBI in his 2007 interview, incorrectly, that he had been in Nisour Square during the incident and had seen gunmen firing from helicopters. The information about the helicopters was false but had been repeated by nearly every Iraqi witness at the men's first trial.

Karim said he had removed the wounded from the square before US officials had arrived—not more than twenty minutes later—and found no bodies but those inside the burning Kia. He had also supervised the collection of physical evidence, and despite the testimony of US military personnel who described seeing more than a hundred shell casings in the square, he had turned over to the FBI one green smoke canister, six shell casings, two rifle magazines, five 5.56 mm casings, five M-240-B casings, two M-203 grenade casings, one smoke canister spoon and pin, and two smoke canisters. FBI investigators never explained what had happened to all the shell casings described by the US witnesses.

Karim's influence over the Iraqi witnesses was so problematic that the FBI had had to "admonish him regarding speaking to the Iraqis [sic] about the substance of the case when he calls to schedule interviews," according to a June 21, 2012, email from Supervisory Special Agent Katrice Jenkins of the FBI to the DOJ's James Walsh and Christopher Gay, the FBI legal attaché at the US Embassy in Baghdad.

According to the government's summaries of the intelligence reports, Karim had been providing a steady stream of information to an undercover agent posing as a Badr Organization insurgent, possibly in exchange for payment, and had been dealing with a Mahdi Army informant as well.

Not only did Lamberth stonewall on the underlying intelligence reports turned over to the defense, he told the Williams & Connolly attorneys that they could not even mention the summaries to the jury to cast doubt on the government's investigation.[3]

Latcovich considered asking Boslego about the allegations that Karim had been working for Iranian-backed militias, but without the intelligence reports there was no way to evaluate the quality of the information. Anyway, Boslego could simply deny having known about the allegations that Karim was doing so.

The defense attorneys also faced an uphill battle to keep alleged victims from testifying about shots that had nothing to do with Nick's murder charge. They feared that the jury would find him guilty because they believed that all the shots fired that day were bad—and that none of the Blackwater team should have been shooting. Although they believed to their core that Nick was innocent of the murder charge, the they were moved by the tragic stories of the victims and aware of the prejudicial effect of their testimony.

The government's other star witnesses, Ridgeway and turret gunner Matt Murphy, tried to bolster the prosecutors' theory that Nick had had a track record of inciting unprovoked killings of Iraqi civilians in previous engagements by testifying about a Downed Aircraft Recovery Team (DART) or "downed helicopter" mission that Raven 23 had responded to about a week before the Nisour Square incident.

Murphy testified that he, Slatten, Ridgeway, and other Blackwater personnel had been flown by helicopter into a location to cover US troops trying to recover another downed helicopter in a Baghdad neighborhood. He also testified that Nick had falsely claimed to see an insurgent training a gun on them from a nearby building and then firing into the building to incite the Blackwater gunmen to fire into it. "And although he doesn't know necessarily why they start firing, there's an Army person present, and then the Army starts firing. And then what? They demolish that structure on his word. On his wink and nod," prosecutor Fernando Campoamor-Sanchez told the jury.

That account of the DART mission was not just ludicrous on its face—with a 25-year-old Blackwater contractor exerting mind control over seasoned Blackwater combat veterans and army troops—it was fiction, and Murphy and Ridgeway should have known it. But with no way to dispute it, the defense had no choice but to let it stand as fact.

More than a year later, on August 2, 2019, a former Blackwater contractor named Darren Hanner emailed Jessica Slatten a State Department document that included real-time accounts from army participants in the DART event. The report said that "Army forces were taking incoming fire from insurgent threats before the Blackwater team arrived at the site."

Jessica immediately forwarded the document to Nick's attorneys at Williams & Connolly, who filed a motion for a new trial based on new evidence that eviscerated the government's "false and inflammatory version of this event."

A few weeks later, a former Blackwater contractor named Charles Rolling saw a news story about Nick's August 14, 2019, sentencing and figured he had some information that the defense attorneys might like to hear. Rolling was a Blackwater aviation mechanic who had been part of the team that had sanitized the downed helicopter during that DART mission. He contacted Jessica Slatten via email on August 28, 2019, with a second document that no one on the defense team had ever seen. Before receiving his email, neither defense counsel nor Jessica had heard of Rolling. His email contained a document titled "(NON-COMBAT EVENT) ACCIDENT RPT BY BLACKWATER-65: 2 CIV WIA 3 AIF KIA."

Based on the military jargon and the use of the acronym SIGACT (for "significant activity report"), the defense team assumed that the report had originated in either the State Department or the army. It included the contemporaneous observations of the army participants in the DART mission and proved, the defense would later allege, that the government's two main witnesses had lied on the stand and that the prosecutors had probably known that they were lying. But the allegations of perjury by the main witnesses in both Raven 23 trials, as well as the appearance of suborning perjury by prosecutors, were not investigated.

The army report showed something very different from Murphy's testimony in both the 2014 and 2018 trials. "But what the government did not tell the jury, the Court, or Mr. Slatten was that these same two witnesses gave sworn statements the day after the DART incident in 2007 that irreconcilably conflict with their later trial testimony," the defense alleged in a motion for a new trial.

Murphy told investigators in 2007—that army personnel had already been engaged in a firefight when the Blackwater personnel rolled up and that the army, not Nick Slatten, had identified the buildings that contained armed combatants. Nick had fired only after seeing someone point a scoped rifle at the team, and the army had called in the combat helicopters that had destroyed the building.

So, based on the above documents, every single one of the government's key witnesses—Monem, Karim, Ridgeway and Murphy, and the Iraqis Karim had directed to "go left or right"—either had lied on the stand or had major credibility problems.

The DART report should have toppled the case against Nick, and the perjury by the government's three main witnesses should have resulted in a new trial for Dustin, Paul, and Evan as well. But again, Lamberth denied the motion for a new trial.[4]

"Even if this information does have impeachment value, Mr. Slatten has not demonstrated that the government's withholding of these materials resulted in prejudice," Lamberth wrote in his August 6, 2020, ruling. "The evidence regarding what happened on September 16, 2007, alone was sufficient to prove the charges against Mr. Slatten. The evidence showed that Mr. Slatten chose to pull the trigger of his sniper rifle with no threat present, resulting in the death of Ahmed Al-Rubia'y."

The defense turned the case over to the jury on August 7, 2018, and hoped for the best.

The jury deliberated for more than a month, and during the wait, the defense attorneys took turns sitting with Nick in his holding cell in the courthouse basement. They spent many hours talking about life, their families, and Nick's hopes for his life after the trial. They came to love and respect Nick, especially for the cool he exhibited in the courtroom as the prosecutors painted him as an evil racist. He would tell them, "Don't worry, God has a plan for me." But the worried defense team wondered whether that plan was a life sentence for a crime he had not committed.

On September 5, 2018, the sixteenth day of deliberations, the jury of seven women and five men deadlocked. Lamberth ruled it a mistrial and dismissed the jury. Nick should have been a free man, but the prosecutors asked Lamberth to keep him imprisoned until at least September 14, when they would decide whether to try him again. Despite Butswinkas's repeated pleas to allow Nick to stay at his home in Maryland while they awaited the government's decision, Lamberth decided that Nick would stay locked up.

Before the trial, the DOJ had offered Nick a ten-year plea deal, meaning that he could walk out of prison after serving a couple more years. He had refused. After the mistrial, his attorneys asked him to take a polygraph to dissuade the government from trying him for a third time. He took the polygraph and passed it. A short time later, the government came back with a five-year plea offer. Again Nick turned them down. "I'm innocent," he said.

Then the Bureau of Prisons started moving him around from jail to jail and was "relentless" in their treatment of him, he told me during those months while we waited to hear if there would be a third trial. "It is definitely by design," he said. "They have a term for it. It's called 'diesel therapy.' Basically, if you won't go along with what they're offering you, they'll just move you from place to place. They call it diesel therapy because you're breathing in fumes from the bus." He began to picture himself being shot in the back of the head as he was being transported. "It would have been a lot neater for them instead of having to try me again," he said. But strangely, he was at peace with that prospect.

It was not the first time he had been abused in prison with the apparent intent to force him to take a plea deal. After the appellate court had thrown out his conviction and ordered a new trial in 2017, the government had offered him a plea deal as he sat in Northern Neck Regional Jail in Warsaw, Virginia. He had refused. The next morning, he had been transferred to Piedmont Regional Jail in Farmville, Virginia.

He had been singled out starting with the intake process. He had had no disciplinary issues with jail staff or inmates but repeatedly been handcuffed for upwards of twelve hours and sprayed with mace. On one occasion, guards had asked him to "cuff up"—submit to handcuffing—then ordered him to lie on the ground. Then they had sprayed him with mace.

The guard had come over and kicked his legs a few times, then dragged him into the shower. As they'd sprayed him with water, the guard had told him to take the deal the DOJ was offering him. "They were wanting me to snap out and hurt somebody," he said. "I told them, 'God bless you.' One of them uncuffed me and gave me a cup of cold water."

He was calm when talking about the escalating abuse, but it brought fear and a sense of desperation to his family and all of us who were trying to find a way to free him. The DOJ informed Nick and his attorneys that it would try him for a third time in November 2018.

It was time to act. What was happening to Nick made it clear that all four men were in physical danger, and the defense attorneys were leery of calling attention to the abuse for fear that it would escalate. They cautioned Mike and me to wait until after Nick's third trial and the resentencing before going public with any criticism of the judge or the government. In the meantime, we quietly gathered our forces.

Before the government tried Nick a third time, it transferred him again to Northern Neck Jail, about two and a half hours from the Washington, DC, courthouse. Every morning during the seven-week trial, the guards woke him at 3:00 a.m. to shower and dress for the courtroom. He wore shackles all day, except when he was sitting in front of the jury. Every time he left the courtroom, the guards put the shackles back on his ankles, and he was in constant pain throughout the day.

He returned to jail each evening at 8:00 p.m. The constant

sitting in shackles was hard on his legs. One day, one of his legs swelled so severely that the trial was stopped so he could be taken to the emergency room. After that, he was moved to DC Jail. "They put me in the worst jail you could be in for preparing for a trial," Nick told me later. "People are always fighting, and it's really violent.... They just put you in worse and worse places as you're going to trial to get you to take a deal."[5]

The inmates at the DC Jail had a weekly tradition they called "Friday night fires." They used batteries and pieces of aluminum foil to create sparks that they used to set toilet paper and then their sheets on fire. The guards would come and spray the inmates with mace, whether they had participated or not, and drag them to a different unit while they put the fires out. The inmates would then have to sleep on metal bunks with no mattresses or blankets for several nights in a row. Nick became so exhausted and stressed due to lack of sleep that it was almost impossible for him to help with his own defense.

He lost weight due to lack of food. He was given one sandwich each day during the trial, until his attorneys asked permission to give him protein bars during the trial.

"Everything is designed to try to break you physically and mentally," he said. "It's an effort that is put forth by the court and the prosecutor just to try to break you down. Because nobody can function on four hours of sleep for an extended period of time, and that's essentially what they're counting on. They want you to be off balance when you go in there."

When opening statements began in Nick's third trial on November 5, 2018, it was still possible that all four men could walk away free. Lamberth had postponed the resentencing of Dustin, Evan, and Paul until after Nick's trial. All the Williams & Connolly team had to do, they felt, was hold on to their winning strategy. A new jury, they felt, would see that Nick had not and could not have killed the Kia driver and that Lamberth could and should sentence the other three to time served—a fair outcome, I thought, considering that Ridgeway had already served his yearlong prison term and been released. At least, that was what we all hoped for as Nick's third trial got underway.

During discovery in Nick's first solo trial, the government had handed over an email from Dr. Haithem Al Rubia'y, the father of the Kia driver, to FBI agent Bryan Finnegan. In the June 4, 2018, email, Finnegan urged Al Rubia'y to come to the United States to testify against Nick. In his reply, Al Rubia'y refused to testify, telling the FBI agent, "History is important: as I read in several newspapers and had been told and talked more than once to US teams, I met in the green zone in Baghdad, that Paul Slough had killed my son and Jeremy Ridgeway had killed my wife. The first had clearly confessed in a protected statement within hours of the incident and the latter pleaded guilty on Friday, in the U.S. District Court in Washington to voluntary manslaughter and attempting to commit manslaughter and is cooperating with the government."

He continued, "This run [sic] true for several years. Changing these charges to others, a serious and risky drift, may put doubts on the honesty of these trials. As far as the US DOJ ignored the significance of informing me with these horrible events, I believe those persons are capable of achieving their targets without engaging me in this play."

In other words, Dr. Haithem Al Rubia'y told the FBI to count him out. Prosecutors filed the email with the court two weeks after they received it. When the defense asked to introduce clear evidence that the government knew that Nick had not killed Ahmed Al Rubia'y, Lamberth refused to allow it to be shown to the jury.

The defense team wanted to strengthen their argument that Paul had shot first, without having to risk calling him and exposing him to more charges. There was another way for the defense to prove that Paul had shot first and to destroy the government's theory that Nick had incited a massacre by killing the Kia driver for no reason: They could call Evan Liberty, who, as the driver of the command vehicle, had been closest in proximity to Nick that day. Evan could testify about the order of shots and could affirm Paul's four sworn statements that he had fired first. They asked the government to grant Evan immunity so that he could testify without risking further blowback from the DOJ. Instead of opposing the motion, as the defense team expected, the government immediately agreed to the immunity request and transferred Evan from Schuylkill to the federal lockup.

Although the government had Evan transferred to Washington, DC, neither side called him to testify. The defense rested on December 10, 2018, and both sides made their closing arguments the next day.

One day, as Evan sat in a cell in the DC Jail, he saw US marshals bring Nick in from court and put him in a cell in the front of the jail. It was the first time they had seen each other in three years, and they sat and talked over the wall between them. "Hey, man, I don't think we're going to call you tomorrow," Nick said. "We closed our case today, and we think everything's going to work out."

Evan figured he would return to Pennsylvania within days, but the next morning, the marshals told him he was going to court. "I don't think I have to go to court," he told them. "They closed the case."

But he was on the witness list, so he was taken to the federal lockup and put into the same holding cell to which he and the others had been taken after they were convicted. He stayed in the DC Jail in segregation for about three weeks. On his way back to Schuylkill, he stopped at Piedmont Regional Jail in Farmville, Virginia, where Nick told him about having been beaten up by the guards.

When he arrived at Piedmont, Evan finally was allowed to make a phone call. He called his mother, Deb, and learned that Nick had been convicted. "I was so upset because they didn't call me. I figured I could help. I just could not believe they convicted him," he told me later. "I thought, you just cannot win. My worst night in prison was probably that one."

The defense team shared feelings of hopelessness in the wake of the conviction after just four days of jury deliberations. They joined the rest of us in thinking "Nick, Evan, Dustin, and Paul are in prison, and I'm here with my family, getting ready to celebrate Christmas."

The defense team never spoke to the media to point out the prosecutors' misdeeds, so the coverage of the verdict was the same as it had been since 2007: Blackwater, mercenaries, massacre.

The conviction was a blow, but it left us finally free to make a big noise.

CHAPTER FOURTEEN

——— ★★★ ———

GOVERNMENT KILLING MACHINES

We must always take sides. Neutrality helps the oppressor, never the victim. Silence encourages the tormentor, never the tormented. Sometimes we must interfere.

—ELIE WIESEL, NOBEL PRIZE ACCEPTANCE SPEECH

AS THE DOWNLOAD NUMBERS for my 2018 Wondery podcast, *Business Wars: Netflix vs. Blockbuster vs. HBO*, climbed into the millions, I finally twigged to how we could get exposure for the Raven 23 story. Mike and I got to work about a month after Nick's final trial.

At Mike's suggestion, I collected sound files from the men and their parents, partners, and friends talking about their personalities and lives before Nisour Square. He wanted to know what they did in their downtime, what kinds of music and books they liked, their morning rituals, their favorite parables, whether they followed sports teams.

"Sorry to ask all of these questions but as I read all of the accounts of these folks, there is hardly a single humanizing portrayal of these guys," he wrote in a February 21, 2019, email. "At best they are lobotomized government killing machines, at worst cold-blooded murderers. The kid in 'Serial' was guilty as hell in my opinion. But they painted him in a human light, and they showed the suffering that his family endured."

I sent the list of questions out to the families and the men and was astonished at the answers they provided; they were a kind of rough poetry. "When I was knee high to a grasshopper, I would go pump oil leases with my Papa," Dustin wrote in response to the questions. "Everyday at noon we would stop everything to listen to Paul Harvey (WBAP 820 AM—This is Paul Harvey and this is the rest of the story. . . . I can still hear it like it was yesterday). I learned to drive on the back roads going from lease to lease checking on pump jack and oil tanks. We spent many days like that."

Paul Slough's parents, Ricky and Vivian West, and his sister, Laura, drove two and a half hours each way from Dickens, Texas, to Olney one Saturday so that I could interview them in person and get a better-quality recording than I could have if I had interviewed them over the phone. Ricky, a rancher, and Vivian had informally adopted Paul, whom they had nicknamed PJ, when he was thirteen, and their love for him and their pain over his situation spilled out in the recording.

"PJ was working at the café washing dishes, and I was fixing to start working cattle one weekend, and I just asked him if he wanted to come help, and he jumped on it like a dog on a bone," Ricky told me. "He didn't know what direction the sun come up from. And he put up with me and my tail eatin's and whatnot, and the kid would listen to whatever I had to say and do whatever he needed to do to get the job done, and he was willing to learn, so I put him to work, and the kid did good."

One day, Ricky pulled up to the Slough home to drop Paul off after work, "and all of his stuff is laying out in the yard, and I just told him, 'Come on, PJ, you can just stay at the house with us.' And that's how he come to live with us."

The interviews were so emotionally compelling that it was easy to forget that we had an uphill battle—not just because of the government's misconduct but because of the men's connection to Blackwater and Erik Prince. Jessica Slatten made it clear that the defense was still struggling with how to address that prejudice. "Nick lost in front of a DC jury because he worked for Blackwater and because of the prejudicial evidence about the incident as a whole that had nothing to do with Nick but that the judge allowed to be introduced even though the law is clear it should be excluded. . . . In short, Nick is guilty by association with the public perception of Blackwater," she wrote in a February 22, 2019, email that accompanied the first in a stream of post-trial motions to appeal Nick's conviction.

There may not have been any legal grounds for the lawyers to discuss the prejudicial effect of Blackwater, but Mike and I decided that we should explore whether Prince and Blackwater were villains or something else in the story. "I never liked 'Mr. Prince' . . . but I wanted to have an episode that discussed Blackwater and showed that these guys were sacrificial lambs," he told me. "Call me a Marxist, but I tend to look at everything through a class lens. Prince, the billionaire, profited hundreds of millions of dollars. . . . And our working-class veterans got screwed."

We later learned that Prince had asked Trump to pardon the men.

While I tracked down Prince and tried to get an interview, Mike researched the billionaire auto parts scion and his company to try to figure out where they fit into the narrative. He found that Prince had pushed aggressively to extend the Blackwater brand into new businesses in the year or so before the Nisour Square incident: Blackwater Armor and Targets, Blackwater Security Consulting, Blackwater K9, Blackwater Maritime Security Solutions, Blackwater Armored Vehicle, even Blackwater Airships and a Blackwater video game.[1]

Prince was not shy about self-promotion. He was all over the media and not in a humble or self-effacing way. He would not be an asset to our efforts, Mike decided. "He must know it puts his men in increased danger with the Enemy and makes them easy targets for a press desperate to present the war on terror in the most cynical light," he wrote me in an email.

That was not a popular line of inquiry with the Raven 23 men, who acknowledged the negative connotations of the brand but would never criticize its maker. But Mike and I were seized with a sense of urgency. "I am starting to feel like Saint Peter will stop me at the gates of Heaven if I don't do everything in my power to fight such an obvious and evil injustice," he told me.

We were shaking the trees, and unexpected things were falling out. Harrison and Jaso had started distributing the pardon packet. I filed requests with the federal prisons in Memphis and El Reno to film interviews with Dustin Heard and Paul Slough. Both turned me down, citing unspecified "security threats." But then FCI Memphis threw Dustin into the Special Housing Unit (SHU) for weeks without telling his family or his attorneys where he had gone. I was starting to get pissed because the prison would not disclose his whereabouts and I needed to interview him.

"Well, I had a very interesting experience this morning. I called FCI Memphis again to ask where Dustin is, and they were quite rude and said they couldn't help me. Then I called Congressman Tim Burchett's office and talked to them for the second time, sent this email, and amazingly, got a call about ten minutes later from FCI Memphis asking when I wanted to interview Dustin and what number did I want him to call me on," I wrote to Mike on May 22, 2019. About an hour later, I got a call from a frantic Stacey Heard. Dustin had resurfaced from the SHU and asked Stacey to give me a message. "He wants you to keep beating the doors because he was instructed when he came out of the SHU, 'Do not call Gina Keating,'" he told me. "They told him, 'Under no circumstances, or you'll go back in the SHU.' Do not let up. He wants you to put the hammer down."

But I needed that interview for the podcast, and pissing off the warden would not make it happen. I decided instead to recruit

Dustin's younger brother Dylan to do my interview using a digital recording app on his phone and coached him on how to pause after asking each question so as not to step on Dustin's answers. It worked well, and I had Dylan interview Dustin a few times before the Bureau of Prisons allowed him to call and email me again.

In keeping with Dustin's request, the pardon team and Mike and I opened the bomb bay doors just before Memorial Day 2019 and prepared to smoke the government's corrupt case against the men of Raven 23.

The same month, a high-level military officer who had served with Nick mentioned the case to President Trump during a brief meeting in the Oval Office. And on May 18, 2019, *The New York Times* reported that President Trump was considering Memorial Day pardons for Army Major Mathew Golsteyn, Navy SEAL Eddie Gallagher, and Nick Slatten.

On May 20, *The Washington Post* editorial board predictably weighed in, declaring that "Trump's war-crime pardons would insult millions of service members.

"Each case is distinct," the newspaper said, "but taken together, such pardons would send a message of disrespect for the laws of war and for the larger values that the United States' fallen service members have so nobly defended. War is hell, but there *are* rules."

CBS This Morning joined in with a story about the fact that President Trump was considering pardoning "accused war criminals," including Nick Slatten. The report had the feeling of a preemptive strike to create public outrage to prevent innocent veterans from receiving pardons, meaning that the source of the report had to be someone at the DOJ.

Mike was furious. "Was Chelsea Manning called 'a war criminal'? Was Bo Bergdahl called 'a war criminal'?" he asked. "The hypocrisy is outrageous. We need to separate the Nisour Square folks from the other ones and in doing so take the media to task for being so lazy and lumping them together."

He became nearly apoplectic a week later when John Walker Lindh, known as "the American Taliban" was freed from prison after serving seventeen years of a twenty-year sentence for providing support to the Taliban ahead of the September 11, 2001, attacks. *The New York Times* reported that he "continued to advocate for global jihad and to write and translate violent extremist texts." "This murderous traitor is getting released and there is barely a peep of protest," he told me.

"I guess if the Raven 23 guys fought for the Taliban, they would be free now. They made the mistake of actually fighting against our enemies instead of for them."

At that time, we started consulting a close friend of Mike whom I will refer to in this account as "the Fixer." That highly placed attorney had one of the best Rolodexes in Washington, DC, and was happy to help us but wanted to remain below the radar. As soon as Mike briefed them about the Raven 23 case and the pardon effort, the Fixer devised a campaign to counter the anti-pardon faction with an aggressive push to disseminate the facts outlined in Harrison and Jaso's pardon packet, "The Unconstitutional, Politically Motivated Prosecution of Military Veterans Paul Slough, Dustin Heard, Evan Liberty, and Nicolas Slatten."

The Fixer reached out to a list of journalists and opinion writers who could be persuaded to review the flawed trials and make a case for the pardons. The targeted news personalities included David French, a senior columnist at *National Review*, Laura Ingraham of Fox News, William McGurn of *The Wall Street Journal*, Matt Drudge of the Drudge Report, and a few others.

But the Fixer set our sights on *Fox & Friends Weekend* host Pete Hegseth, an Iraq War veteran and veterans' advocate who had a close relationship with Trump and who openly used his morning show to advocate for the release of vets unfairly caught in the military criminal justice system. He seemed to speak directly to Trump through the show, media watchers said. The Fixer provided

Hegseth's email address to David Harrison and Christin Slough, who had met in Washington, DC, a week before Memorial Day to pass around the pardon packet and meet with members of Congress.

The timing of the pardon request was a problem, Christin learned. They were distributing the pardon packet nearly two years before the end of Trump's first term, and the pardon season was traditionally at the end of a term, after an election. Harrison tried to temper her expectations about whether and when a pardon could occur, but both agreed that the Trump administration was not like any other. "It always felt like something can happen any second," Christin told me. "[Pardons] don't come until the end of term, but Trump was an anomaly. He did not give a shit. He would [say], 'I'll just pardon somebody on a Tuesday if I feel like it, like any old Tuesday.' I loved that about him."

Mike and I raced to assemble an elaborate and dramatic trailer for the podcast in time for Memorial Day to conform with the expected date of the rumored pardons. In the trailer, we wanted to share the voices of the men and their loved ones so that listeners would recognize them as normal people living through extraordinary circumstances—not the bogeymen created by the government and the media.

Even the government did not buy its own portrayal of the Raven 23 defendants. At a hearing before the 2014 trial, Assistant US Attorney T. Patrick Martin had walked up to Paul Slough and introduced himself. "Who is this fine-looking young man?" he had asked the then-thirty-five-year-old veteran, sticking out his hand.

"I'm Paul Slough, sir—one of the men you're trying to kill."

"Oh," Martin said, taken aback. "You don't look the way I thought you would."

Paul later told me about this exchange.

As we worked on the trailer in late May, Jessica, Christin, and the attorneys followed the Fixer's outreach plan. A forty-minute phone call between David French, an Iraq War veteran, former JAG, and public policy professor, turned into a May 28, 2019, column titled "Pardon the Men of Raven 23."

"They've been unfairly lumped in with different men who face punishments for very different incidents," French wrote. He emailed the link to Mike the day it was published, telling him, "I've been reading court documents, media reports, and talking to folks. I share your view of the case."

Even as *The New York Times* allowed Defense Department bigwigs to bitch in its pages that pardons of convicted combatants would undermine the chain of command, *Washington Post* columnist Charles Lane likened Trump's supposed support for "war-crime pardons" to President Richard Nixon's about-face in the Vietnam War–era case of Army Lieutenant William Calley. Calley was convicted in 1971 of twenty murders for his part in the My Lai massacre and sentenced to life in prison but served only three days before Nixon pardoned him. "President Richard M. Nixon did not see this as an opportunity to drive home the point that U.S. soldiers must follow the laws of war and that deviations are not only morally wrong but counterproductive militarily," he wrote on May 20, 2019. "Rather, Nixon decided to exploit a groundswell of sympathy for Calley. In 1971, millions of Americans vilified Calley as typical of a corrupt and violent policy; yet millions more saw him as a dedicated soldier being scapegoated for the failed policies of others."

During the week before Labor Day, which fell on September 2, Jessica Slatten appeared on various national radio shows talking about the three Raven 23 trials; Buck Sexton and Lars Larson spent entire episodes analyzing the case. Christin Slough appeared on *The Ingraham Angle* on May 23, 2019, thanks to intervention from Mike and the Fixer, who were personal friends of Fox News host Laura Ingraham.

The years of knocking on doors and learning to pitch products for SeneGence paid off in the greenroom at Fox News studios in Manhattan. As Christin waited to go on, she started talking to a gray-haired man in a suit. She did not recognize Trump's chief of staff, Mark Meadows. They chatted, asking each other what they would be talking about with Ingraham. Christin explained her plight, and he introduced himself. "Well, I can tell you one thing that I know for sure: The president will be watching this show tonight," he told her.

"No pressure!" Christin said.

"No pressure," he told her.

Before he went on, he gave Christin his cell phone number. For the next eighteen months, she occasionally texted Meadows with updates but never received a response. She was getting used to the black hole that was DC communications and wondered if all the motion was having any effect.

A few days after the flurry of pardon stories ran, Nick Slatten called his sister, Jessica, from the Rappahannock Regional Jail in Stafford, Virginia. He had been incommunicado for several weeks after the inmates had rioted, breaking the sprinklers, setting fire to the microwave ovens, and running the guards out of the unit. Throughout the mayhem, Nick had sat on his bed and read his Bible while his cellmate had gone out to participate. Another inmate had shut his door, and it locked from the outside. When the guards returned to restore order, Nick was spared the worst of the punishment, but he was not unscathed. "They didn't feed us much for seven days," he told me later. "They brought us trays, that way it looked good for the camera, but there was just a tiny amount of food on the tray. We were hungry, and I was laying there calling out to God."

He read Psalm 91, a prayer of protection in times of hardship, every day. One particular verse stood out to him. He drew a box around it and recited it every day: "Surely, He will save you from the fowler's snare," it said. He prayed, "You're my Father . . .

you're saying this, you're going to save me from the fowler's snare. That's where I'm at. When are you going to do this? I need you to help me."

One day, as he recited the prayer, a voice came over the speaker box in his cell: "Slatten, pack your stuff. You got a presidential pardon." He thought he was losing his mind from the lack of food. When he was finally able to make a phone call a few days later, he called Jessica.

"Have you talked to anyone?" she asked him.

"No," he said.

"Well, *The New York Times* reported that President Trump was considering pardoning soldiers accused of war crimes, and it mentioned you by name."

After that day, Nick Slatten had no doubt that God had a plan for him.

CHAPTER FIFTEEN

─── ★★★ ───

SENTENCING

They're talking about things of which they don't have the slightest understanding, anyway. It's only because of their stupidity that they're able to be so sure of themselves.

—FRANZ KAFKA, *THE TRIAL*

THE WHITE-MARBLED COURTROOM AT the E. Barrett Prettyman U.S. Courthouse was packed when I arrived for Nick Slatten's sentencing on August 14, 2019. Nick's family and comrades from the 82nd Airborne Division and Blackwater talked quietly together, waiting for Judge Lamberth to arrive. I had met Jessica, Reba, and Darrell Slatten and their family and friends at a nearby hotel the evening prior, and we had talked about the statements each would make the next day, pleading humbly for mercy for Nick.

Nick's attorney, Dane Butswinkas of Williams & Connolly, was first to stand at the lectern before Judge Lamberth and may have been speaking for all of us in that courtroom about our disillusionment with a system that was not working. "I have wanted to be a lawyer since 1969, 50 years, since I was 8," he said calmly. "And for 30 years I have practiced; and I have always worked hard at it . . . and I always leave every case with a little bit more passion for the next one. . . . But most of all, I am inspired by a system, however imperfect, that ultimately serves democracy; a system that protects our citizens like Mr. Slatten from oppression, one that does its level best to ensure justice is served. And it's a system that works hardest in the most unpopular case, the cases most prone to bias."

He paused, wrestling with emotion. "As I left this case this past winter, I, for the first time in 30 years, questioned whether I belonged as part of this system. And so I even, for a brief period, stepped aside from this position. But I could hear my late mother saying, 'Think of something positive and do your part.' Even my mom would have been challenged by this chronology."

He expressed his admiration of Nick "not just for his service to this country . . . but his unbroken faith in a system that, from his vantage point, probably hasn't earned it; for the strength of his human spirit to endure what he has endured; for his friendship; for his . . . devotion to and faith in God." He vowed that Nick was "someone that we will stand proudly beside until the day when, in our view, respectfully, until justice is done."

He went on to list the reasons that the case was fatally flawed: "There are four eyewitnesses who had no relationship with Mr. Slatten who said he was innocent. There was a Raven 23 member who admitted to this incident four times almost contemporaneously with the incident. There was ballistics and reconstruction evidence that suggests he's innocent; there were members of the State Department who said so; the top career former FBI polygraph expert said so. And the Government said so to the victim's father, so poignant that he refused, as you know, to be part of this trial when asked."

Then came a procession of family, friends, and military comrades standing at the lectern and pleading with Lamberth to free Nicholas Slatten, an innocent man. Among them was Nick's army comrade Johnny Ivanovich Nuñez.

"I am Nick's brother from another mother; I am sure you guys can tell the resemblance," Nuñez told Lamberth. "I am here to share a few words in support of Nick Slatten who was my team leader in the Army in 2005. We have been close ever since. . . . While we are from very different backgrounds, we quickly created a bond while serving in the military. Nick is a man of character and principles who does the right thing even in the face of intense pressure." He told how Nick had protected him from hazing "even when higher ranking soldiers tried to intervene and pulled rank on him, he prevented it. He stood his ground and said: 'This will not happen on my watch.'"

The testimonials went on for ninety minutes, creating an atmosphere that was defiant yet akin to a wake. There was not an empty seat or a dry eye in the courtroom. Patrick Martin cowered at the prosecutor's table, his movements rabbity. He refused to look out into the gallery. The judge had pasted a thin smile on his slick, chinless face.

Then Nick's father, Darrell Slatten, tall and lean, walked to the lectern. The fifth-generation Tennessee farmer and twenty-year reservist addressed Lamberth: "When I look at my son Nick, I see someone that this Court, these prosecutors, and the jurors that are not here fail to see; I see an innocent man. I see a patriot. I see a soldier and a protector of our great America. I see a man unlike many in here, including this Court and the jury that are not here today, that have never been down a range, have never been in combat, ain't got a clue. It's tough. It's tough to watch our system at work.

"I see a man who went to war for our country. I see a man that served two combat tours in Iraq serving in one of America's most elite divisions, the 82nd Airborne. I see a man that watched many of his brothers be wounded and die at the hands of Iraqi insurgents, most of whom didn't even wear a uniform. One minute, they were your friend, the next minute they shot you in the back.

"Nick, please accept my apologies for what your country has done to you. The country and people that you were willing to die for. I know you're innocent, this Court knows you are innocent;

and the jury would know you were innocent if they had been allowed to hear and see all of the evidence.

"Rest assured, my son. Rest assured, we will fight until hell freezes over to correct this total failure and travesty of justice," he concluded. "Nick, thanks for your service; and I love you."

Darrell Slatten's rough eloquence caused the judge to come completely unwound. Rather than consider the life sentence he had helped engineer and was about to hand down or the family that had suffered for so long at his incompetent hands, he took exception to the existence of men of far greater valor. "The defendant's father made a statement that the Court has no experience with combat. I served a year myself in Vietnam; I do know the situation in combat," he said, jowls quivering indignantly. "And I reject the idea that I don't know what I am doing; that I don't understand combat situations. I do. . . . And I was in many situations myself that were very dangerous. But I was in a situation where we depended upon each other to carry out our orders and to ensure that innocent people were not needlessly killed, and we followed the combat rules."

Except when you "fired like hell" near a Vietnamese village because you were terrified of nothing, I thought as I listened to him blather on.

Finally he got to the point: Nick would be sentenced to life in prison for murder because he had failed to help the prosecutors out of the predicament in which their own incompetence had landed them. Yet even though the government had twice dismissed Nick from the case for lack of evidence, Lamberth insisted that the vindictive murder charge was appropriate.

"There was no incoming fire at the time that shot was fired. . . . The jury got it exactly right, and this was murder. It meets any definition of murder," he said.[1]

"I agree that it's unfortunate that there is a disparity in the sentence of the other defendants," he continued. "I agree that, were this an ideal world, manslaughter might have been a better outcome. The defendant had the opportunity for that and turned it down and went on to gamble and take all or nothing, so he gets what he gambled for."

In an opinion he issued about two weeks before the sentencing hearing, Lamberth denied a motion for acquittal for Nick and compared the Nisour Square shootings to the 1770 Boston Massacre, after which the British soldiers who killed American colonists were acquitted of murder charges by a colonial jury who found the colonists had provoked the soldiers. Ignoring the mountain of evidence and testimony that the Raven 23 men had been shot at by at least eight insurgents in the world's most dangerous city, Lamberth concluded that "history will not be so kind to Nicholas Slatten. . . . And unlike the British soldiers two centuries and a half a world apart, Slatten and his teammates shot without any provocation."

At last Nick was allowed to speak. He stood up from the counsel table and turned to face Lamberth. Even exhausted and dressed in a khaki prison jumpsuit, he exuded dignity and peace. "Does the truth matter? The members of my jury have never been to combat, so there was no way for me to get a fair trial, especially when prosecutors and key witnesses were allowed to lie to my jury. This is a miscarriage that will not stand," he said. "Judge, you know I am innocent. I am asking you to throw out this case. If you don't, Judge, I forgive you for killing me for something I did not do. May the Lord bless you, sir."

Lamberth did not look Nick in the face as he handed down his sentence: life in prison.

"I have to reject the statements that the defendant himself makes that he is innocent," Lamberth said. "The Court's own view of the evidence is the same as that of the jury; that, in fact, the defendant committed this offense; the defendant is guilty of this offense; the defendant, in fact, committed this crime and fired this shot into the white Kia and shot the decedent, Ahmed Al Rubia'y between the eyes, and killed him before that car ever moved forward; that the statements of Mr. Slough that he did it were fictitious, and were in an effort to mislead authorities and were never true and . . . were an effort to mislead authorities at the time as to what was going on. . . . The Court is in full agreement that the defendant is in fact guilty of the offense."

Nick was taken away to the courthouse lockup. We drifted outside the courtroom to comfort one another. As I stood talking to Evan's childhood friend Chris Buslovich and Brian Liberty, the prosecutor, Patrick Martin, hurried past. I fell in behind him, trying to get his attention. He ignored me, then turned rapidly to say that he had no comment about the case.

I called Mike and unloaded. "It's not going to go any better for Paul, Dustin, and Evan," I said. "We need to use everything we've got against Lamberth and the prosecutors. I honestly believe it can't get any worse. This judge is totally crazy, and everybody has finally realized it."

We were desperate to churn out more episodes of the podcast—to do something, anything—before the other three men were sentenced. "This thing needs to be out by September 5," I told Mike.

The last week of August, I boarded a plane bound for Spain to attend my brother's wedding and was not able to attend the September 5 sentencing of Dustin, Evan, and Paul, but I heard all about it when I returned. It was as big a debacle as Nick's sentencing had been—partly because of a letter sent to the court by a group of Texas lawmakers led by State Senator Drew Springer, who represented Dustin's and Paul's hometowns.

For several years after her husband had gone to prison, Christin Slough had booked him a plane ticket whenever she and Lily had taken a trip. She would make sure that her hotel room had a sofa bed where Lily could sleep in case Paul somehow was freed in the time between booking the tickets and taking the trip.

When she arrived in Washington, DC, for his September 5, 2019, sentencing hearing, she brought her family and friends, as well as Paul's driver's license and wallet, his clothes, and his watch. Five years after the original trial, the entire courtroom filled, as did an overflow room; that, even after Lamberth had switched the sentencing hearing date from August 14 to September 5, 2019, at the last minute, costing the families and friends thousands of dollars in airline and hotel change fees. If Lamberth and the prosecutors had been trying to minimize attendance at the hearing, it had not worked.

Paul, Nick, and Evan saw one another for the first time in almost five years at the courthouse lockup. They were so pleased to see one another that the US marshals remarked that they had not acted like men who were facing the specter of having to beg mercy from a judge who had put them into prison for crimes they had not committed.

Prosecutor Patrick Martin was the first to speak, asking Lamberth to sentence Paul to thirty years in prison, Evan to twenty-five years, and Dustin to twenty-five years. "This case is not like any other and that's why these sentences, while severe, are perfectly appropriate, given the loss of life and the maiming of countless innocent civilians," he said. He read letters from the alleged victims, urging Lamberth to apply the maximum sentences after their rigged victory.

Next, Paul's attorney, Brian Heberling, spoke in an echo of Butswinkas. "Your Honor, to say that this case has haunted everyone on this side of the courtroom for the last five years would be a significant understatement. We have all struggled to come to terms with what happened in Nisur Square and what happened in this courtroom.

"You have the power to send Paul home to do the little things his family so sorely misses, to make breakfast together, to attend the tea party that Lily so desperately wants him to come home to attend, to rejoin his community in west Texas that so badly needs him home. I submit to you that Paul has earned that opportunity."

Person after person got up to petition the judge for mercy for Paul, Evan, and Dustin. When Christin Slough's turn came, she told Lamberth of a pact made by the four men right after they had been sentenced: "Evan turned to the guys, including Paul, and said, 'There is no way we are going to walk away from this without changing, so we simply have to choose whether we're changing for the better or for the worse.

"'All we can say is that we are so sorry for all of the grief and the loss that have resulted and we just pray that you see that the answer to this question is not more grief and loss.'"

Stacey Heard spoke, asking Lamberth to sentence Dustin to time served. Then Dustin's fifteen-year-old daughter, Hannah, got up and addressed her dad. "I love you, Daddy. I've always looked up to you, and you are so openly caring of me and Quinn," she began, talking about memories they had made since he had gone to prison when she was nine years old. "But I have also experienced so much without you, too. One was my first formal. I wish you could have been there to give me a hard time for getting dressed up. . . . I went from intermediate school to middle school to high school while you've been in, and although they've been pretty good years of my life, it's been hard not having you around. . . . When I turn 16, I want you to be there to celebrate with me. And most of all, I would like you to be there for my high school graduation."

Chris Buslovich came to court again to speak for Evan, and Evan's brother, Aaron, summed up the bitterness permeating the entreaties for mercy to the troglodyte on the bench: "Years from now, I often wonder what I would tell my kids if either of them came to me and said, 'Dad, I am considering joining the military. I wish I could tell them that their service would be appreciated and rewarded with unwavering support from a country that stands behind them. I wish I could tell them that if they joined the military, they would be given the benefit of the doubt if they were forced to rely upon their training and experience to make split-second decisions that nobody wants to make. I wish I could tell them that nobody would ever second-guess them for these decisions when things don't go according to plan. But I am no longer that naive."

Evan's attorney, Bill Coffield, was the last of the defense to speak. "I have to say that this case has shaken me like no other," he said. "At the original sentencing, I said this case haunts us. Four and a half years, it still haunts us. I still wake up at night, and I wonder 'what could I have done to help Evan?'" Then, like the other speakers, he asked Lamberth to sentence the men to time served.

When the defense attorneys mentioned the outpouring of support for the men in the courtroom and in letters addressed to the court, Lamberth again burst into defensive indignation. He went on a tirade about the letter sent to him by Springer and the Texas lawmakers, urging him to sentence the men to time served not only because they were innocent but because the trial had so obviously been rigged to appease the Iraqi government. "Again, I have to totally reject any notion that my sentence in this case is to appease an ally, as the congressman and senators are raising with me in the letter yesterday. I am not here to appease an ally," he said.

In one of the most heartbreaking moments of the sentencing, Paul Slough rose to address the court—and to apologize for having shot Ahmed Haithem Al Rubia'y, the driver of the white Kia: "Your Honor, this time and this experience has been crushing and I am beyond horrified that innocent life was taken that day. Your Honor, I take full acceptance for my own actions, and I thank God for his providence that Mr. Rubia'y knows who I am and that some day I might find forgiveness in his eyes and the two of us may, indeed, be healed.

"Your Honor, by God's grace, I, too, am a father, a son, a brother, a husband, and an uncle. And it is crippling to even consider losing my wife, our daughter, my parents, my in-laws, brothers, sisters, and their siblings. But just as crushing and horrifying and crippling, Your Honor, is being forever branded with this loss of life."

Dustin spoke of his desire to be back with his children, who had lived most of their lives without him at home. "Please give me a chance to be their father before they're grown," he appealed to Lamberth. "I would appreciate your consideration. I'm ready to get back to the life of being a father, a son, and just being with my family."

Dustin, too, regretted "any innocent life lost due to my actions that day." In his statement to the Court, he echoed, poignantly, what Joe Bob had told me about his childhood values: "I got the order from my team leader to return fire. I did not. I didn't have a target. So I'm not going to take shots blindly. . . . I only engaged threats that day. I did what I thought I had to do under the circumstances, and I understand the jury found that I was wrong. I accept that."

He begged Lamberth to free him from prison that day, for the sakes of Quinn and Hannah.

Evan spoke of his desire to serve and to "find a way to give back if given the chance."

"I sincerely regret that innocent lives were lost on September 16, 2007," he told the judge. "I never intended that any innocent lives be impacted. This is something that will weigh on my conscience for the rest of my life."

He had changed, he said. "I believe I am more thoughtful and considerate. I am closer to my family and value my friends more," he told Lamberth. "I have come to realize that the most important thing in my life is the positive impact I can have on others."

One thing that had not changed in the twelve years since the

Nisour Square incident was the love he had for the United States of America, he said. "I am proud that I had the chance to serve, and I would serve again right now if I could. I know further military service is not possible for me, but I intend to find a way to give back if given the chance."

Lamberth rejected their request for a sentence of time served—the seven years of virtual imprisonment while the DOJ had tried to get the case off the ground, plus six years and two months of actual prison time. But, according to Lamberth, the Raven 23 men had not exhibited sufficient guilt to win leniency.

"I don't like comparing a cooperating person like Ridgeway at all," Lamberth said when defense attorney Brian Heberlig objected to the twelve-months-and-one-day sentence handed down to Ridgeway. "You can't compare cooperators who fully come forward and agree that they did wrong, who have changed their lives, you can't compare how a Court sentences them to how a Court sentences your client."

Lamberth also took umbrage at the men's continued insistence that they were innocent.

"First and foremost, I squarely reject any notion that . . . there is any question as to the factual guilt of each of the three defendants . . . each of these defendants was found guilty by a jury after a fair trial that I conducted. . . . There is a message, though, that this Court in sentencing does consider, and that is, what kind of country is the United States. We hold our Armed Forces and our contractors accountable for their actions. We did in cases I worked on in Vietnam sometimes as a defense attorney. . . . We believe in the rule of law in our country. We believed it in Vietnam, and we believed it in Iraq, and our courts try to enforce the rule of law, and I believe as a judge my duty is to enforce the rule of law," Lamberth said.

Instead of time served, he sentenced Dustin Heard to twelve years in prison, Evan Liberty to fourteen years, and Paul Slough to fifteen years. "Although there were mistakes made along the way by the government, by and large, the government found and exposed and delivered to the world a trial where the truth of what happened in Nisour Square came out and was there for the world and the public to see, and I think the government of the United States deserves great credit for how the truth came out in this case and this trial," he concluded.

After the hearing ended, Christin Slough was devastated. Lamberth's resentencing had taken no account of each of the men's spotless records in prison and beforehand. "Where do we go from here?" she wondered. The only chance was a presidential pardon. The outcome of the hearing had been catastrophic, she felt; it was the worst-case scenario that she and her SeneGence tribe and her family had gamed out before they arrived. "There was the fact that it was thirteen years. I thought that was insane," she said later. "Even though we went from thirty to thirteen years . . . it was hard for it to feel like a win because . . . a win would've been putting him on a plane home with me."

CHAPTER SIXTEEN

───── ★★★ ─────

MORDOR

Only those who will risk going too far can possibly find out just how far one can go.

—T. S. ELIOT, PREFACE TO *TRANSIT OF VENUS*

MIKE CAME UP WITH a title for the podcast—*Raven 23: Presumption of Guilt*—and we released the trailer on June 15 to quite a bit of attention; it actually charted and racked up about three hundred views each hour for the first week or so.

As he and I worked on the first four podcast scripts, we wondered how to approach the story and draw listeners in when worldwide public opinion was so divided—and set—over what happened in Nisour Square. "I think we need to tell the audience *why* they should care," he said.

The Raven 23 story was unfolding in real time, as we wrote. On a philosophical level, the story was about how war teaches us about both the best and the worst sides of human nature. For every virtue on display, there is an equal and opposite reaction. Loyalty is met with betrayal. Courage is met with cowardice. Sacrifice is met with selfishness. And the truth is met with deceit.

On a practical level, the US government spent trillions of dollars and thousands of lives to try to bring democracy to a lawless country whose citizens hated us and wanted us gone. By the time the Nisour Square incident happened, it was becoming clear that Iraq was already a vassal state of Iran—even if the State Department and the US military did not want to admit it. The Shi'a Iraqis' and Iranians' strategy was simple: put the United States into as many lose-lose positions as possible to force a withdrawal. Once we withdrew, the Shi'as could finally use their newly gained power to exterminate the Sunnis. The US government's continued prosecution of the Raven 23 men was perhaps a way to distract the public from the hard truth that we had poured American lives and treasure into a neocon delusion that we could spread democracy around the world and had nothing to show for it.

While I gathered the first-person accounts of the trial and aftermath from the families, Raven 23 team members, and the men in prison, Mike went after interviews with the political and military leaders who had made the decisions that had resulted in the Nisour Square incident. Since we had no expertise in audio production, Mike called his godson, Kyle Hartford, and asked him to help edit, produce, and master the podcast. Kyle, a college student at the time, agreed instantly.

Dave Harrison had his first conversation with Pete Hegseth a couple of weeks after the brainstorming session with the Fixer at the Washington, DC, law office of Nick's original trial counsel Steptoe. "I was driving home with my kids from a soccer game, and he called, and we talked for an hour about the case, and he said, 'I'm in,'" he later recounted.

Harrison asked if Mike and I could go on *Fox & Friends Weekend* a few days before the sentencing to promote the podcast and bring attention to the pardon effort ahead. Of course, we agreed, and we doubled down to try to finish the first four episodes before we appeared on Hegseth's show.

Mike and Kyle uploaded the first episode to Buzzsprout just

hours before Mike drove from Boston to Manhattan to meet me at the Fox News studios in Manhattan in the predawn hours of August 11, 2019.

I had flown up to New York from St. Louis the night before our appearance and the next morning took the limo that Fox sent to its headquarters on Avenue of the Americas. It was still dark as I stood in Fox Square, holding a couple of dresses in a plastic bag and looking up at the building. I might as well be entering Mordor, I thought. The voices of my agent and some of my friends, warning me to stay away from the story, kept running through my mind. *There's no going back after this*, I thought. I would be stuck on that ride until it ended with all four men exonerated, however long that took.

Fox security checked me in, and soon I was sitting in a makeup chair, chatting with the makeup and hair ladies and waiting for Mike to turn up. The podcast episode, titled "Saving the Pentagon from Itself," was delivered to Fox less than an hour before we aired. The greenroom at Fox was familiar territory for Mike, who had appeared on several Fox News shows during his time at Walden Media to talk about his movies. We met in the greenroom just minutes before we went on—the first time we had seen each other in person since the *Narnia* junket fourteen years earlier.

I was extremely nervous while waiting for our segment to begin, thinking about how to describe the intricacies of the case in the limited time we would have. Mike and Pete were pros and deftly led the short discussion in a way that allowed us to hit all our points. It was over before I realized it. Mike's best contribution was finding the video clip of Joe Biden discussing "Key-sore Square" with the Iraqi president. Knowing that those segments were limited, he knew he had to find something under ten seconds to illustrate our point that Biden had been clueless about what had actually happened there. What better way to do that than to show that he didn't even know the name of the place where it had occurred, despite claiming that he had been following the case closely.

We changed back into street clothes and, with our heavy TV makeup still on, walked down the street to the Pret a Manger sandwich shop to talk. Mike said that our hit-and-run appearance with Hegseth had felt like "an out-of-body experience." "Every other time I had been on the show, it was part of a plan that a publicity team put together months in advance, and I was always accompanied by a publicist who made sure all the clips were in place," he said.

We were both in shock that it had gone as well as it had, and after a few minutes, the conversation pivoted to "Will this help the boys get out?" and "What do we do next to move the ball forward to get them out of prison?"

As we considered that, I got a call from the producer of *Fox & Friends First* with Carley Shimkus, who asked us to appear the next morning at an even earlier call time. Having both pulled all-nighters, we retreated to our respective hotels.

We had barely walked out of the studios when Media Matters for America, a nonprofit website funded by progressives, including the billionaire George Soros, and "dedicated to comprehensively monitoring, analyzing, and correcting conservative misinformation in the U.S. media," weighed in on our Fox News appearance.

Mike was energized by the attention, but I felt wounded and angry. The "analysis" posted below a video of our appearance reiterated all the incorrect reporting from *The Washington Post* and *The New York Times*, which had been based entirely upon the government's vindictive and unconstitutional prosecution in a round robin of misinformation. It did not bother me that the Left had not immediately believed me, but the fact that it was not even the slightest bit curious about the NACDL amicus brief or the documents that we had posted from the trial was infuriating and depressing. The reaction of that supposed guardian of progressive media was not just closed-minded, it was aggressively reactionary. It was the first of many, many times that I would yell in frustration at my phone or a computer screen, "I'm liberal, too, idiots!"

Fox dropped the trailer, and it skyrocketed up the charts, finding a place in the top twenty of all podcasts for a couple of days. Suddenly our phones started to ring with offers from various companies that specialized in podcast advertising. We made the decision that we would not accept advertising, as it would be a distraction from the serious message we were trying to convey. We did not want anything to break the momentum that we could feel building, especially a commercial by a company hawking protein powder or another podcast.

After the second Fox News appearance, Mike went back to Boston to oversee production on the next few episodes, while I boarded a train at Penn Station to Washington, DC, to attend Nick's sentencing two days later.

As I rode the train, I got a call from Joe Bob. A year earlier, he had quit his college studies in St. Louis to work in the Permian Basin near Midland, Texas, where oil field workers were making bank in the shale oil revolution. He had told the guys on his crew that his girlfriend was on Fox News, and he had showed them the clips of our interviews.

The Fox News appearance was definitely provocative; in addition to internet trolls, I heard from someone who shared with me a copy of the State Department's original report on the Nisour Square incident, written on September 16, 2007. The email also contained a photo of then Senator Barack Obama wearing sunglasses and surrounded by his Blackwater guard detail in Iraq.

I shared the email with Mike. "Damn! I love this photo of Obama with the Blackwater squad in Iraq that was assigned to protect him in 2008," I wrote. "He is so damn cool. Why did he have to turn on them? Kind of blows it for me."

When we first began the podcast, we went directly to Blackwater founder Erik Prince. We felt that Blackwater was not represented fairly in the press, and we wanted to get his perspective on Nisour Square. It turned out that there were reasons for him to keep his distance—at least publicly—from the criminal case. I chased Prince for about a year before I could finally get him on the phone in July 2019. It happened that I got my one and only chance to speak with him while sitting in my car outside the El Reno prison, where I had just visited Paul Slough. Prince and I spoke for about an hour, and I learned a couple of important facts: First, Prince was well aware that the Raven 23 men had suffered from association with him and Blackwater. He was right: The jury foreperson who had voted to convict Nick in his third trial had told *The Washington Post* not to print his or her name for fear of retribution by Blackwater. By that time, the company had not existed for almost a decade.

The second most important revelation was that Prince had commissioned a report about the Nisour Square incident by the former chief prosecutor of Iraq, who had retired after helping the US government prosecute Saddam Hussein. Prince's disclosure of the report was not news; he had mentioned it in a YouTube video of an appearance he had done at Oxford University. Blackwater had hired the man to investigate the people who had claimed to be victims and who were suing the company for solatia, or "consolation," and condolence payments. The ex-prosecutor had visited the families of eleven alleged victims from Nisour Square.

"We don't know that they were all killed by a Blackwater round," he told me. "We know that they were killed in the Nisour Square incident. There was a lot of other people that were injured—wounded—and brought to American military facilities to seek treatment, and when they would remove the bullets, they would find that it is a 762 bullet that weighs 123 grains—which is exactly what an AK-47 round weighs. And it's very hard to misinterpret that as any other round because none of our men were shooting anything like an AK-47 round that day—or ever."

The Muslim requirement of burying the dead within twenty-four hours had prevented detailed autopsies from being performed, but Prince said he had seen medical reports from a number of cases in which enemy bullets had been taken from the wounded. I never got to see that report.

The main thing that bugged me about Prince was that despite his purportedly enormous wealth, the men and their families were having to sell T-shirts and hold spaghetti suppers and bake sales to fund their never-ending legal case. Dustin had started making leather purses in prison, and his parents were selling them in their café in Olney so he could afford to call his children and buy personal items and food from the commissary.

The financial pressure was relentless; it cost money to visit the prisons, the men had to pay the prison for each email they received, and we were charged by the BOP when the men called us on the phone. Kelli Heard sold their home in Maryville and bought a smaller house; she also sold Dustin's boat and fishing gear to stay afloat. That became a flash point in their marriage—a sign to Dustin that she no longer believed he would be released. To Kelli, it sprang from the reality of raising two children alone on a teacher's salary and not being able to see the end of the debt.

I had numerous conversations with Prince's aides about helping with his former employees' defense costs, but none of the conversations resulted in actual money. To this day, I am not aware his providing any aid to help clear their significant post-pardon legal debt.

The four lawyers who defended Dustin Heard, Evan Liberty, Paul Slough, and Nick Slatten in the first trial shared a pot of somewhere between $1 million and $4 million provided by Prince and Blackwater's liability insurance policy. But that sum was made to stretch to four defendants in a thirteen-year legal battle in two countries—against the government's unlimited resources.

On the cost issue, I talked to a few private trial attorneys, and they said that the costs of a half-dozen government attorneys, three full trials, forty-six foreign witnesses brought to the United States for court appearances—without background checks, I might add—and other expenses would probably total up to $40 million to $50 million. I have been trying to get the real numbers from the Department of Justice since August 19, 2019.

CHAPTER SEVENTEEN

PETE HEGSETH

We are but warriors for the working-day;
Our gayness and our gilt are all besmirch'd
With rainy marching in the painful field.

—WILLIAM SHAKESPEARE, *HENRY V*

PETE HEGSETH WAS A KID from Forest Lake, Minnesota, who wanted to be a professional basketball player. His dad coached high school basketball, and his mom was a homemaker. Pete was the valedictorian of his high school class and saw no reason why he should not attend Princeton University and play for the Tigers and ultimately the NBA. He also applied to the US Military Academy at West Point.

When both institutions offered him a spot in their freshman classes, he opted for Princeton for a shot at playing in an NCAA tournament. "I didn't even know how hard it was to get into Princeton," he told me. "Honestly, I mean, in retrospect, I probably wouldn't have tried if I knew my chances, but I was naive enough to think I could get in, and somehow it happened." That impulse to draw a line between where he was and what he wanted was powerful—and effective beyond dreams of athletic accolades.

He mostly rode the bench but for a glorious game right before his graduation in 2003 in which he led a rally that clinched a game-winning basket against Columbia University. Princeton Athletic Communications noted that Hegseth had "made the best of his opportunity, draining a pair of three-pointers and assisting on the game-winning basket to lead the Princeton men's basketball team to a 44–40 victory in front of 5,205 fans at Jadwin Gym."

In his sophomore year at Princeton, Hegseth joined the Reserve Officer Training Corps to satisfy a yearning to serve. The Hegseths were not a military family, nor even a family that thought much about politics. But he loved patriotic events, and watching the veterans march in Memorial Day and July 4 parades in Forest Lake had imprinted on him the idea that "those men walking down the street did something special for their country, something brave, and hopefully someday I could do something brave."

He joined the Army National Guard out of college on a three-year contract and went to Guantánamo Bay, Cuba, in 2004 as a reserve infantry officer with the Minnesota National Guard. He volunteered to deploy to Iraq in 2005 and ended up in Samarra with the 3rd Battalion, 187th Infantry Regiment, 101st Airborne Division, known as the "Iron Rakkasans."

It was in Samarra with the Rakkasans (a nickname meaning "falling-down umbrella men" that had been given to the unit by Japanese civilians in World War II when they had seen US troops parachuting out of airplanes) that Hegseth discovered the true vicissitudes of the Iraq War and found a personal mission defending the indefensible. He was assigned to Charlie Company—which would come to be known as "Kill Company" for its high body count—as a platoon leader in Samarra, then switched to a counterinsurgency role working with local governments just before his company embarked on a disastrous mission called Operation Iron Triangle.

There, a number of civilian casualties and criminal cases against soldiers resulted arguably from army leaders' failure to understand the situation they were facing in Iraq and communicate it to their soldiers.

When Operation Iron Triangle led to the prosecution of some members of Charlie Company, he spoke publicly to *The New Yorker* magazine about the incorrect command decisions that had led to the civilian deaths. He told the magazine that the men on the ground had been put into life-threatening situations by their higher-ups. They hadn't chosen that particular battle, yet they had been burdened with the full weight of responsibility for any incident that went sideways. The government and the press seemed to him to be giving a free pass to the decision makers and demonizing the men on the ground risking their lives.

"I knew the leadership there. I knew the people there. I knew the ethos there. . . . what was done to them . . . was a persecution of guys who were simply out there trying to defeat the enemy and given orders by their higher-ups to do so," he told me. "It left a terrible taste in my mouth. And the reason I did the interview with the reporter was to try to humanize a few of the guys who were being so mischaracterized in the article, and I just remember thinking 'Okay, so this is how we treat those that go over there to do an impossible job in really dangerous places.'"

That sense of urgency never left him, and when he joined Fox News Channel's *Fox & Friends* morning show in 2014, he saw criminal cases against the military veterans begin to pile up. The press largely ignored the cases. When journalists did pay attention to the growing number of criminal cases involving combat-related incidents against lower-ranking officers and GI Joes, they failed to question the military justice apparatus or strategies by Washington, DC, bureaucrats that had led to the incidents. So Hegseth invented his own beat, drawing attention to the number of veterans who were unfairly being prosecuted and trapped in the military legal system—on every platform he could leverage.

"I'm with the war fighter every time. War is messy and war is difficult, but there are those who go fight it on our behalf. Considering the enemy that we're up against, who ignores all semblance of rules of war, I'm going to side with the guys who went over there and did the job and oftentimes are mischaracterized or impugned for the way in which they fought it," he told me in an interview for this book.

In President Donald Trump, he found a commander in chief who was willing to give those cases a second look, one who unfailingly tuned in to Hegseth's show. Hegseth was amazed that a sitting US president would take on an issue that had zero political upside and would only create more negative press for his embattled administration. The constituency was not one that could deliver a meaningful number of votes or generate positive press to boost the president's approval ratings.

"There are just so many politicians who would say, 'Okay, why would I open that mess up when I don't have to? Just leave it be. Let them languish in prison. Not my problem,'" Hegseth told me. Like Trump, Hegseth did not worry much about political blowback. He was still that high school kid from Minnesota applying to Princeton. He didn't pay attention to the odds, the doubters, or the friends who thought that taking such a stand would kill his career. He was going to take his shot.

By the time we met him in 2019, he was using every platform he had to argue for pardons for Chief Petty Officer Eddie Gallagher, Major Mathew Golsteyn, and First Lieutenant Clint Lorance. "Most people who bring the criticism over advocating for guys like Raven 23 have no idea what it's like to pull the trigger in anger, in combat, with their life on the line, trying to protect people and get out and get their brothers out safely," he said. "It was personal, based on my own experience but also in the macroenvironment of these wars, which are so misunderstood, saying 'I don't want anybody that I can help sitting in jail for difficult decisions they made.'"

Lorance's case had struck close to home. In 2012, Lorance, a first lieutenant in the infantry with the 4th Brigade Combat Team of the 82nd Airborne, had been convicted by court-martial of two counts of unpremeditated murder for ordering his men to open fire on three Afghanis on a motorcycle. He had suspected that the men were Taliban scouts.

"That's a team leader that could have been me," Hegseth said. "I went out on many missions as a platoon leader and had to make the call on whether to pull the trigger or not. Was it an enemy truck? Was it not? Was it a bad guy? And sometimes you made the right decisions. And sometimes we didn't, but . . . I'm with the guys who were willing to do it, and I'm not going to second-guess them and leave them behind."

The same thinking extended to the Raven 23 case, although the fact that they had been military contractors would lend complexity to the story he needed to tell. Private contractors had been a critical component of the war strategy, and their involvement had been conceived by the Department of Defense and supported by both the Bush and Obama administrations, Hegseth thought.

He knew that when Obama had visited Iraq, he had requested Blackwater protection, and when Biden had found himself and others stranded on a mountain during a snowstorm, their first call for help had been to Blackwater. Hegseth had worked with contractors in Iraq, and to him, they were patriots who had stepped up to serve their country, knowing that they would never get the accolades or welcome home that conventional troops enjoyed. "They were often left to do the jobs that no one else wanted to do or no one else wanted to admit was being done or no rules of engagement would allow conventional troops to do because we had special operators doing so many other things," he said.

Hegseth was in an ideal position to bring a soldier's perspective to the Raven 23 case and others, both as a journalist and as a veteran. He arrived in Iraq in 2005 and was stationed in Samarra in 2006. He returned to Iraq twice as a journalist, in 2007 and 2008. He was a senior counterinsurgency instructor in Afghanistan in 2011–2012, sending troops from his "finishing school" to their battle spaces, knowing that "the things we were teaching... wasn't reflected in what reality was." Often, troops were "playing into the hands or bowing to the decisions of certain elements who don't have our interests in mind."

He knew, even then, that the institutions he was helping build up were never going to last beyond the US occupation. "In Iraq and Afghanistan, they briefed really nicely, but they did not reflect the reality on the ground," he said. "By the time you fast-forward to these cases, I'm realizing these guys in every case did the best they could in impossible circumstances with leaders who had no idea what they were doing, as if we're going to unleash democracy across Iraq and Afghanistan." The soldiers, he reflected, had been "cast off as fodder for a failed experiment."

He vowed to leverage the Fox News platform and President Trump's attention as long as he had both to try to free every worthy war fighter he encountered because there was "so little knowledge about what actually went down there."

During their initial conversations, Hegseth told Dave Harrison to contact California Congressman Duncan Hunter, who headed the Justice for Warriors Caucus. A few months after we started exchanging information, Justice for Warriors celebrated big wins with the presidential pardons of Golsteyn and Lorance. Lorance had been serving a twenty-year sentence in Fort Leavenworth for actions he had taken in combat in Afghanistan and had been court-martialed in 2012. Conservatives had rallied around him and presented a petition to President Obama demanding a pardon. Obama had demurred, but President Trump, who had followed the case on Fox News, pardoned him on November 15, 2019.

When Harrison contacted Hunter, Justice for Warriors was deeply involved in helping change the Uniform Code of Military

Justice to protect veterans from "predatory prosecution" and providing legal help to soldiers prosecuted for battlefield incidents. Its charter did not extend to helping military contractors.

The caucus members met with Harrison and Williams & Connolly's Simon Latcovich for a briefing about the Raven 23 case. The lawyers asked the caucus to support a formal pardon request, as it had for Lorance. "They were all very enthusiastic about supporting our efforts," Harrison recalled later. The group of congressional veterans—Louie Gohmert, Paul Gosar, Ralph Norman, Bill Flores, Brian Babin, Michael Burgess, Daniel Webster, Steve King, and Ted Yoho—voted to amend their charter and then began assembling an airtight case to persuade the president of the United States to relitigate the most notorious incident of the Iraq War.

CHAPTER EIGHTEEN

NEVER READ THE COMMENTS

Let all you do be done in love.

—1 CORINTHIANS 16:14

PRODUCTION OF THE PODCAST ground to a halt for two months after the sentencing; our editor, Kyle, had returned to college, and we could not find production services we could afford. On November 6, 2019, as I was preparing to attend the Lone Star Film Festival in Fort Worth for the screening of my documentary *Netflix vs. the World*, Mike shot me an email with the solution to our problem. "Please meet our guardian angel and our close family friend—Mitchell Weinbaum," he wrote. "Mitchell just happens to be a director that also graduated from the Connecticut School of Broadcasting! Praise God!"

Mike pitched the Raven 23 story to twenty-four-year-old Mitchell, a former Walden Media intern who was also his best friend's nephew. Sitting at his aunt's kitchen table down the street from Mike's house in Lexington, Mike took Mitchell through a presentation about the case on his laptop and handed him a sheaf of printed-out articles and summaries.

He explained what we were trying to accomplish: "We really need somebody that can take this and run with it in a creative way."

They listened to a few examples of how the podcast should sound, documentary-style investigative shows such as *Up and Vanished*.

The fact that Mike was so passionate about it meant something to Mitchell, who later confessed to having found the project a little crazy. "I've only ever seen him get really passionate and enthusiastic about stuff that at the end of the day kind of matters," he said. "I did my own kind of research on it . . . and I started to realize what was the bigger picture here. And I felt like the best way to get involved was to just help."

The weekend I was at the film festival, I made arrangements to finally meet Tommy Vargas, the Raven 23 follow vehicle commander, in person. He came to my hotel the evening before my film screened, and when he arrived, he pulled out a thumb drive. He told me a story about how twelve years earlier, an army investigator named Tony Guerrero had given him the thumb drive immediately after the Nisour Square shootings. In fact, Guerrero had told him as he pressed the thumb drive into Vargas's hand in the Green Zone, "Whatever you do, don't open it in country. When you get home, take a look at it. But I want you to hold on to it because I think they're trying to fuck your guys."

Vargas had taken the storage device home, uploaded the files to his home computer, and forgotten about them after the case was dismissed in 2009. He did not like thinking about Nisour Square, so it had taken talking to me for the podcast for the memory to resurface. "It took me a year to find it because I remember when I saved it, I saved it under a different name." he said. "I finally found it after half a bottle of Tullamore D.E.W. I went through my hard drive and found it under 'Sports.'" Guerrero had died in a diving accident a few years earlier, so Tommy had never had a chance to ask what had inspired him to hand over the thumb drive.

I wanted to record the moment when Vargas opened the files for the first time, so I called Mitchell and asked him what to do. Using my phone, I recorded his impressions of the videos and stills that Guerrero had preserved—of army investigators walking on the roof of the bus shelter in Nisour Square and finding AK-47 shell casings.

We immediately called Toby Romero at Williams & Connolly to explain what Tommy had found, and Tommy dropped a copy into the mail the next morning. There were several videos on the thumb drive, and at least one had not been turned over to the defense. The videos provided even more evidence that the Nisour Square incident had been a gun battle and that every investigating agency had known it.

The recording I made of Tommy and me looking at the footage became my favorite episode. Mitchell, however, found the audio "creepy" because Tommy's phone periodically vibrated on the table while we were talking about the videos. "I felt like I was listening to something that I shouldn't be, and so every time it would get interrupted by the vibration, I'd almost jump in my seat a little bit as I was editing it."

My film won Best Documentary at the Lone Star Film Festival that weekend, so there was a lot to celebrate.

By Christmas, we had six episodes up on the website, including an interview with Clint Lorance, who was now actively lobbying for the Raven 23 pardons. The episodes definitely got traction, even though the Nisour Square incident was then thirteen years old and the trial had happened six years earlier. We had plenty of listeners who complimented our storytelling, saying they had learned a lot about the incident. Then we had the haters. My favorite comment from the die-hard anti-contractor bunch was that we were "whitewashing a massacre." Somebody started an online petition to stop Fox from promoting the podcast. The rest of the media ignored us, which I had expected.

"I got some news that a very well known vlogger has come across the podcast—or at least the story—and is accusing Fox News (and us) of 'whitewashing' the 'massacre,'" I wrote in a December 2,

2019, email to Mike and Mitchell. "Yeah, I stewed about it for a while and then realized that we just need to put out the facts—call them out on their laziness—and let it go."

Mitchell had the brilliant idea of making an audio salad of the comments, read by actors, and addressing them at the top of the next episode. We tried to respond thoughtfully to the most common complaints, but it was frustrating that most people simply saw the name "Blackwater" and flipped out without actually listening.

Mitchell shared my frustration. "It feels like we're putting in all this work and nobody was even actually listening to what we were saying and what the message was."

But the podcast began to wake up decision makers. Jessica Slatten told me the next day that a Tennessee state representative "who had ignored the Slattens for years finally reached out to them to ask what he can do to help," I wrote to Mike and Mitchell. "Darrell Slatten was so pissed that he won't reply, but I'm going to." It seemed as though an army was slowly materializing, I told them.

"It does seem like things are moving in the right direction, and the podcast is definitely helping to change the momentum," Jessica told us. We were not the only voice on the airwaves—Lauren McLaughlin and Derrick Miller, the communications director and executive director at Justice for Warriors, put the full weight of their operation behind the Raven 23 men, helping us get an interview with Clint Lorance on December 10, 2019.

When we had appeared on his show, Pete Hegseth had called the men "The Biden Four." The name was an ideal way for them to stand out in an election year among thousands of other pardon seekers. I did not love the idea as much as most everyone else working on the plan did because it felt like pandering, but there was no doubt that Joe Biden had played a huge part in the wrongful convictions of Dustin, Evan, Paul, and Nick.

"I spoke to [voice-over actor] Ash [Smith] who is all in to get this over the finish line," Mike wrote to Mitchell and me two days before Christmas. "He happens to love 'The Biden Four' as well. He is pretty plugged in and he thinks as the show gets to Biden's involvement that we will have more press than we know what to do with."

The "Biden Four" proponents wanted to take advantage of the election news cycle, starting January 2 and running until election day. "February 3 is the Iowa caucus. From January 2 to that day, it will be in the news 24/7," Mike said excitedly. "Biden is the front runner. Impeachment is the top subject. Everybody wants to bring Biden down. And he is weakest on his corruption. So I have been furiously assembling that." He had learned from exit polling "that you can't buy attention until the Monday after New Year's. So we will be ready to move then."

As I worked to complete interviews and scripts, Mike dived into the political intrigue swirling around the cases. Every few days he came up with a new way to ratchet up the pressure on Lamberth and the prosecutors, ideas that were usually vetoed by me or the lawyers. One of them—the idea of buying Raven 23 billboards beside the federal courthouse in San Antonio, where Lamberth occasionally sat at trial—kept coming up even after Dave Harrison swatted it down.

But even I urged the lawyers to consider it after Lamberth denied Nick's motion for a new trial or an acquittal based on the rediscovered DART mission report. Lamberth responded to a litany of defense complaints with one word: "harmless." He applied it to the prosecution's withholding of the DART report from the defense; to the lies told by Murphy and Ridgeway that prosecutors had used to establish Nick's intent to commit murder; to his own prejudicial conduct toward the defense lawyers in front of the jury.

On Sunday, March 15, 2020, the world stopped when covid hit. We had no idea how long the lockdown would last.

And there was another factor that made me nervous: Two weeks before the lockdown, Joe Biden and Bernie Sanders had been duking it out after Super Tuesday for the Democratic Party's presidential nomination. Biden led with 10 states and 726 delegates to Sanders's 4 states and 505 delegates. Sanders, then seventy-eight, had had a heart attack in late 2019 and was deemed to be too liberal for the Democrats' only agenda item: Beat Trump. So it would be Biden as the nominee—a bad sign that put a ticking clock on our pardon efforts. No way would Biden pardon the Raven 23 men he had condemned just a decade earlier in front of the international media. So it would have to happen before January 21, 2021. That gave us nine months.

During my time at Reuters, I had learned a great deal about how adverse events affect entertainment companies, especially from writing my book about Netflix, which had posted enormous growth in the wake of the September 11 attacks and the 2008 banking meltdown because consumers wanted to stay home and "cocoon." Now they would be forced to do so. On March 16, 2020, I wrote to Mike and Mitchell, "I hate to say this—but we have a great opportunity to re-launch our podcast at a time when people are going to be looking for ways to entertain themselves."

We produced some of our best work in the first few months of the covid pandemic, taking deep dives into the case files and putting the government's behavior into context with episodes about the Code of Hammurabi, the Bush administration's push to outsource DOD functions to contractors, and the politics behind the "surge."

It was getting harder to speak with Dustin, Evan, Nick, and Paul by telephone because they were locked in their cells almost 24/7, except for a shower once a week. I could contact all of them but Dustin via email.

Somewhere along the line, Paul got access to a contraband phone, which I learned when I got a video call from him one day over Facebook. Nick had access to a tablet and could read the news but not communicate. Up to that point, none of them had heard an entire episode of the podcast—just snippets that we had played them over the phone during our fifteen-minute calls. I had been sending them the scripts before we recorded them for the sake of accuracy and to ensure that we were not endangering their appeal or their families.

Before lockdown, they had had no access to the internet, so they'd had no idea what was being said about them or their case other than brief mentions on cable news. Ironically, lockdown gave them a window to the wider world.

We soon realized a frightening dimension of covid: The men were captives inside an ideal incubator for the illness. As they described the conditions inside the prisons, we became terrified for their health and safety. The Bureau of Prisons had established a program for early "compassionate" release for inmates who were ill or nearing the end of their prison terms. When Dustin let me know how dangerous the conditions were getting at USP Atlanta, Lauren and I got together to apply for his release through that program. I had all his medical records among the case files, so we wrote a letter and she sent it to the Attorney General's Office under Representative Louie Gohmert's letterhead.

I went back and forth with the BOP in phone calls and emails to make sure we had all the documents it needed to make a decision as soon as possible. Dustin was suffering from some preexisting conditions that made him especially susceptible to covid, and the conditions at the prison were not on his side.

"You replied to my questions with an unresponsive form letter," I emailed the BOP in Washington, DC, on April 2, 2020, requesting an interview with BOP Director Michael Carvajal. "Therefore, I'm going to ask again: First, there are still three men per two-man cell in Atlanta. That is not only illegal, it is dangerous during a pandemic. How do you respond to this, and what do you plan to do to mitigate the situation?"

Later that day, a representative from the prison actually phoned me to discuss Dustin's situation, but I was never able to contact her again, and Dustin was not released. The BOP provided a handy map showing the number of active cases at each prison so I could helplessly watch the numbers climbing. USP Atlanta remained one of the worst hotbeds of covid—but all we could do was redouble our efforts. Every holiday, we hoped for news from the White House, but the cavalcade of misfortunes that overtook the world during those months started to dent our confidence.

Mike and Mitchell and I started to have long Zoom calls that had a lot more to do with our terror of getting the virus and worry over what was happening with the pardons than writing and recording the remaining scripts. Joe Bob had been declared an essential worker and was driving oil field trucks in the Permian Basin, returning to St. Louis only once every few weeks. I was alone a lot of the time, but it did not seem to help my writing—or thinking—at all.

The pardon team and Justice for Warriors were reaching ever higher into the Trump administration to line up support from the people around the president. Mike had a connection with Vice President Mike Pence through Pence's daughter Charlotte, who had interned at Walden. In September, he reached out to Pence, suggesting that a pardon would be a great way to show loyalty to the troops ahead of the election.

Amazingly, the world's lassitude had not affected the Justice for Warriors caucus. Although Lauren and Derrick had been working with us behind the scenes for months, the caucus had not officially endorsed the pardon.

On May 12, 2020, Representative Louie Gohmert took a few minutes at the end of a Fox News appearance about covid to announce that the caucus had sent a letter to the White House, asking President Trump to pardon the "Biden Four." "Following a firefight that resulted in the tragic death of a number of Iraqis, the media portrayed Nick, Paul, Evan, and Dustin as killers. The corruption and prosecutorial misconduct uncovered over the last twelve years, paints a very different picture," the letter said. "We write to respectfully request a Presidential Pardon for these fine men who served when our country needed them the most."

It was enormously satisfying to see the case laid out, supported by evidence, and endorsed by members of Congress. Less satisfying was the reaction to the pardon request by the national news media—except for the conservative outlets. "They should have medals on their chests, not be behind metal bars," Hegseth told Gohmert. "The Biden Four—we are going to carry this story."

CHAPTER NINETEEN

--- ★★★ ---

HOW TO GET DONALD TRUMP'S ATTENTION

I have fought the good fight, I have finished the race, I have kept the faith.

—2 TIMOTHY 4:7

PETE HEGSETH GOT TO work on the Raven 23 case very soon after making contact with Dave Harrison in May 2019. He had written about the cases of Gallagher, Golsteyn, and Lorance on the Fox News website, and his advocacy had led to a flood of inquiries from people who had similar cases or were already incarcerated in Leavenworth. He spent a lot of time evaluating the cases, knowing that only a limited number could penetrate the public consciousness and win Trump's attention and a possible pardon.

Hegseth knew that Trump would accrue no political capital from pardoning military convicts and that plenty of people with a lot more political capital were clamoring for pardons. He knew that he would need to be intimately familiar with the facts of each case to make the president comfortable that freeing convicted soldiers accused of grisly crimes would not come back to haunt him.

Hegseth did not know the odds at the time, but in the end Trump would grant only 2 percent of the pardon requests he received during his first term, fewer than all but two other presidents, according to the Pew Research Center.

After researching the Raven 23 case, he was convinced that it was "exactly the type of case that should be elevated and publicized." He talked through the case with Dave Harrison and the author Don Brown, a former Navy JAG officer and best-selling military author who was also drawn to the case.

Hegseth was not involved in Trump's first presidential campaign in any formal way, but he openly supported the Republican contender during the 2016 election. He was vetted for secretary of veterans affairs and interviewed for the role several times in 2016. Later, he interviewed to be White House press secretary in 2017 and 2018 after the departure of Sean Spicer. He ended up taking neither position but remained an ad hoc adviser to Trump on veterans and military issues. Although the media portrayed Hegseth as having ready access to Trump, he actually spoke with the president "when he wants to talk to me," Hegseth later told me. "It depended on the issues," he said. "If there was something really going on, like these cases, it was frequent. If there wasn't, then it would be when my phone rang."

To keep the pardons top of Trump's mind, Hegseth had several ways to communicate with him. "One is directly," he said. "And then two was over the airwaves, and we were careful about it, but because I was a vet and because these are issues I'm passionate about—rules of war, supporting war fighters, all of that—it was a no-brainer to highlight these cases that were up for consideration and highlight them on *Fox & Friends*. So this case and the other three I mentioned, that would lead to attention in the media, which regularly would get his attention and then could lead to personal conversations about the cases."

Trump wanted to know what the soldiers had faced on the ground—and he relied on Hegseth to give him the information. "We would talk through some of the ins and outs of 'What was the situation that Clint Lorance was facing as a platoon leader there?' These are rough guys, and we would talk through the case a little bit, and he'd ultimately say, 'Yeah, but they don't deserve to be treated this way.'"

Trump shared his frustration with Pentagon leaders, who discouraged him from pardoning rank-and-file soldiers accused of war crimes. "He would talk about the institutional types inside the Pentagon that would be in his ear saying 'Sir, you can't pardon this person because it would undermine the chain of command.' And he would do so in a way that was sort of mocking," Hegseth said.

Trump would ask, "Hey, Pete, what's the right thing to do for these guys that we sent to fight these wars?"

"I got to see a real personal patriotic side of the president, who understood that he would be unpopular at some level but also understood it was just the right thing to do," Hegseth said. "In the case of Raven 23, they were political giveaways of years ago when [the government] threw Americans in jail for doing their job. He just had this sense that that wasn't right."

The wrinkle in the Raven 23 case was one that had dogged the men since the first trial: their association with Blackwater and Erik Prince. Prince was a high-profile Trump supporter, and his sister, Betsy DeVos, was Trump's secretary of education. Pardoning the embattled Prince's former employees would come off more like political cronyism than patriotism. But Hegseth never spoke to Prince about the pardons, nor did he have any sense that the Blackwater founder was actively involved in freeing his men.

With the pardons of Lorance, Golsteyn, and Gallagher achieved by Veterans Day, Hegseth turned to the Raven 23 case in late 2019.

The new year, 2020, began with the controversial drone killing of Iran's second in command, General Qasem Soleimani, and Trump's Senate impeachment trial in January and went downhill from there. Washington, DC, seemed to reel from one crisis to the next.

In March, covid shut down the US economy, and the unemployment rate quickly soared to its highest level since the Great Depression. Congress passed a record-breaking $2.2 trillion stimulus package and embarked on a race for a vaccine. In mid-April, the price of oil on the US market fell below $0 as sellers had to pay to get rid of it, in its worst trading day in history.

In May, mass protests rocked more than two thousand US cities after police in Minneapolis killed George Floyd, a black man arrested for allegedly passing a counterfeit $20 bill at a convenience store. The protests rolled on all year, sparked by the police shootings of Jacob Blake in Kenosha, Wisconsin, and Breonna Taylor in her Louisville, Kentucky, home.

Over the summer, wildfires in America's western states burned 8.2 million acres, a drought gripped the Southwest, and numerous tropical storms hit the coastlines. Trump negotiated the withdrawal of US troops from Afghanistan as violence in that country rose. Supreme Court Justice Ruth Bader Ginsburg died and, after a battle with Senate Democrats, was replaced by Amy Coney Barrett.

Trump brokered a deal to have the United Arab Emirates, Bahrain, and Morocco recognize Israel in return for the Jewish state's pledge not to annex territory in the West Bank. Diplomatic relations with China soured over scrutiny of its handling of the covid pandemic. Turkey retaliated against Syria for alleged Russian-sponsored attacks on Turkish soldiers.

The constant crises engulfing the country and the Trump administration made it hard for Hegseth to gauge the progress of the pardon requests, so his goal became "just to keep it alive." He took to mentioning the Raven 23 case every time he spoke with Trump.

"I was very careful not to call and bother and badger but when given the opportunity," he said. "He was always right there, but with so much going on and frankly not a lot of interest amongst his staff or the White House, of all the things they could be encountering or dealing with, they probably looked at that and [said], 'Why would you? What's the upside?'"

For Trump, the pardons were "a very personal thing for him, I felt like." He agreed with Hegseth that the case looked like a political persecution of Americans who were doing the job they had been trained and sent to do. It did not hurt Raven 23's cause that the people who had put them there had been Biden, his opponent in the upcoming 2020 election, and Hillary Clinton, whom he had bested in the 2016 election.

As they went over the case, Hegseth had the sense that Trump wanted to make sure that the pardons had no hidden pitfalls that could weigh on his reelection chances. "It became more clear that this is something he wanted to do. It was just a matter of getting to the place where it was time to do it," he said. As the months passed with no commitment, the case began to weigh on him, but he kept on pushing Trump every opportunity he had.

Trump began to preempt talk of Raven 23 before Hegseth mentioned the case. "Yeah, we're still working on it," he would say. "Everybody felt the crucible of the time frame," Hegseth told me.

The November 3, 2020, election put a hard end date on the pardon process. Trump lost and contested the election result that had put Biden into office.

In late November, Trump personally called Hegseth. "I'm going to do it for these guys," the president told him. Hegseth turned to his wife as he hung up the phone. "I think it's going to happen," he told her.

He felt an enormous sense of relief. He had been hanging on tightly to any strand of hope throughout those tumultuous months. His next call was to Dave Harrison. The pardons are happening, he said. You can tell the families with the condition that no one knows when they will happen. And they can't tell anyone else.

Harrison hung up with Hegseth and dialed Christin Slough. When she heard what he had to say, she burst into tears.

CHAPTER TWENTY

★★★

BRAVO ZULU

Little children, let us not love in word or talk but in deed and truth.

—1 JOHN 3:18

IN MID-DECEMBER, DAVE HARRISON called Christin to say that something was afoot. He thought it would take a week for the pardons to take place. She and Lily informed Paul when he called for a video chat on his contraband iPhone that evening. "I got to tell him and Lily at the same time," Christin said later. "It was just our own little private moment, just with the three of us on video."

Next, Christin called Kelli Heard and then Stacey Heard with the news. Williams & Connolly was next and then Evan's attorney, Bill Coffield. In the fifteen months since the resentencing, Christin and Paul had agreed to divorce, based on the long odds of getting a pardon. She had filed the papers shortly before covid shut down the courts in Texas and had never really followed up. She met a man and moved with Lily to Florida to be with him, but the relationship soon cratered. A few days before she heard the news about the pardons, she had decided to move back home to Texas as soon as Lily's school year ended. "We're thinking it's going down . . . on the eighteenth [of December], Friday, after hours," she said. "Well, the eighteenth was Lily's last day of school. So I literally go to her little beach Christmas program, load her up, take her to the airport, drop her on the airplane to send her back to my mom."

Christin and her dad accompanied the movers, driving back to Texas through the night, thinking that the pardon could come at any minute. Paul's sister Robin and her husband, Steve, settled in to wait at a hotel near the federal prison near Bastrop, Texas, to which Paul had been moved after his resentencing.

Halfway across the country, Stacey and Lawana Heard and Lawana's son, Brandon, sat in a cabin outside Atlanta, waiting for word that Dustin had been released from USP Atlanta.

At around 5:00 p.m. Eastern Standard Time on December 22, 2020, Christin Slough's phone rang. It was Harrison. "It's happening right now," he told her. Before she could react, her phone beeped with an incoming call. It was the last call she would ever get from the Bastrop prison. It was Paul, telling her to come bring him home.

Stacey Heard had returned to Olney to go back to work, but Lawana and Brandon raced from the cabin to USP Atlanta to pick up Dustin.

In Sparta, Tennessee, and Washington, DC, Nick Slatten's parents and his attorney, Amy Mason Saharia, got the word and started driving to Rappahannock Regional Jail in Stafford, Virginia, to pick up Nick. Harrison alerted Bill Coffield, who arranged to pick Evan up in Schuylkill, Pennsylvania.

Trump had issued four full pardons, reversing the wrongful convictions in the 2007 Nisour Square incident. In his pardon message, he cited broad public support for the pardons and the men's long record of service to their country. Finally, the government admitted—more than ten years after the fact—that the lead Iraqi investigator, who had told US prosecutors that there had been no insurgents in the square that day, "may have had ties to the insurgency himself." Of course, that fact never made it into the news coverage of the pardons.

Paul Slough was forty-one years old and many miles and years from the twenty-eight-year-old turret gunner who had ridden into Nisour Square on September 16, 2007. That evening, he had given up on hearing about the pardon as he waited in line for the prison phone to call Christin and Lily and say good night. He heard a woman's voice in the unit—and heard his name called. Another inmate came over to him. "Hey, you're being called into the cops' office," he said. He walked into the office, and the officer told him to close the door.

"Well, ma'am, what's this all about before I close the door?" he asked.

She handed him a document. It read, "Executive Grant of Clemency, Donald J. Trump, President of the United States of America."

He stared at it. "Can I hug you?" he asked.

"No! I need a phone number," she said.

"Can I give you a high five?" he tried again.

"No, I need a phone number! You can't be here. You have ten minutes to leave the premises. So I need a phone number right now!" she said.

He went to retrieve his possessions from his cell. On the way back to the offices with bags in hand, he ran into his boss at the commissary. "Hey, where are you going?" the man asked.

"Sodhi, it's real. It happened," he said, scarcely able to believe it.

"No shit?" the man asked incredulously. He started crying and hugged Paul. "I'm so proud for you guys," he said.

News of the pardon traveled like lightning through the prison. Paul slid the document under the door while he waited for the corrections officer to finish his paperwork. "The guys saw it, and there was an eruption on the tier," he told me later. "People were banging on doors. Oh, my God. It was pretty cool."

When he finally stepped out of the gates of Bastrop a free man, his first thought was "This could be a setup. They're going to shoot me from the tower." But then his sister Robin swooped in and grabbed him, hugging him so hard he could barely breathe. She took a photo of him with her phone and sent it to Christin with the caption "Package secured." They drove into the night toward Sanger, where Christin and Lily waited with what Paul often described as his coming-home meal: steak and yellow cake with chocolate icing. That night, he lay in bed watching his wife and daughter sleep.

Dustin got the call as he stood in his cell in a pair of shorts and shoes while he was getting dressed and eating a burrito after his weekly shower.

"Well, it's your lucky day," the corrections officer told him.

"Oh, yeah?" he said.

"They said you're getting immediate release," the CO said.

"Under what circumstances?" Dustin asked, curbing his elation.

"I don't know," the CO admitted.

"I want to make sure that all my guys got out," Dustin said.

"I can't show you that," the CO said.

"I don't care about seeing, you can just tell me if three other names are in there," Dustin said.

He listed the names: Evan Liberty, Paul Slough, and Nick Slatten.

They're there, the CO said.

The first I heard of the pardons was at 5:31 p.m. on December 22, when Dustin's dad, Stacey, called to tell me the news. I could barely understand what he was saying because he was so excited.

Next, I got a text from Christin Slough in all caps: IT'S HAPPENING RIGHT THIS SECOND. THEY'RE GETTING PICKED UP RIGHT NOW.

Dustin got a hero's welcome when he arrived back in Olney on December 23. The whole town came out, mustering every fire engine and police vehicle it had. People lined Main Street and cheered as Lawana and Brandon drove the surprised Dustin into town. They had stopped in Sparta to say hello to Nick and pressed on to Maryville to pull his children out of bed, to their surprise and delight.

When I saw Dustin on that bright, cold day on Main Street in Olney, he looked a bit lost amid all the joy—pulled in a thousand directions. He was thirty-nine years old with a fifteen-year-old daughter and nine-year-old son. He had been just twenty-six with two tours of duty in Iraq and Afghanistan under his belt when the Nisour Square incident had happened.

When I called to congratulate Brian Liberty on December 22, he couldn't believe that his son, Evan, was finally free. He said he wouldn't accept it until Evan was standing in front of him. It would take a couple of months for Evan to return home to New Hampshire because he had caught covid in prison. He had turned eighteen years old in Marine Corps boot camp in 2000. He was thirty-eight years old when he walked out of the Schuylkill Federal Correctional Institution.

Evan had been out of the loop on the pardon efforts because Schuylkill had been shut down for the entire month of December to stop the spread of covid. He had not communicated on the phone or by email with his family in weeks. He knew that they were in crunch time: If the pardons did not happen by January 20, "That was it." He coped as he always had: by sticking with his routine. He had been moved after his cellmate had tested positive for covid and he had tested negative. The corrections officers had given him a job as an orderly, spraying down the showers, and left his cell door open all day. "I was free to be out. I pretend I'm cleaning. I do my workouts. . . . I was out all day long, but it kind of turned into me running around doing favors for all the guys locked in because they want to pass shit back and forth . . . running around and doing that, like checking on people, trying to be a nice person because . . . you know how bad it sucks to be stuck in the cell and alone."

He was joking with the guards about an inmate who had received a compassionate release but could not leave because he'd had no address to give the prison officials. "I [said], 'I've got twenty addresses. I'm ready to go right now," he said. He spent the rest of the day trading little favors such as getting other inmates hot water or passing notes between them for little bags of sunflower seeds that came in the inmates' Christmas bags that had been handed out that day.

Later, as he lay in his bunk, the corrections officer he had been joking with entered his cell. "Liberty, sit down," he said.

"I am sitting down," Evan told him. "I'm lying down."

The man was excited. "Are you ready for this?"

"Yeah, what?" Evan said.

"Full presidential fucking pardon," he said. "Pack your shit."

"No way!" Evan said. "He did it?"

"He fucking did it," the guard said.

Evan took only a list of Spanish vocabulary words he had made, a photo of his grandfather, and a book he had been reading. He forgot the sunflower seeds. In the office, he asked to see the stack of pardons and was relieved to see pardons for Nick, Dustin, and Paul along with his own. As the guards walked him out of the unit, news of the pardons came over the prison televisions and the inmates started yelling "He did it!" "I told you he would fucking do it, Liberty!"

Evan said, "A couple of [the guards] probably weren't supposed to do it, but they shook my hand and they're like 'Man, good luck. I'm glad this happened for you.'"

He called his astonished brother, Aaron, and told him to get his room ready. "I'm going to show up later," he said. One of the corrections officers dropped him off at a hotel in Harrisburg. Coffield drove up the next day and delivered him to his brother.

I heard from Nick, Paul, and Dustin that night as they drove home through the darkness—all of them astounded at their second chance at life. It was pretty striking to me that the first thing that Evan, Paul, and Dustin had wanted to know when they heard about their pardons was whether Nick Slatten would be going home as well.

Nick was thirty-seven years old and a free man at last after enduring three trials and drawing a life sentence for a shot that he had not taken. He learned that he had been pardoned when another prisoner slid a note under his cell door that read, "Four contractors pardoned by the president."

It was about 7:00 p.m., and Nick was the last to be released. As the news spread around the prison, inmates began kicking the cell doors and yelling. The police officer on duty almost called for backup.

Nick led a Bible study class that evening, focusing on the Gospel of Matthew, chapter 7, about fathers: "If your son asks for bread, would you give him a stone?"

"It was just really fitting that that was the last Bible study that we did because God will give us all good things when we ask him," Nick told me later. "Thousands of people had been praying that we would get this pardon, and God answered us. So it was definitely amazing. And all those guys that came to that Bible study for weeks and months, sometimes for a year in that little unit that I was in, it was a testimony to them that that prayer works and that God is listening to us. It was really good."

Nick took only his Bible, personal photos, and legal work from his cell and left the rest. He waited on the sidewalk in a button-down shirt and sweatpants that the prison had issued him. "I was so happy to be breathing free air," he said when I asked whether he had gotten cold standing there.

Saharia arrived just a few minutes after he was released. She started crying when she saw him. They drove through a fast-food joint and picked up a hamburger, then waited at a hotel for a friend to come drive him to Sparta. His parents had taken off as soon as they'd heard the news. They caught up with each other at a gas station later that evening.

"I felt blessed, but I didn't feel any different," he told me a couple months later. "I don't know if that's a normal response. The only thing that was different to me was when we got out and went into the gas station, everybody had masks on because of covid, and I think, 'This place is getting robbed.' No, it was just covid."

His first night at home, he stood outside his little house in the fold of a hill on his family's land. "I'm just standing in the freezing cold. I'm just staring at the stars that I had not seen in six years, thinking of the things that you take for granted, the birds and the trees. It's just amazing, the things that I was missing out on: the smells and the sights, the sounds. Tennessee is lovely. God has really blessed me for sure."

Because Nick's conviction was still on appeal, the Williams & Connolly team got the DC Circuit Court to vacate it. They had been disappointed not to be able to celebrate the pardon with Nick. Instead, they had a celebration at Butswinkas's home about a month later, sitting outside on the patio furniture in their winter coats under outdoor heaters.

CHAPTER TWENTY-ONE

★★★

THE WAY FORWARD

And so long as we are still able to dream, we are truly alive.

—ROD NORDLAND

WITHIN A YEAR, Nick Slatten was back in jail, but not as a prisoner. Life had moved quickly from the night he had arrived home. For one thing, Whitney Judd, a high school agriculture teacher from Sparta who had fallen in love with him by letter and then email, phone, and in-person prison visits, was waiting at his modest house when he arrived. Whitney is a solid, strong woman of faith and deep common sense—the type of person who puts everyone in a room at ease.

"Lord willing, I'll just stay here, get married, have a bunch of kids," Nick told me a few weeks after he was pardoned. He and Whitney married, and almost nine months after he was released from Rappahannock Regional Jail, their daughter, Willa Grace, was born.

Nick's days are filled with caring for Willa and keeping body and spirit together by reading his Bible, attending church, and practicing jiujitsu when he is not farming with his dad. "It's a simple life. I just want to live at peace with all men. Hopefully I could spend the rest of my life helping people; that's what I really want to do."

Once a week, Nick goes back to jail—the White County Jail up the road—to work with inmates who have been unjustly incarcerated and seek their release, and to help those who committed crimes transition back into society. His main goal is to start a reentry program for inmates. "A lot of these guys, they're locked up for drug-related offenses and they have burned every bridge they have so they don't have anywhere to go," he said. "When they get out, they just fall right back into the old trap. They need Jesus, they need a place to live, they need employment. So hopefully we can set something like that up."

The years of prison abuse and stress took their toll on Nick's mental and physical health, but he is surprisingly uninterested in lingering in the past. "There comes a point in your life where you kind of set that aside after you fought for so long," he said. "The things that happened to us, it would be real easy to be bitter towards your government or towards the people in charge, but you just gotta love them and forgive them."

He often tells me something that I still struggle with when I think about this case: "Flesh will always let you down. It doesn't matter whoever it is. If you put your hope in people, they will let you down. If you hang out with me long enough, I'll definitely let you down, but God won't. So you just love and forgive and don't dwell on the past. Just focus on the day, focus on God, and then the next day, do the same thing. God is going to take care of you if you seek His face."

* * *

HANNAH HEARD CROSSED THE stage of the Maryville High School football stadium in her black-and-red cap and gown. She thought about college and her future as she returned to her seat, diploma in hand, waiting for her classmates to cross the stage. The day was a blur, not bittersweet exactly, because she had gotten exactly what she wanted most for her graduation. She rose with her classmates and threw her tasseled mortarboard into the air. The people in the bleachers descended on the field. When she saw her father, Dustin, and he caught her up in his arms, a wave of emotion hit her. *I actually get to hug him right now*, she thought. *This isn't just a phone call where I say, "I graduated," and I get to share the moment in person instead of through letters or over the phone.* She buried her head in his neck. "I love you, Daddy."

* * *

EVERY FRIDAY, PAUL SLOUGH sits at the beach with his daughter, Lily, and her classmates and their parents and thinks about the durability of dreams and whether it is possible to recapture innocence and joy. In prison, he dreamed of joining Lily and Christin in the sand and waves because he knew how much they loved the beach.

Now in the cleansing sunshine, surrounded by a diverse community of supporters who know about their journey to freedom, they can start to unpack. "A lot of our previous anxiety and toxic stuff is being worked out for all of us," he said. "It is a continuous journey to work through the layers of stuff that happened during a fourteen-year period and unpack that and come back together as a family. Sometimes it can be messy, and other times completely filled with joy."

Christin and Paul recently visited New York City—part vacation and part thank-you tour. They visited the National September 11 Memorial & Museum and sat with Pete Hegseth in his studio. Together, they filmed a short video thanking Donald Trump for "a second chance at life from a president who saw us as people rather than some number."

Trump posted the video on his Truth Social account. Paul sees similarities in Trump's litigation struggles and what he and his Raven 23 comrades endured. "To see what he is going through now, we feel like the machine is really ramped up," he reflected. "We are not all cookie-cutter people. There are things we disagree about on policy, but at the end of the day we agree this never should have happened. It is an affront to our judicial system. The veil is being torn, and people are able to see behind the system. Not just the Justice Department, it is the panorama of our government system."

He and his brothers, Dustin, Evan, and Nick, are still tight. They speak to one another frequently and have a bond that surpasses distance and their individual experiences. Whereas Nick has journeyed into stillness and peace, Paul struggles to accept that what happened to them was intentional, carried out for political gain and with utmost cynicism. "At one time, there was an acceptance that everybody was operating on their best intentions," he said. "Sitting on the beach and hearing the waves crash over, I don't know that I will ever experience peace like when I was a kid. It's just like you are trying to recapture some innocence that you can't regain."

* * *

EVAN LIBERTY SPENT A year after his release from prison doing security jobs in Washington, DC, as the world recovered from covid. He was not sure what the rest of his life would hold; he was in peak physical condition after recovering from covid but too old to join the Navy SEALs. He spent his first months of freedom revisiting old haunts: the streams in and around Rochester, where he had gone fly-fishing with his grandfather, and the mountain lanes where he and his parents had trained for road races, his family home. At last, it was time to start again. He packed his belongings into two suitcases and boarded a plane in Washington, DC. He connected in Panama and landed in Cali, Colombia. He arrived alone. For the first time in fourteen years, he truly felt free.

* * *

THE FIRST PERSON I called after Stacey Heard told me about the pardons on December 22, 2020, was Micheal Flaherty. The road had been so long that I wanted him to savor every second of the joy that he had helped create. Next, I called Mitchell, who had already received a text message from Mike's wife, Kelly, promising "really big news."

Then I called Joe Bob in the Permian Basin. "We did it," I told him. "They're out."

We were all pretty shocked, and after we exchanged the news, conversation subsided as we took it all in.

Mitchell later told me that he had sat on his bed after talking to me and Mike and thought, *Wow, this is real. This is actually happening right now.* "I never thought that was going to be the outcome," he told me. "It seemed so out of reach at the time."

A few weeks later, I got everyone together on a Zoom call. Evan, Dustin, Paul, and Nick talked about the overwhelming feeling of being free: the technology they now had to learn, the readjustment to having endless freedom and endless choices. Dustin commented that he had been overwhelmed by the toothbrush selection at the local Walmart. They seemed a little fragile, and we all hoped they would prosper.

The news coverage of the pardons was exactly what I had expected and not much worse than the nasty missives I was getting on social media. I tried rebutting the worst of the misinformation by posting highlighted pages from the trial transcript on my social media accounts but gave up after the United Nations decreed the pardons "an affront to justice."

New York Times columnist Michelle Goldberg typified the idiotic reaction in her December 24, 2020, column, titled "Trump's Most Disgusting Pardons." Michelle, who "[tries] to seek out stories that challenge my preconceptions," apparently did not do much research before penning those thoughts. "It was perhaps not surprising that the president acted to free the mercenaries; Trump's enthusiasm for war crimes is well known, and last year he pardoned three men accused or convicted of them," she wrote. "Because of Biden's words in 2010, some conservatives called the perpetrators of the Nisour Square massacre the 'Biden Four,' giving Trump an extra incentive to let them go. Erik Prince, who founded Blackwater, is a close Trump ally and the brother of his education secretary, Betsy DeVos.

"Neither the predictability of these pardons, however, nor our dulled capacity for shock, lessens their grotesqueness."

As a liberal journalist who had entered this story with a very similar attitude, I was not surprised—just tired by and disillusioned with my peers. There is nothing fun about being called names or having your reputation questioned by the people at the highest levels of your profession. Journalists' basic function is to watch and tell the truth in plain terms about what we see, not regurgitate the utterings of the powerful forces in this country that require the most scrutiny. My fellow St. Louisan, the newspaper publisher Joseph Pulitzer, put it bluntly: "A newspaper should have no friends."

That is the job, and if you don't have the heart for it—do something else because the fate of the nation depends on the press doing its job and doing it well. "Our Republic and its press will rise or fall together," Pulitzer also said. "An able, disinterested, public-spirited press, with trained intelligence to know the right and courage to do it, can preserve that public virtue without which popular government is a sham and a mockery. A cynical, mercenary, demagogic press will produce in time a people as base as itself."

What went wrong with the Raven 23 case is that journalists just like me saw what I saw and choked. I don't blame them; it took me almost a year to decide what to do about it. I'm no different in wanting to stay in the good graces of the "cool kids," especially in the cancel culture era. But I learned something else: Reconciliation is possible, and everyday grace is all around us if we choose to focus on it.

I am thankful to have traveled this path with Americans in four small towns that opened to me because of Dustin, Evan, Paul, and Nick and their families. In the 2,079 days between Jessica Simpson stealing that newspaper and their pardon, I witnessed the immense strength and courage of the powerless to demand that those in power redress an injustice. That gives me hope.

* * *

CODA: ON MARCH 20, 2024, I got my final communication from the DOJ regarding my Freedom of Information Act requests filed on August 16, 2019. "To the extent that non-public responsive records exist, without consent, proof of death, or an overriding public interest, disclosure of law enforcement records concerning an individual could reasonably be expected to constitute an unwarranted invasion of personal privacy, . . . this Office is not required to conduct a search for the requested records."

Good night, babe. Love ya.
Semper mecum.

ACKNOWLEDGMENTS

★★★

It has been a long decade—one filled with anguish, persistence, revelation, and, ultimately, grace. There are many people to thank for helping me through one of the most challenging chapters of my life, and certainly the most worthwhile.

To Micheal Flaherty and Mitchell Weinbaum: Thank you for walking down a sometimes tortuous path with unwavering humor and fortitude. You took up my burden when I had no right to ask, and together we created something that echoed across the world. I am forever in your debt.

To Joe Bob: For pushing me out of my comfort zone and for letting Jessica Simpson and me live in your weird, wonderful world.

To the citizens of Olney, Texas: Thank you for enfolding me in your community, even when it seemed I could do nothing for your son, Dustin Heard. To the families and friends of Dustin Heard, Evan Liberty, Paul Slough, and Nick Slatten—your belief in me, even when I faltered, was a quiet and constant strength. And to the men themselves—thank you for your honesty, vulnerability, and trust. Your courage taught me what it means to truly stand by one's convictions.

To Jonathan Friedland, for your sharp eye and clearer mind: Thank you for finding the soft spots in the manuscript and helping me discover its true shape. To Hannah Long and the team at HarperCollins/Broadside, for embracing this project with such heart and commitment. And to Michael O'Connor at Williams & Connolly, for representing it with care and conviction.

To Shawn Ryan, for giving us a forum to discuss the Raven 23 case and the pardons and for sharing clips and photos from your show to help us get the message about this injustice into the world.

To everyone who shared with me how this tragic incident seared their souls—your words and witness carried me and shaped this book.

And finally to my family—especially my parents, John Sopuch and Margaret Romero: Thank you for never once arguing or contradicting me when I insisted, year after year, that I would help free four men the world had written off as war criminals. Your faith gave me the strength to hold my ground.

This book is for all of you.

From the Men of Raven 23

We extend our deepest gratitude to the many loyal, courageous, and steadfast individuals who walked this long road with us—often in silence, often at great personal cost. You were our strength when ours was gone, our voice when we had none, and our hope in the darkest hours.

To our families, our brothers in arms, and our Blackwater family: Thank you for standing beside us through it all. You bore burdens you never signed up for, and still you never wavered. To those who wrote to us, visited us, sent books, magazines, prayers, commissary money, and encouragement—your kindness made the unbearable more bearable. Even strangers, whose names we'll never know, reached out in solidarity. Every letter mattered. Every gesture mattered. You reminded us that we were not forgotten.

To those who showed up at our sentencing hearings and dared to speak truth in hostile spaces: Thank you for your courage. To the army of supporters that never gave up—and to those individuals who went above and beyond to help us rebuild our lives in ways big and small—our release is your victory as well. You know who you are.

We especially honor Jim Phelps, the first journalist to see past the headlines and tell our side when no one else would. When we were a "hot topic" for all the wrong reasons, Jim stood up and fought for us. You were there from the beginning, and we will never forget it.

To Christin Slough: You defied the odds with unrelenting grace, faith, and resolve. You were told it was impossible, and still you made it possible. Not just once, but four times over. Your strength reminds us of Deborah, the warrior-prophetess. You are a lioness, and we are in awe.

To Pete Hegseth—a brother-in-arms and a relentless advocate: You carried our cause into the halls of power and kept it alive. You ensured our names were heard by the one man who could restore our lives. Your commitment to justice and dedication to the war fighter reflects the very best of the ideals of our Republic.

To President Donald J. Trump: We are profoundly grateful for your decision to grant us full and unconditional presidential pardons—the action that speaks to your commitment to justice, truth, and the foundational freedoms that define the American spirit. Through your courageous action, you restored our futures, reunited our families, and returned to us the freedom that had been unjustly ripped away. Your decision not only righted a grave injustice but also reaffirmed the power of executive action to uphold the very ideals on which this Republic stands.

To attorneys Dave Harrison, Eric Jaso, Dane Butswinkas, Barry Simon, Tobin Romero, Simon Latcovich, Amy Mason Saharia, and Krystal Commons: Your belief in liberty and justice never faltered, even as the odds stacked high. You led us through the legal gauntlet with honor, dignity, and tenacity, securing not only legal victories but moral ones. Together, you set the gold standard for principled legal defense in our Republic.

To Lauren McLaughlin and the team at Justice for Warriors: Thank you for your unwavering support and for never letting the story die.

To Drew Springer, your boldness in speaking truth—even when it wasn't popular—had a profound impact. Thank you for standing in your stirrups with us.

To Gina Keating, a woman of principle, grit, and uncommon integrity: Thank you for walking this journey alongside us with unwavering strength. Your friendship and courage will always be honored with deep respect and lasting gratitude.

To Joni Rogers-Kante, whose unwavering dedication, personal resolve, and deep empathy motivated her to use her donor influence to open critical doors to members of Congress and the White House.

From Micheal Flaherty

To the men of Raven23 and their families: You are proven men of valor, but I love you for teaching me about resilience, grace, and forgiveness. You and your families daily reflect the fruits of the spirit—love, joy, peace, patience, kindness, goodness, faithfulness, gentleness, and self-control. (And thank you, Emma, Alicia, and Mia for teaching me about the fruits of the spirit at Camp of the Woods!)

To Gina Keating and Mitchell Weinbaum: Thank you for letting me experience what it is like to work with people I truly love for a story about people who I grew to love. Together, we discovered the new medium of podcasting, which has become my most beloved form of media and journalism.

To my wife, Kelly: My Proverbs 31 Brooklyn girl whose steadfast love and quiet strength are the foundation beneath every page. "An excellent wife, who can find? She is far more precious than rubies." Like Penelope, you waited with grace and faithfulness—even if I was off chasing windmills more than fighting Trojan wars. And thanks for blessing me with the most thoughtful in-laws, who have always loved me like their own family. Barbara and Harold, you were always my guardian angels. John and Kim, thanks for loving me like your own brother and enabling me to become close friends with your spouses—Marissa and Bill, respectively.

To my parents, Francis Xavier and Margaret Maureen: Thank you for teaching me that the substance of faith is a hope in the unseen. Dad, thanks for teaching me to always fight for the underdog. Mom, thanks for taking me to Robbins Library when I was five years old to get my first library card. You were right: As long as I have a book, I will always have a friend.

To my older brothers, Chip and Peter, who encouraged me to stay in the game when I wanted to bench myself: As John Steinbeck wrote, "A guy needs somebody—to be near him." You have never left my side. Even when I ballooned to 240 pounds, you always lived the mantra "He ain't heavy. He's my brother."

To William M. Bulger: Thank you for being more than my first boss but my first mentor and writing teacher. Most of all, thank you for modeling that loyalty is the holiest good in the human heart. Even when you were unjustly targeted by those forces of "unsleeping malevolence," you never lost your rebel heart for righteousness. Or your sense of humor. The fun is in the fight.

To Chai Ling: A prophet is never appreciated in their own land. Yet the cry for freedom you courageously voiced in Tiananmen Square in the spring of 1989 echoed worldwide and through eternity, inspiring countless people and nations in ways you may never fully know.

To Phillip and Nancy Anschutz: Thank you for showing me more kindness, generosity, and confidence than anybody outside my family. Your modesty is equally praiseworthy and is the reason that more people may never know all that you have done to make the world a better place. You have transformed the culture and impacted more lives for the common good than anyone will ever know. And I respect you even more for wanting it to be that way.

To my best friend, George Hartford: Thanks for having my back since 1983. Without your wife, Vicki, and your son (and my godson), Kyle, this podcast never would have been made. I love you.

To all of my mentors in media: Matthew Scully, Jack Fowler, Bill McGurn, Bill Bennett, Carl Cannon, David Feith, David French, Nancy French, Cal Thomas, Laura Ingraham, Lauren Greene, Jonathon Bock, Jim Braude, Margery Eagan, Bart and Tina Graff, Kathie Lee Gifford, Kirsten Powers, Naomi Schaeffer Riley, Dick Lehr, Jason Reilly, Clark Gilbert, Rachel Joy Victor, Timothy Dalrymple, Sheri Dew, and David Feith.

To all the healers who have literally kept me alive these past two decades. To everybody at the Lahey Clinic, thank you for saving me from a heart attack and Stage 3 cancer. To everybody at McLean Hospital, thank you for saving me from depression. To Dr. Feldman, thank you for saving me from discouragement. To Dr. Nineberg, thank you for saving me from despair. To Dr. Bill Hurlbut and Dr. Erica Goldman, thank you for volunteering for the thankless job of being my concierge doctors and close friends. To Grace Chapel and my church family, thank you for always covering me in prayer. Most important, thank you to my Lord and Savior Jesus Christ, for giving me new life—in this world and the next.

NOTES

INTRODUCTION: THE CASE OF THE VANISHING INSURGENTS
1. *United States vs. Slough*, etc. Jury Trial Transcript, Day 25. Criminal No. 08-360, and *U.S. vs. Slatten*, Criminal No. 14-107 (D.D.C. June 17 and 3, 2014). Unless otherwise noted, all evidence or testimony cited are from this trial.
2. Tom O'Connor, "FBI Team Leader: How I Know the Blackwater Defendants Didn't Deserve a Pardon from Trump," CNN, December 24, 2020, https://www.cnn.com/2020/12/24/opinions/blackwater-defendants-pardon-trump-opinion-oconnor/index.html.
3. Defense exhibit by Schertler & Onorato, drafted May 21, 2009, "Investigation and Collection of Evidence at Nisour Square."
4. Testimony of US Army Captain Peter Decareau, August 12, 2014.

CHAPTER ONE: CATCH-23
1. Terry McCarthy, interview with the author, September 20, 2024.
2. Radio log, Defendants' Motion In Limine to Admit Tactical Operations Center (TOC) Log into Evidence, filed July 7, 2014. AK-47 casings; witness statements: Peter Decareau testimony, August 12, 2024. Bullet strikes: Testimony of Tyler Hall, August 8, 2014.
3. "Brief of Amicus Curiae National Association of Criminal Defense Lawyers in Support of Appellants, Support Reversal," National Association of Criminal Defense Lawyers, February 8, 2016, pp. 14, 17, 38, https://www.supportraven23.com/s/As-Filed-NACDL-Amicus-Brief.pdf.
4. "Attorney General Loretta E. Lynch Hosts the 63rd Annual Attorney General Awards Honoring Department Employees and Others for Their Service," press release, US Department of Justice, October 29, 2015, https://www.justice.gov/archives/opa/pr/attorney-general-loretta-e-lynch-hosts-63rd-annual-attorney-general-awards-honoring.

5. Judge David B. Sentelle: "I would like to see prosecutors quit getting themselves and the country in these Brady violation problems when they do not turn over evidence that is favorable to the defense. And then they turn up, I don't know if you're familiar with the trial Royce has going on now but there was some dramatic exculpatory evidence for the Blackwater defendants that was not turned over." Frederick, David, "Oral History of the Honorable David B. Sentelle, Seventh Interview," Historical Society of the District of Columbia Circuit, August 7, 2014, https://dcchs.org/sb_pdf/interview-7-sentelle/; Defense Motion for Relief to Cure Brady Violation with Exhibits, filed July 28, 2014.

CHAPTER TWO: SOMETIMES THEY REALLY ARE OUT TO GET YOU

1. Don Terry, "Rackets Law Can Be Used Against Police in Los Angeles," *New York Times*, August 30, 2000, sec. A, https://www.nytimes.com/2000/08/30/us/rackets-law-can-be-used-against-police-in-los-angeles.html.
2. Joseph Low IV, interview with the author, January 15, 2020.
3. Gary Baum, "Anthony Pellicano Wiretap Lawsuit Nears Settlement," *Hollywood Reporter*, June 5, 2013, https://www.hollywoodreporter.com/business/business-news/anthony-pellicano-wiretap-lawsuit-nears-562721/.
4. Sleeping: Reba Slatten interview. Jail threat: Opening statement, first trial.
5. "Blackwater USA II Perceived Threat Statements," PowerPoint presentation prepared by defense attorneys for 2014 trial.
6. Jeremy Ridgeway plea agreement required him to share these emails. Letter from US Attorney Jeffrey A. Taylor to Ridgeway's attorney William Sullivan, dated November 15, 2008, Subject: Criminal investigation of Nisour Square shooting.

CHAPTER THREE: WHAT ACTUALLY HAPPENED IN NISOUR SQUARE

1. Testimony of Mia Laczek-Johnson, August 25, 2014.
2. Jimmy Watson's testimony, July 29, 2014. Nick Poulos comments: FBI interview (FD-302), transcribed November 30, 2007. Evidence in trial.
3. Tommy Vargas, interview with the author, November 7, 2023.

CHAPTER FOUR: THE FRAME-UP BEGINS

1. Gina Keating, "Resurrecting Belmont," Los Angeles *Daily Journal*, July 31, 2001.
2. Jimmy Watson denies firing his weapon. His testimony, July 28, 2014.

3. Evidence in trial, provided to author by defense lawyers.
4. Jeremy Scahill, *Blackwater: The Rise of the World's Most Powerful Mercenary Army* (New York: Bold Type Books, 2008), p. 24.

CHAPTER FIVE: THE GOVERNMENT IS (ALMOST ALWAYS) OUT TO GET YOU

1. *U.S. v. Slough* No. 08-0360 (D.D.C.), Memorandum Opinion Granting the Defendants' Motion to Dismiss the Indictment (Blackwater Case).
2. FBI 302, interview with Ridgeway, December 1, 2008.
3. PTSD: Jeremy Ridgeway's testimony, July 31, 2014, pp. 94, 5.
4. Jeremy Ridgeway's testimony, August 4, 2014, p. 9.
5. Steven McCool, "Letter from McCool to AUSAs," *Legal Times*, March 12, 2013, https://legaltimes.typepad.com/files/dwb-doj.pdf.
6. FBI 302, Ridgeway.

CHAPTER SEVEN: JUDGES MAKE ALL THE DIFFERENCE

1. McCool letter.
2. Scahill, p. 15.

CHAPTER EIGHT: HOW WIKILEAKS REVEALED THAT HILLARY CLINTON MADE THE RAVEN 23 MEN POLITICAL PRISONERS IN THEIR OWN COUNTRY

1. Expanding of drone program: "Procedures for Approving Direction Action Against Terrorist Targets Located Outside the United States and Areas of Active Hostilities," *FOIA Library*, May 22, 2013. Declassified documents: https://www.justice.gov/oip/foia-library/procedures_for_approving_direct_action_against_terrorist_targets/dl.
2. "Obama authorized two Central Intelligence Agency drone strikes in northwest Pakistan, which, combined, killed an estimated one militant and 10 civilians, including between four and five children." Micah Zenko, "Obama's Embrace of Drone Strikes Will Be a Lasting Legacy," *New York Times*, January 12, 2016, https://www.nytimes.com/roomfordebate/2016/01/12/reflecting-on-obamas-presidency/obamas-embrace-of-drone-strikes-will-be-a-lasting-legacy.
3. "More than 2,400 dead as Obama's drone campaign marks five years." Bureau of Investigative Journalism, January 14, 2023, https://www.thebureauinvestigates.com/stories/2014-01-23/more-than-2-400-dead-as-obamas-drone-campaign-marks-five-years; "Obama authorized two Central Intelligence Agency drone

260 NOTES

strikes in northwest Pakistan, which, combined, killed an estimated one militant and 10 civilians, including between four and five children" from ibid.; "A Wedding That Became a Funeral," Human Rights Watch, February 19, 2018, https://www.hrw.org/report/2014/02/19/wedding-became-funeral/us-drone-attack-marriage-procession-yemen; Obama drones strike Pakistani funeral: Pir Zubair Shah and Salman Masood, "US Drone Strike Said to Kill 60 in Pakistan," *New York Times,* June 23, 2009, https://www.nytimes.com/2009/06/24/world/asia/24pstan.html.

4. Frank James, "Obama Warned by Ex-CIA Director," NPR, September 18, 2009, https://www.npr.org/sections/thetwo-way/2009/09/obama_warned_by_excia_director.html.
5. John Fund and Hans Von Spakovsky, *Obama's Enforcer: Eric Holder's Justice Department* (New York: Broadside), p. 97.
6. "Rahm Emanuel on the Opportunities of Crisis," *Wall Street Journal* YouTube, November 18, 2009, https://www.youtube.com/watch?v=_mzcbXi1Tkk.
7. Originally a confidential cable written by Robert Ford. "Public Outrage Over Blackwater Decision Generating Heavy Fallout," Wikileaks, January 4, 2010, https://wikileaks.org/plusd/cables/10BAGHDAD20_a.html.
8. "Hillary Clinton Email Archive: Blackwater," Wikileaks. December 31, 2009, http://wikileaks.org/clinton-emails/emailid/692.
9. Robert Ford, interview with the author, November 3, 2019.

CHAPTER NINE: THE GUILTY CONSCIENCE OF AMERICAN WARMONGERS

1. Stewart Baker, *Skating on Stilts* (Stanford, CA: Hoover Institution Press, 2010), p. 39, https://www.google.com/books/edition/Skating_on_Stilts/CrRIhcZFyd8C?hl=en&gbpv=1&kptab=overview.
2. Ibid.
3. The U.S. Senate Select Committee on Intelligence, and U.S. House Permanent Select Committee on Intelligence, "Report of the Joint Inquiry into the Terrorist Attacks of September 11, 2001—by the House Permanent Select Committee on Intelligence and the Senate Select Committee on Intelligence," Congress.gov, December 2002, https://www.congress.gov/107/crpt/srpt351/CRPT-107srpt351.pdf.
4. Ibid.
5. Lamberth: "I was in the carpool lanes there by the Pentagon when the plane hit the Pentagon. My car was enveloped in smoke and I couldn't move." Interviewer: "The FBI had to come get him out. By the time they arrived, Lam-

berth had already approved five wiretaps over his cell phone. Lamberth said it's important to get wiretaps up immediately after an attack takes place." Ari Shapiro, "Judge Remembers Time on Top Secret Bench," NPR, June 24, 2007, https://www.npr.org/2007/06/24/11342056/judge-remembers-time-on-top-secret-bench.

6. Carrie Johnson, "Ex-FISA Court Judge Reflects: After 9/11, 'Bloodcurdling' Briefings," NPR, July 3, 2013, https://www.npr.org/2013/07/11/198329788/fisa-court-judge-reflects-after-sept-11-bloodcurdling-meetings-and-briefings.

7. The 9/11 Commission, *Final Report of the National Commission on Terrorist Attacks Upon the United States* (Washington DC: National Commission on Terrorist Attacks Upon the United States, 2004), p. 353, https://govinfo.library.unt.edu/911/report/911Report.pdf.

8. Richard J. Pierce, "Judge Lamberth's Reign of Terror at the Department of the Interior," *Administrative Law Review* 56, no. 2 (2004): 235–62, http://www.jstor.org/stable/40712173.

9. Associated Press, "Judge Orders Interior to Shut down Net Connections," NBC, March 15, 2004, https://www.nbcnews.com/id/wbna4535644.

10. Erik De La Garza, "Family Can't Sue Police for Son's Beating Death," Courthouse News Service, March 19, 2025, https://www.courthousenews.com/family-cant-sue-police-for-sons-beating-death/.

11. Thomas Bednar, Judicial Profile of Judge Royce Lamberth. *Federal Lawyer* (published by the Federal Bar Association), May 2008, https://www.fedbar.org/wp-content/uploads/2019/10/LamberthMay2008-pdf-3.pdf; "One or more of the Rangers later boasted over a few beers that, after killing the enemy soldiers, they had 'cut open the bodies from throat to groin and stuffed them with rice' from the 100-pound burlap bags strapped to the enemy bicycles. This 'calling card' was intended to strike fear into any enemy who later happened upon the dead men." Frederic L. Borch III, *Judge Advocates in Vietnam: Army Lawyers in Southeast Asia, 1959–1975* (Fort Leavenworth, KS: U.S. Army Command and General Staff College Press, 2016), pp. 98–100, https://www.armyupress.army.mil/Portals/7/combat-studies-institute/csi-books/judge-advocates-in-vietnam.pdf.

12. "Reassignment of Criminal Case." *US v. Slough et al.* (PACER June 8, 2012).

13. Pierce, *Administrative Law*.

14. Defense Motion to Compel Production of Evidence, filed April 4, 2014.

15. 395—Slatten's Motion to Stay Pending Emergency Petition for Writ of Mandamus, Case 1:08-cr-00360,filed March 6, 2014.

16. US Court of Appeals Order Granting Slatten's Writ of Mandamus, April 7, 2014.

CHAPTER TEN: JUDGE LAMBERTH TIGHTENS THE KNOT

1. Ridgeway's trial testimony, July 31, 2014.
2. Jury selection and instructions, trial transcript, June 17, 2014, p. 13.
3. Defense closing argument, trial transcript, August 27, 2014.
4. "Approximate Locations of Victims Around Nisour Square" diagram and victims list filed as exhibits with the December 4, 2008, indictment.
5. Boslego: "We had two veteran army officers who knew this space like the back of their hand who went there. They went there to see what was going on. And I told you about those individuals, they went there for the very purpose of determining how could this have happened, and for finding the evidence that would show that there was a hostile force out there that had caused it all. They didn't find anything like that." David Boslego testimony, trial transcript, August 13, 2014.
6. David Frederick, "Oral History of the Honorable David B. Sentelle, Seventh Interview," Historical Society of the District of Columbia Circuit, August 7, 2014, https://dcchs.org/sb_pdf/interview-7-sentelle/.
7. Defendants Motion for New Trial, filed April 27, 2015.

CHAPTER ELEVEN: VERDICT

1. Nicholas Slatten Arraignment for Murder, hearing transcript, May 12, 2014.

CHAPTER THIRTEEN: THE PERSECUTION OF NICK SLATTEN

1. FBI 302, interview with Ridgeway, July 22, 2009.
2. David Boslego cross-examination by Simon Latcovich, trial transcript, July 2, 2018, p. 46.
3. Author's interview with Williams & Connolly attorneys.
4. Memorandum Opinion Denying Slatten's Motion for New Trial, *USA v. Slatten*, Case No. 1:14-cr-107, filed August 6, 2020.
5. For more on conditions in this DC jail, see: Lamont Ruffin, "U.S. Marshals Service Nov. 1 Memo to D.C. Dept. of Corrections re: D.C. Jail Inspection," *Washington Post*, November 2, 2021, https://www.washingtonpost.com/context/u-s-marshals-service-nov-1-memo-to-d-c-dept-of-corrections-re-d-c-jail-inspection/1ecd5c89-1655-4e86-9ccc-28f432af78c5/; Madeleine Carlisle, "The Crisis at the D.C. Jail Began Decades Before Jan. 6 Defendants Started Raising Concerns," *Time*, November 8, 2022. https://www.congress.gov/118/meeting/house/116626/documents/HHRG-118-JU10-20231205-SD003.pdf.

CHAPTER FOURTEEN: GOVERNMENT KILLING MACHINES

1. "During our rapid rise, the company created numerous affiliates, branching far beyond Blackwater Lodge and Training Center, Blackwater Armor and Targets, and Blackwater Security Consulting. One early addition was Blackwater K9, which trained law enforcement dog units in Moyock and deployed nearly one hundred teams around the world with bomb-sniffing German shepherds and malamutes. For water-based practice and antipiracy protection in the Gulf of Aden, we created Blackwater Maritime Security Solutions. . . . We figured Blackwater Armored Vehicle might sell three hundred of the trucks a year. Then we built a blimp. No joke. So Blackwater Airships prototyped a 170-foot-long remote-controlled blimp that could hover for days, for half the price of a fixed-wing UAV." Erik Prince, *Civilian Warriors: The Inside Story of Blackwater and the Unsung Heroes of the War on Terror* (New York: Portfolio, 2013).

CHAPTER FIFTEEN: SENTENCING

1. "There was no incoming fire at the time that shot was fired. There was no basis for firing that shot. The jury got it exactly right, and this was murder. It meets any definition of murder." Sentencing of Nicholas Slatten, hearing transcript, August 14, 2019, p. 38.

INDEX

★★★

Abd al-Mahdi, Adil, 111–12
Abernathy, Pierre, 122
al-Awadi, Hussein, 141, 167–68
al-Awlaki, Abdulrahman, 104
al-Dabbagh, Ali, 110
Allen, Bill, 153–54
al-Maliki, Nouri, 97–98, 110, 111–12, 161–62
al-Mihdhar, Khalid, 119
Al Rubia'y, Ahmed Haithem, 2–3, 179
American war zone reporters, 56–57
Anschutz, Philip, 86
appeals court
    appellate court's answer to, 83–84
    case dismissal, 91–95
    case reassigned to Lamberth, 124–25
    Court of Appeals rejecting Urbina ruling, 123–24
    defense argument for, 34–35, 69
    gun charge, 83–84
    media coverage on Urbina's ruling, 95
    NACDL amicus brief, 17–18, 29, 69, 127, 130, 207–8
    oral arguments, 83
    Urbina ruling, 91–95
Apuzzo, Matt, 95
Ashcroft, John, 118
Asuncion, Anthony, 136

Baker, Stewart, 116–20
Ball, Donald, 43, 63, 93–95
Belmont Learning Center, 54–56
Bennett, William J., 86

Biden, Joseph, 98, 104–6, 206–7, 223–24
"Biden Four, The," 222–23
Blackwater K9, 263n
Blackwater Maritime Security Solutions, 263n
Blackwater USA. *See also* Prince, Erik
    affiliates, 263n
    Clinton firing, 97
    defensive role of, 61
    Heard joining, 10
    hiring criteria, 78–79
    Iraqi government revoking license, 59
    negative brand connotations, 184–85
    prejudicial effect of, 184, 230
    providing Obama protection in Iraq, 208
    unfairly blamed, 114
Boslego, David, 140–42, 166–70, 262n
Brady violations, 142–43, 258n
Brown, Don, 229
Bulger, James "Whitey," 85, 87–88
Bulger, William M., 85
Bureau of Prisons
    compassionate release program, 225
    diesel therapy, 176
    FCI Coleman, 37
    FCI Memphis, 30
    FCI Schuylkill, 32
    inmate visitation protocols, 22–23
    prisoner abuses, 176–78, 185
Burgess, Michael, 160

Busch, Anita, 23
Bush, George W., 65
Business Wars (podcast), 182
Buslovich, Chris, 96, 199–200
Butswinkas, Dane, 152, 156, 192–93

Calley, William, 189
Campoamor-Sanchez, Fernando, 166, 170
Carpenter, Theodore, 58
Carvajal, Michael, 225
Childers, Daniel, 43
Cipollone, Pat, 162
Civilian Warriors (Prince), 33
Clinton, Bill, 105
Clinton, Hillary, 73, 97, 104–6, 109
Coalition Provisional Authority, 112
cobelligerents, 87
Coffield, William, 32, 62, 96–97, 147, 156, 200, 234–35
condolence payments, 111, 114, 209
Connolly, Tom, 133, 144–45, 152
Cooley, Steve, 68
Court of Appeals, 29, 121, 123–24, 149
covid-19 lockdowns, 223–25
Crocker, Ryan, 60
Crosthwaite, Arlen, 9

DART report, 173–75, 223
Decareau, Peter, 52–53, 133, 142
Department of Justice
  alleged pretrial harassment by, 74–76
  alleged prosecutorial misconduct, 69–71, 91, , 93–94, 153–54
  interagency battle with State Department, 71–72, 109–10
  McCool and, 94–95
  needing different set of facts, 90
  plea deals, 23
  possible professional ethics violations on, 69–70
  prosecution team, 125–26
Department of the Interior, 120–21
DeVos, Betsy, 230
diesel therapy, 176

Downed Aircraft Recovery Team (DART) mission, 173–75, 223
Downie, James, 104
drone campaign, 231, 259–60n

Emanuel, Rahm, 107–8
England, Gordon, 35, 130–31

false testimonies, due to plea-bargain push, 77
Fattah, Rodeina, 41–42, 51
Federal Bureau of Investigation (FBI), 72–77
FISA court, 118–19
Fishback, Brett, 138–39
Flaherty, Francis X. "Chip," 85–86
Flaherty, Michael
  background, 84–86
  conservative friends of, 86–87
  Fox & Friends Weekend interview, 205–7
  Keating and, 84–90, 197
  on media's reaction to potential pardons, 186–87
  on movie marketing/political campaign fusion, 88
  post-pardon, 246
  Jessica Slatten and, 152
  Christin Slough and, 152
  Walden Media and, 85–87
  Weinbaum and, 222–23
Ford, Robert, 110, 111–13, 116, 260n
Foreign Intelligence Surveillance Court (FISC), 116–19
Forward Operating Base Prosperity, 52
Fox & Friends Weekend, 205–7
Freeh, Louis, 118
French, David, 86, 189
French, Nancy, 86–87
Frost, Adam
  accepting government immunity, 64–65
  at Nisour Square incident, 43, 50
  Slatten confronting, 64
  testifying against teammates, 64–65
  testimony, 134–35

Gallagher, Eddie, 215
Gates, Robert, 66
George, Keith, 51, 52, 58
Gettysburg National Military Park, 30–31
Gohmert, Louie, 226–27
Goldberg, Michelle, 247
Golsteyn, Mathew, 215, 217
government obfuscation, evidence of, 22
Grace Chapel, Lexington, 86–87
Granat, Cary, 85–86
grand jury, 69–73, 80, 92–94, 126
Guerrero, Tony, 220

Hanner, Darren, 173
Harris Wiltshire & Grannis, 152
Harrison, David
  case review, 109, 116
  Coffield and, 235
  Hegseth and, 205, 217–18, 229, 233
  on Lamberth's rulings, 161
  Christin Slough and, 157, 234
  See also Spiro Harrison & Nelson
Hartford, Kyle, 205
Heard, Dustin
  author's initial visit with, 22–30
  background, 8–10, 25
  on case dismissal, 99
  covid pandemic and, 225–26
  DSS interview, 73
  family visit at FCI Memphis, 24
  Joe Bob and, 8–9
  joining Blackwater, 10
  nickname, 26, 27, 42
  Nisour Square incident and, 42, 50–51, 52, 58
  opinion of government's motive to prosecute, 27–28
  personality profile, 183
  on plea and immunity offers, 29–30, 74
  podcast interview, 185–86
  post-pardon, 244
  prison abuses, 185
  prison release, 235, 237–38
  resentencing of, 197–98, 201
  return to the United States, 62–63
  sentencing of, 10
  tattoos, 30
  trusting his own judgement, 26
Heard, Dylan (brother), 185–86
Heard, Hannah (daughter), 24, 199, 243–44
Heard, Kelli (wife), 13, 24, 146–47, 234
Heard, Lawana (stepmother), 13, 235
Heard, Quinn (son), 24, 99
Heard, Stacey (father), 13, 23, 58, 199, 234, 235
Heberlig, Brian, 133–34, 137, 198–99, 202
Hegseth, Pete
  arguing for pardons, 215–16
  athletic dreams, 212–13
  background, 212–13
  calling the men "The Biden Four," 222
  evaluating Raven 23 case, 228–29
  Gohmert and, 227
  Harrison and, 205, 217–18, 229, 233
  joining *Fox & Friends*, 214
  leveraging Fox News platform, 217, 229
  military background, 213–14
  on military private contractors, 216
  Slough and, 233, 244
  Trump and, 229–30, 231–32
  on veterans caught in military criminal justice system, 187–88
Hill, Christopher, 112
Hill, Dustin, 43
Hill, T. J., 51–52
Holder, Eric, 105, 106–7, 154
Hunter, Duncan, 217

Ingraham, Laura, 86
intelligence world, atmosphere in, 117–19
Iraqi government
  political pressure from, 2, 108–9
  response to Urbina ruling, 110–13

Iraqi government (*continued*)
  revoking Blackwater USA license, 59
  wanting guards to face trial in Iraq, 95
Iraqi National Police (INP), 58, 115, 140–41, 166–68
Iraq war
  Low defending US servicemen and women in, 21–22
  military jargon in, 165–66
  Nisour Square (*see* Nisour Square incident)
  public opinion of, 15
  Shi'a strategy, 205

Jaso, Eric, 108–9, 116, 157
Jenkins, Katrice, 172
Joe Bob (author's boyfriend)
  background, 7
  encouraging author's investigation, 11–12
  as essential worker, 226
  Gettysburg National Military Park visit, 30–31
  Heard and, 8–9
  Keating and, 6–7, 11–12, 83, 208, 246
  views on merits of war, 31–32
Judd, Whitney, 242
Judges' Club, 125
Justice Department. *See* Department of Justice
Justice for Warriors Caucus, 217–18, 222, 226

Kajima Urban Development, 54–55
Karim, Faris, 140–41, 168, 171–72
Kastigar hearing, 100, 164
Keating, Gina (author)
  Flaherty and, 84–90, 197
  on FOIA request, 248
  Fox & Friends Weekend interview, 205–7
  Gettysburg National Military Park visit, 30–31
  grandfather of, 7–8, 19
  initial visit with Heard, 22–30
  initial visit with Liberty, 32–35
  initial visit with Slatten, 37–38
  initial visit with Slough, 35–37
  Joe Bob and, 6–7, 11–12, 83, 208, 246
  journalism background, 5–6
  Netflix vs. the World (film), 219–21
  Netflixed (book), 84–87
  pitching Raven 23 story, 87–88
  podcast (*see* Raven 23 podcast)
  Prince, Erik, and, 209
  reviewing trial transcript, 14–17
  seeking publisher for the book, 38–39, 69
  Soliah story, 68–69
  views on merits of war, 31–32
  working at Los Angeles *Daily Journal*, 29
Khalilzad, Zalmay, 60
Kinani, Mohammed, 142
Koh, Harold, 109
Kohl, Kenneth, 70, 72, 74, 92
Krueger, Jeremy, 43

Laczek-Johnson, Mia, 42–43
Lamberth, Royce
  alleged bias, 144
  attitude toward prosecution, 168, 170
  background, 117–19
  Brady violations, 142–43
  Court of Appeals orders to, 83–84
  denying new trial motion, 223
  disbelief in Military Extraterritorial Jurisdiction Act, 130–31
  as FISA court judge, 118–19
  Interior Department and, 120–21
  on Monem's testimony changes, 148–49
  postponing sentencing, 178
  reputation and influence, 120–21
  and Ridgeway, 150–51
  September 11, 2001, attacks, 117–19, 260–61n
  Vietnamese episode, 122–23, 261n

Lane, Charles, 189
Latcovich, Simon, 167–70, 218
Leon, Richard, 124
Liberty, Aaron (brother), 129, 147, 199, 239
Liberty, Brian (father), 96–97, 147, 238
Liberty, Evan
 author's initial visit with, 32–35
 background, 33–34
 calling mother, Deb, 57–58
 on case dismissal, 96
 on CNN special report, 57–58
 Coffield and, 32, 62
 nickname, 42
 at Nisour Square incident, 43, 49, 51
 Paola, relationship with, 99–100
 physical appearance of, 32–33
 post-pardon, 245–46
 prison experience, 33
 prison release, 235, 238–40
 rejecting FBI plea offer, 74
 resentencing of, 197–98
 return to the United States, 62
 sentencing of, 10
 sentencing testimonial, 201–2
 on witness list, 180–81
Lindh, John Walker, 187
Ling, Chai, 87
Lorance, Clint, 215–16, 217, 221
Los Angeles Police Department, corruption of, 19–21
Los Angeles Unified School District (LAUSD), 54–55
Low, Joseph, IV, 21–22, 76, 166
Lynch, Loretta, 17

Martin, T. Patrick, 26, 132–33, 135, 165, 188, 194, 197
McCarthy, Terry, 56–57
McCool, Steven, 93–94
McGurn, William, 86
McLaughlin, Lauren, 222
Meadows, Mark, 190
Mealy, Mark, 43, 45, 65, 135–36
Media Matters for America, 207–8
Military Extraterritorial Jurisdiction Act (MEJA), 34–35, 81, 130–31

military-media industrial complex, 88
Miller, Derrick, 222
Monem, Sarhan Dheyab Abdul, 147–48
Murphy, Carolyn, 73
Murphy, Matthew, 43, 65, 173–75

National Association of Criminal Defense Lawyers (NACDL)
 alleged Constitution violations during trial, 149
 amicus brief, 17, 29, 69, 127, 130, 207–8
 on the trial penalty, 76–77
National Registry of Exonerations, 77
Nelson, Jermaine, 21
Netflixed (podcast series), 84–87
Netflix vs. the World (film), 219–21
news media
 reacting to 2014 trial sentences, 151
 reaction to potential pardons, 186–87
 reaction to sentences, 151
Nisour Square incident
 army investigations, 4, 220–21
 Blackwater convoy driving to, 42–45
 car bomb explosion, 41
 command vehicle, 43, 49
 convoy retreat from traffic circle, 50–51
 Decareau gathering evidence at, 52–53
 deterrent actions taken, 47
 emergency response vehicle, 43
 evidence collection, 16, 52–53
 Hill assessing convoy vehicle damage, 51–52
 insurgents firing on Blackwater convoy, 46–49
 Iraqi government's pressure for convictions, 2
 Kia sedan approaching, 47–48
 lead vehicle, 43
 motorists approaching Blackwater convoy, 45–46
 official narrative of, 2–4

Nisour Square incident (*continued*)
  Prince commissioning report on, 209–10
  returning Fattah to Green Zone, 41–42
  shielding team members from gunfire, 49–50
  Thorp's investigation of, 39–40
  US Army assistance at, 52
  Watson's disobedience, 44, 51
Nuñez, Johnny Ivanovich, 193–94

Obama, Barack, 72–73, 97–98, 103–4, 106, 110–11, 208, 259–60n
O'Connor, Thomas, 3
Olson, Sara Jane. *See* Soliah, Kathleen Ann
O'Melveny & Myers, 54–56
Operation Iron Triangle, 213–14
Opsahl, Myrna, 68
O'Quinn, John, 91

Pace, Peter, 168
Panetta, Leon, 107
pardons. *See* Raven 23 pardons
Patarini, John, 72
Pellicano, Anthony, 23
Pence, Mike, 226
Petraeus, David, 66
Pierce, Richard J., Jr., 120–21, 125
plea bargains, US criminal justice system's push for, 75–77
Posillico, Michael, 73
Poulos, Nick, 51, 52
Powell, Robyn, 80
presidential pardons, media's reaction to potential, 186–87. *See also* Raven 23 pardons
Prince, Erik, 33, 60, 87, 112, 209–10, 230. *See also* Blackwater USA
Professional Appointee Court Expenditure (PACE), 68
prosecutorial misconduct, 69–71, 91
Pulitzer, Joseph, 247

Rampart scandal, 19–21
Randall, Eddie, 42, 47–48, 50

Raven 22, delivering Fattah safely, 51
Raven 23 case
  association with Blackwater, 184–85, 230
  Hillary Clinton reviving, 104–5
  CNN special report on, 56
  government's narrative, 56
  Justice for Warriors Caucus briefed on, 218
  Obama administration's motive to push, 105–12
Raven 23 convoy at Nisour Square. *See* Nisour Square incident
Raven 23 defendants
  assault weapons charge, 72–73
  DOJ's attempts to indict, 69–70
  filing After Action Report, 58
  financial pressure on family of, 210
  first prosecution attempt, 71–72
  government's and media reports' support of, 59
  government's legal costs to prosecute, 211
  Heard and (*see* Heard, Dustin)
  indictments on, 80–81
  Liberty and (*see* Liberty, Evan)
  media glare fracturing, 63–64
  non-guilty pleas, 81–82
  pretrial harassment, 74–76
  return to the United States, 61–62
  Slatten and (*see* Slatten, Nicholas)
  Slough and (*see* Slough, Paul)
  State Department interviews, 58
Raven 23 pardons
  campaign to counter anti-pardon faction, 187–89
  Flaherty ratcheting up pressure, 223
  Gohmert's support letter, 226–27
  Justice for Warriors support for, 226
  news coverage of, 246–47
  pardon packets, 161–62, 185
  timing of, 188
  Trump's call to Hegseth on, 232
Raven 23 podcast
  assembling trailer for, 188–89

criticisms for, 221–22
decision makers aware of, 222
gathering first-person trial accounts, 205
halt of, 219
Hartford's assistance with, 205
Lorance interview, 221
political and military leaders interviews, 205
relaunch of, 224
"Saving the Pentagon from Itself" episode, 206–7
trailer release, 204
resentencing hearing
for Dustin Heard, 197–203
for Evan Liberty, 197–203
Lamberth's decision, 196, 202–3, 263n
Lamberth's denial for acquittal, 196
Lamberth's indignations, 195–96, 200
Lamberth's rejecting time served sentence, 202
for Nick Slatten, 192–97, 263n
for Paul Slough, 197–203
testimonials, 193–95, 198–200
Rhodes, Kevin, 43
Rice, Condoleezza, 61, 97
Ridgeway, Jeremy
addressing false media reports, 63–64
background, 77–78
and Lamberth, 150–51
nickname, 42
at Nisour Square incident, 44, 48, 50–51
plea agreement, 4, 75, 82, 258n
plea hearing transcript, 77–79
return to the United States, 63
testimony, 79–80, 130, 136–38
version of events, 79–80
Rogers-Kante, Joni, 160
Rolling, Charles, 174
Rowan, Patrick, 81

Saharia, Amy Mason, 156, 235, 241
Salman, Hassan Jaber, 139
San Antonio Police Department, 121–22
Sanders, Bernie, 223–24
Satterfield, David, 61
Scahill, Jeremy, 66, 97
Schertler, David, 150
Scollan, Agent, 92–93
Second Amendment of the US Constitution, 16
self-incrimination, 72, 91, 109–10
Senate Armed Services Committee, 60–61
Sentelle, David, 143, 258n
September 11, 2001, attacks, 116–20, 260–61n
Shimkus, Carley, 207
Skinner, Jeremy, 43
Slatten, Darrell (father), 194–95
Slatten, Jessica, 130, 145, 152, 155–56, 174, 184, 189
Slatten, Nicholas
author's initial visit with, 37–38
background, 37–38
Connolly as trial attorney for, 152
during covid pandemic, 224–25
faith in God, 190–91
FBI agents following, 74–75
first trial (*see* trial, first [2014])
Frost confrontation, 64
indictment dismissal, 100
leading Bible study, 240
losing CIA dream, 100–101
new indictment on, 126–27
nickname, 42
at Nisour Square incident, 43, 48–49, 50
plea offers, 176
post-pardon, 242–43, 245
prison abuses, 176–78
prison release, 240–41
return to the United States, 62
second trial (*see* trial, second [2018])
sentencing of, 10, 192–93, 262n
third trial (*see* trial, third [2018])
updating sister from prison, 190–91

Slatten, Reba (mother), 129, 144
Slough, Christin (wife)
    at 2014 trial, 129
    on Biden condemning her husband, 98–99
    confronting Nick on abrasive behavior, 140
    distributing pardon packet, 188
    Flaherty and, 152
    Harrison and, 157–58, 161–62
    Hegseth and, 233
    on husband's sentencing, 197–98
    on *The Ingraham Angle*, 189–90
    on judge's decision, 203
    Keating and, 36–37
    in market for new attorney, 157
    Meadows and, 190
    on pardon update, 234–35
    recruiting people to her cause, 160
    sentencing testimonial, 199
    side hustle, 159–60
    suffering anxiety and panic attacks, 159
Slough, Lily (daughter), 36–37, 244
Slough, Paul
    author's initial visit with, 35–37
    on case dismissal, 96
    DSS interview, 58, 73
    on government appealing Urbina's ruling, 99
    hiring Harrison and Jaso, 116
    nickname, 42
    Nisour Square incident and, 43, 47–48, 50, 57
    parents of, 36
    peaceful pilgrimage, 128
    personality profile, 183
    post-pardon, 244–45
    prison release, 235, 236–37
    resentencing of, 197–98
    return to the United States, 62
    sentencing of, 10
    sentencing testimonial, 200–201
    sister Robin, 237
    thank-you video to Trump, 244–45
Smith, Ash, 222

Soleimani, Qasem, 231
Soliah, Kathleen Ann, 67–68
Soros, George, 207–8
Sparacino, Ryan, 75
Spiro Harrison & Nelson, 157, 161–62, 185. *See also* Harrison, David; Jaso, Eric
State Department, 58, 59–60, 71–72, 109–10
Status of Forces Agreement (SOFA), 110
Stevens, Ted, 70, 153–55
Sullivan, Emmet, 154
Symbionese Liberation Army (SLA), 68

Talabani, Jalal, 98
Tavernise, Sabrina, 59
Thorp, Harrison, 39–40
trial, first (2014)
    body counts and, 140, 149–50
    Boslego testimony, 140–42, 262n
    Brady violations during, 142–43, 258n
    casualty list count presented at, 28
    criminal procedure rules violations, 133–34
    defense argument, 13, 144–45
    discovery, 179
    errors at, 29
    family members at, 128–29
    Fishback testimony, 138–39
    foreign witness testimonies, 139
    Frost testimony, 134–35
    judge's actions at, 29, 144
    jury deliberations, 146
    Karim's omnipresence at, 142
    Kinani testimony, 142
    Mealy testimony, 135–36
    Monem testimony, 147–48
    opening statements, 132–33
    pretrial hearings, 137
    prosecutors' behavior, 129–30, 133–34, 143–44
    Ridgeway testimony, 136–38
    sentencing hearing, 147–51
    star witnesses' testimonies, 137–38
    venue rules, 129–30

verdict, 146–47
Washington, DC, press corps coverage of, 11–12
trial, second (2018)
Boslego testimony, 166–70
defense attorneys' uphill battle, 172–73
government's intelligence reports' summaries, 171–72
judge presiding over (*see* Lamberth, Royce)
jury deliberations, 174
Karim's influence over government's case, 171–72
mistrial, 176
Murphy testimony, 173–75
new trial motion, 174
pretrial hearings, 170–71
prosecutor's strategies in, 165–66
trial, third (2018)
convictions, 181
jury deliberations, 181
opening statements, 178
sentencing (*see* resentencing hearing)
witness list, 180–81
trial appeal. *See* appeals court
trial penalty, 76–77
Trump, Donald
considering pardons, 186
Hegseth and, 229–30, 231–32
pardoning Raven 23 men, 3, 235–36
Trump administration, crises engulfing the country during, 231–32

Uighurs, 90–91
Uniform Code of Military Justice, 217–18
United States Agency for International Development (USAID), 41–42
Urbina, Ricardo, 69–70, 90–95, 105, 158
US military
failure with Iraqi Army and National Police, 66
Forward Operating Base Prosperity, 52
press ganging of, 65
recruitment requirements, 78–79

Vargas, Tommy, 42, 46–51, 220

Wagler, Dean, 42
Wainscott, Corey, 43
Walden Media, 85–87
Watson, Jimmy, 43–44, 47, 49, 51, 58, 258n
Waxman, Henry A., 61
Weinbaum, Mitchell, 219–23, 246
West, Rick and Vivian, 36, 183
WikiLeaks, 108
Wilber, Del Quentin, 70
Willett, P. Sabin, 91
Williams, Edward Bennett, 152–53
Williams & Connolly, 152–54, 163–66, 192–93, 221, 241

Yagman, Stephen, 19–20

Zenko, Micah, 259n

ABOUT THE AUTHOR

★★★

GINA KEATING is a longtime investigative journalist, author, and filmmaker. Her most recent projects include the book *Netflixed: The Epic Battle for America's Eyeballs*, the podcast series *Business Wars: Netflix vs. Blockbuster vs. HBO* and *Raven 23: Presumption of Guilt*, and the 2019 award-winning documentary *Netflix vs. the World*. Keating covered finance, politics, and law for three decades at the international wire services United Press International, Associated Press, and Thomson Reuters, and for newspapers in Los Angeles and Austin. Her work has been featured in *The New York Times*, *The Washington Post*, DuJour, *Texas Monthly*, *Southern Living*, *Variety*, and *Forbes* magazines, among many other major outlets.